PERSPECTIVES™ ON
INCREASING
SALES

THE SALES EXPERT
MARVIN N. MILETSKY

THE PURCHASING AGENT
JAMES A. CALLANDER

COURSE TECHNOLOGY
CENGAGE Learning

Perspectives on Increasing Sales
Marvin N. Miletsky and James A. Callander

Publisher and General Manager, Course Technology PTR: Stacy L. Hiquet

Associate Director of Marketing: Sarah Panella

Manager of Editorial Services: Heather Talbot

Marketing Manager: Mark Hughes

Acquisitions Editor: Mitzi Koontz

Series Editor: Jason I. Miletsky

Project Editor: Kate Shoup

Editorial Services Coordinator: Jen Blaney

Copy Editor: Kate Shoup

Interior Layout: Shawn Morningstar

Cover Designer: Mike Tanamachi

Indexer: Sharon Shock

Proofreader: Gene Redding

For product information and technology assistance, contact us at **Cengage Learning Customer and Sales Support, 1-800-354-9706.**

For permission to use material from this text or product, submit all requests online at **cengage.com/permissions.**

Further permissions questions can be e-mailed to **permissionrequest@cengage.com.**

Library of Congress Control Number: 2008935079
ISBN-13: 978-1-59863-874-5
ISBN-10: 1-59863-874-2

Course Technology, a part of Cengage Learning
20 Channel Center Street
Boston, MA 02210
USA

Cengage Learning is a leading provider of customized learning solutions with office locations around the globe, including Singapore, the United Kingdom, Australia, Mexico, Brazil, and Japan. Locate your local office at: **international.cengage.com/region.**

Cengage Learning products are represented in Canada by Nelson Education, Ltd.

For your lifelong learning solutions, visit **courseptr.com.**
Visit our corporate Web site at **cengage.com.**

Printed in the U.S.A.
2 3 4 5 6 7 11 10

This book is dedicated to both Donna and Jason,
without whose support and encouragement it would not
have come to life. When I hit the wall and thought
this endeavor would never be successfully completed,
they were the ones who believed in me most,
picked me up, and gave me the strength to continue.

—MARVIN MILETSKY

Dedicated to my loving wife Ruby,
who has seen me through all the challenges
in our life, especially writing this book.
Without her support, encouragement, and guidance
I'm afraid I could not have finished this endeavor.

—JAMES CALLANDER

ACKNOWLEDGMENTS

I'd like to thank everyone at Cengage Learning who was involved in the development of this book, including Stacy Hiquet and her staff. In particular, I'd like to thank my editor, Kate Shoup, who has been great throughout this entire process. Kate was actually able to translate the language that I spoke into English that could be understood by the reader.

Thanks to Jack Benrubi for the contribution of his expertise in the use of rebate programs as sales tool. Thanks also to Dante Longo for his discussion of customer service and its effect on the sales function. Finally, Jason Miletsky added some great information regarding the benefits of multimedia in a sales environment.

Much appreciation is due to Jim Callander, who co-authored this work from the purchasing viewpoint, and with whom I have enjoyed a professional relationship for many years. (Special note to Jim: If, after reading my answers, you become suspicious that I've tried any of my tricks on you, you'd be absolutely wrong. I'd never do that to you. By the way, you'll still buy from me in the future, won't you?)

My mentor, Alan Rubin, taught me the lessons of hard work, dedication, and commitment very early in my career. I was a young purchasing agent at an electrical contractor when this role model pushed me unselfishly in this right direction. My sincere thanks to Alan, who still checks up on me to this day.

I'd like to acknowledge those buyers and purchasing agents who wouldn't give me the time of day, as well as the receptionists who protected their charges from my aggressive sales pitches by not letting me get past the door. Thanks, too, to the people who promised to give me an order but wound up only using me to compare prices, the people who did finally buy and then cancelled for no apparent reason, as well as the ones for whom nothing in this world could ever be done to satisfy their inane requirements to doing business. You were my school of hard knocks. You taught me what *not* to do with a customer and how to eventually get through to you and be successful.

Lastly, I'd like to thank my employer for these many years, Mac Products of Kearny, NJ, who allowed me this career in sales and stood by me until the orders started coming our way.

—MARVIN MILETSKY

ACKNOWLEDGMENTS

I would like to thank my co-author, Marv Miletsky, for inviting me to participate in creating this book. I also wish to thank Jason Miletsky, who brought our efforts together and managed to manage us compassionately at times of great stress! Thanks, too, to Stacy Hiquet for her support. The person I have come to appreciate most dearly during this process is Kate Shoup, who has the endurance of 10, the pen of Ben Franklin, and a great sense of humor. If I had only known her early in life, maybe I would write better now!

—JAMES CALLANDER

A sales veteran and manager with more than 30 years of experience in the electrical industry, **Marvin N. Miletsky** has been responsible for landing and negotiating millions of dollars' worth of new and continued contracts. Miletsky's visionary approach to new-business development has helped him amass an expansive client network built from some of the largest and most influential decision-makers in his industry. A nationally recognized expert, Miletsky has been a featured speaker at both conferences and universities on topics including techniques for increasing sales and maintaining profitable relationships. In the 1990s, he was a two-term president of one of the industry's oldest and most respected regional trade associations, spearheading the development of a buyer/seller networking system that continues to flourish. Miletsky has been an active member of the advisory council for New Jersey Institute of Technology and a mentor for graduating students seeking to establish themselves in a variety of sales roles. In *Perspectives on Increasing Sales*, Miletsky shares his time-tested new-business techniques with both seasoned and emerging sales professionals. He is also the author of some of the industry's most creative expense reports (but regrettably has left these out of the book).

James Callander is purchasing manager for L.K. Comstock, an electrical contractor that designs and installs electrical systems primarily for the railroad and rail-transit industries. Mr. Callander has almost 30 years of account-management, sales, and purchasing experience. As someone who has experienced sales from both the sales and purchasing point of view, Mr. Callander is uniquely qualified to provide insight into the sales practices that ensure optimal performance. His sales experience includes direct sales for GE Supply, as well as indirect sales for Panduit Corporation. His purchasing experience ranges from on-site project purchasing to the corporate level. Raised and educated in Ohio, he now lives with his wife and two sons in Atlanta, GA.

TABLE OF CONTENTS

Part Two
Developing Prospects and Making Contacts   **55**

Part Three
Pitching, Negotiating, and Landing the Account   **139**

Part Four
Managing the Relationship   221

INTRODUCTION

Walk down the aisles of any bookstore or library and you're bound to see plenty of books written by two or more authors. But sit down and read through it, and it's doubtful you'll be able to tell which author has contributed which information. They've collaborated, shared notes, and have ultimately written the book from a single voice.

But is that the best way to learn about a given topic? Sure, the authors are usually recognized experts in their field and can draw from some unique experiences and insights, but each book only takes into consideration a single viewpoint—one perspective that the reader is supposed to accept as true. That might make for an interesting read, but it only tells half the story. The importance, value, and methodology of sales, for example, may look dramatically different when seen through the eyes of a representative of a sales professional than through the eyes of a purchasing agent or consumer. Each may be seasoned when it comes to the buying and selling, but their approach—and even their fundamental beliefs—could be quite opposite, simply because they work on different sides of the fence.

That's what makes the books in the *Perspectives* series so different from any other books on the shelves. Each offers a true 360-degree learning experience that gives you the opportunity to learn by providing two distinct and often opposing viewpoints. It's a rare chance to get both sides of the story so that you, the reader, can get a more complete understanding of the given topic.

In order to make a series like this work, though, the authors for each book need the freedom to write in their own voice and provide their own opinion, even at the risk of conflicting with their co-author. Therefore, it's important to note that **the authors of this book have not collaborated on their work during the course of their writing.** In fact, neither author will even have a chance to read their co-author's submissions until after the book has been completed. This is what makes *Perspectives* books such a unique concept, and a true opportunity to get both sides of the story.

In *Perspectives on Increasing Sales*, Marvin Miletsky represents the sales perspective, while James A. Callander speaks on behalf of the customer. Through a total of 97 questions divided into five distinct parts, Marvin and James give their expert opinions on important topics including the basic foundations of sales, developing prospects and contacts, pitching, negotiation, and managing the salesperson/customer relationship. Part how-to book, part philosophical debate, *Perspectives on Increasing Sales* covers all the topics that anyone involved in sales would need in order to vastly improve their knowledgebase and skill set.

We hope you have as much fun reading *Perspectives on Increasing Sales* as we had working on it. Sometimes the authors whole-heartedly agreed with each other. In other instances, they couldn't have been more different. There's no question, however, that it's eye-opening to see the different perspective each author provided. But the perspectives don't end in this book. We want to hear your point of view, as well. Visit the blog site for this book at PerspectivesOnSales.com to comment on select content, read questions and answers that don't appear in this book, and let us know whose perspective you agree with more.

Opening Remarks

Marvin Miletsky

It started innocently enough: I was on my summer vacation and realized that I was in need of direction, of some motivation, something to keep my brain challenged and satisfy my thirst for being in the game. My entrepreneurial juices were flowing as I tried to envision a business enterprise that would reward me with the wealth I sought in return for my dedication. I considered what business to open and the best site for its placement. And then, as if by divine intervention, it came to me: a lemonade stand, right in front of my house. I was five years old and I was on my way.

I had it all worked out: The commute was manageable, the raw materials plentiful and cheap (actually, they were free, provided by my family). But it wasn't as easy as I thought it would be. I gave free samples to my friends—only to discover that my sample quenched their thirst, meaning that they didn't need to buy any actual product. The sun's heat warmed my thirst quencher to a point that it was undrinkable and had to be thrown out. I paid a playmate a dime (in advance) to watch the store while I went inside; when I returned, he was gone—and so was all my stock. The worst blow of all came when a kindly officer told me I would have to move to another location as I was blocking the sidewalk.

The products and services have sure changed since those days, and so have the people. And the simplicity of setting up shop without any care or planning has long ago disappeared. Plus, there are threats to a business from angles not even invented when I was hawking my lemonade. But my passion for making the sale, for positioning myself properly, for networking has never waned. In fact, it's more like the story of the hungry lion: The more success I had, the more I wanted.

In writing this book from the sales point of view, I hope to share with you various techniques I've used over the years that have helped in developing leads that eventually turned into negotiations, which led to the ultimate reward: the sale! Along the way, you'll find advice on the importance of relationship-building and the establishment of trust between you and your prospects and clients.

Whether you're at the beginning of your career or just looking to brush up, you should find some interesting advice to sharpen your approach and keep you in the hunt. Happy sales to you!

I was drawn to this project by the perspectives concept. There are always at least two sides to any situation, and selling is no exception. A salesperson who can see things from his or her customer's point of view is more likely to be successful. Your goal must go beyond beating out the competition; you must make it your mission to establish yourself as the person your customer relies on—again and again.

As a salesperson, you should never see yourself as being in a competition with your customer. Taking a predatory or adversarial position with your customer is not productive. Your efforts should be aimed at becoming a valued asset to your customer. In helping facilitate your customer's business, you will be increasing your own. In order to be of help to the customer, you must first gain an understanding of the sales process from your customer's point of view. If your customer is successful, you will be successful.

I hope you will view this book as being like a trip to the grocery store. When you go grocery shopping, you don't put everything you find on the shelves into your cart. You pick and choose the items that suit you. I have tried to take a broad view and write for salespeople in a broad range of businesses and at various stages of their career. Take what you find helpful now. You can always come back and re-examine the answers as your career evolves.

This book is one I wish had been available when I was starting out my career in sales. Now that I am on the other side of the desk, I wish more of the salespeople who call on me would put into practice the ideas we have covered here. The answers in this book were hard-won, and I hope you will benefit from them and maybe avoid some of the mistakes we made.

Ultimately, only you can decide what kind of salesperson you want to be. I hope this book will arm you with the knowledge you need to put that decision into practice. Whether you are just getting started or have been in sales for years, there is always more to be learned and new perspectives from which to view things.

A Special Note from Series Editor, Jason Miletsky

Since about a week after graduating from Brandeis University in 1994, I've owned my own marketing and advertising agency. I started small, working out of my bedroom for the first few months before upgrading to a one-person office in one of those buildings where 30 or so sole proprietorships share a pool of receptionists and half a dozen conference rooms.

Those weren't easy years. I didn't know much about advertising (I was an Economics major) other than that I had always loved watching television commercials. And I knew even less about computers and graphic design at a time when the industry was shifting from drafting boards to the PC. But I had a daily routine: Get to the office by 8:00 a.m., call every number in the *Yellow Pages* to try to drum up any business I could, head out the door by 4:00 p.m. to wait tables so I could generate some cash until about midnight, head back to the office to teach myself Photoshop and Quark until about 3:00 a.m., and then back home for a few hours of sleep before doing it all again.

That went on for a long time. And all the while, I was selling. During the day, I cold-called anyone and everyone, looking for opportunities to get my foot in the door with any small project a company needed. At night, during my restaurant shifts, I'd let every customer I served know that I was trying to get my own company off the ground. Believe me, I played every card I could; I milked the "ambitious young guy struggling to start his own company" thing for as long as I could. When I finally persuaded someone to let me come in and make a presentation, I had to come up with sound rationale as to why they should let a kid just out of college (who had never even taken a marketing class) with no portfolio and no case studies handle the design of their business cards, much less any portion of the marketing efforts.

It was a pretty slow and arduous process, but I loved every minute of it. Selling was such a rush—I loved the challenge of it! I mean, what could be a bigger mountain to climb than starting with so much of the deck stacked against me and having to figure out a way to succeed? By nature, I believe that overcoming challenges is part of a salesperson's DNA—and the bigger the challenge, the better!

So I kept on selling, and apparently I was pretty good at it. As the years passed, my company started to grow, and I found myself taking up more than my share of the spotlight—at least among family and friends. I had published a few books on how to use Photoshop (all those late-night, self-help lessons paid off), was named by *NJBIZ* magazine as one of the "Top 40 Under 40" business people in New Jersey, and even found myself on the cover of *Entrepreneur* magazine one month. The sales efforts I made had, to a large extent, paid off.

Today, my agency, PFS Marketwyse, is consistently listed as one of the leading agencies in New Jersey, with clients including Hershey's, JVC, SecureHorizons, and others. Like any company, we've had some missteps and struggles along the way, but we've seen phenomenal growth and there's a lot for me to be proud of—especially the approach I've taken to sales and my efforts to bring in new business.

But what sometimes gets lost in all of that is how much of the credit I *don't* deserve. I didn't just wake up one day and discover that I was a good salesman; I grew up learning from an amazing teacher. My dad is without question one of the best salespeople I've ever known. He always has a story about something different he did to get a prospect's attention—a method he took to get an order that most others wouldn't have ever thought of. Most often, these involved something funny, witty—something that maybe even ran the risk of making a prospect or current customer stop dead in their tracks and say, "Are you nuts?"

My dad always finds a way to make it work. He knows when to play hardball in negotiations, when to back off and give a little, and how to get the most out of every sale. I remember going to his office, both as a little kid off from school for a day and as a college student working for his company during winter breaks, and seeing how well-respected he was. The owner of the company, other salespeople, engineers, the guys in the warehouse—hell, even the dude who worked in the sandwich truck parked outside every morning constantly told me what a great guy my dad is. I don't know if I've ever told him this, but it always made me feel proud of him.

Even more importantly, though, was the way he kept everything in perspective and had his priorities in order. Sure, he paid a lot of attention to his job. I often saw him at the kitchen table, working on orders at night after dinner, and business trips sometimes kept him away from home for a few days every month. But I don't remember any nights (other than when he was away on business, of course) when I was very little that he didn't read with me before I went to sleep or sit and play a board game with me when I got a little older. I don't think he ever missed one of my little-league games (it didn't seem to matter that I wasn't very good), high-school track meets, or college rugby matches. He found the right balance. In a profession that has been known to totally consume people and claim their identity, my dad never let it take him away from what was really important.

So much of my own success has come from lessons I've learned watching my dad. In fact, many of my early clients were through connections my dad made for me or companies he convinced to give me a try. Even his own company was an early client of mine. All these years later, my dad still tries to sell for me.

He frequently calls me after business trips to say he talked me up with some-one on an airplane who might need some marketing and that I should give the guy a call. Always selling, and always looking out for me.

When I developed the concept for the *Perspectives* series and decided that *Perspectives on Increasing Sales* would be among the first four titles, there was only one person I could think of to write the Sales Expert perspective. It's always been tough for me to say "thank you," to let my dad know that I'm proud of him, and to tell him how much respect I have for him as a salesman and as a father. Hopefully, giving him the chance to share his experiences in this book says it all.

Getting this series launched has been a rough and wild ride, and one of the best parts about it was getting the chance to work with my dad on this title. Great job, Pop! I'm proud of you.

I would of course be remiss if I failed to thank James Callander for being part of this book. His experiences as a purchasing agent (and as a salesperson) have been remarkable, and I believe the contributions he's made to this book will help give truly valuable insight to every reader. Many people don't realize it, but writing a book can be an extraordinarily difficult, time-consuming, and sometimes thankless process, and I appreciate James's commitment to turning in some excellent work in representing the Purchasing Agent perspective.

PART ONE

Getting Down to Basics

Q: WHAT DEFINES A GOOD SALESPERSON?

MARVIN MILETSKY
THE SALES PERSPECTIVE

At the outset of my sales career, something simply wasn't right. I was the entertainer among my friends, co-workers, and prospective clients—the one with enough charm and wit to make them do what I wanted. So why weren't they breaking down my door to do business with me?

For the life of me, I couldn't figure out what the problem was. After all, when you're the life of the party and the guy who always leaves 'em laughing, sales should be snap. This is a field for extroverts, and nobody has ever accused me of being shy. One day, it all became clear. I was in a meeting with a prospective client who just wasn't falling for my style. I was using my best material, positively pouring on the charm, but to no avail. During the meeting, the buyer said that he hadn't been able to find anyone to solve a problem for him, and that it didn't appear I'd be able to, either. This came as a total shock to me—*he didn't think I could do what he needed!*

Then it hit me: My approach to sales was completely wrong. Rather than listening to potential clients to find out what their needs really were, I had been selling on charm—and charm just wasn't enough. So I humbly admitted that I didn't understand what his problem was and asked him to explain it to me again. And I listened—*really* listened—to him this time. As he spoke about his dilemma, I realized that my company actually had something very near to what he needed. When the meeting was over, I went back to my office and asked for advice from my boss, my co-workers—anyone with more experience than I had who could shed some light on how to solve my prospect's problem. As it turned out, the solution was far simpler than I had expected.

This experience changed my whole approach to sales. I no longer went to customers to tell them my story; I went to understand theirs. I listened. I was inquisitive. I stopped selling products and started adding worth. I began to build relationships predicated upon value and loyalty. I stopped *tending* to accounts and started *servicing* them. I became part of a partnership focused on solving problems.

As I changed my approach, my customers changed their attitude. Slowly, over time, *they* started calling *me* instead of the other way around. They asked me to come in rather than me having to beg for an appointment. I made a commitment to them, and they rewarded my efforts by becoming lifelong partners.

That's what really defines being a good salesperson. Be charming and have fun, but don't let that get in the way of the real labor of work and understanding. Pledge yourself to your customers. Make their interests your interests, and revolve your service around their needs. Anyone can talk a big game, but good salespeople prove themselves through actions rather than words, and by listening when it really counts.

JAMES CALLANDER

THE CUSTOMER PERSPECTIVE

The variety of industries needing sales personnel is as varied as the types and styles of selling used today. The million-dollar question for anyone interested in selling products or services in any industry is this: What does it take to be a good salesperson? As a customer, I've worked with an uncountable number of salespeople over the years, and can very quickly distinguish the good from the bad and the ugly.

So…want to know what it takes? Here are a few key points:

- Clients need sales personnel to quickly provide answers to their questions, and a good salesperson must be able to react swiftly—and competently—to these requests. By "competently" I mean that their answers need to be correct and useful. Wrong answers don't do much of anything except waste our time.

- So many salespeople go through the motions of handling business without reviewing their proposals first. I know everyone is anxious to get proposals into the client, but good salespeople will take the time to ensure they conform to the client's actual request. Providing a price is great, but just about anyone can do that. And besides, lead times, shipping terms, and other factors are often equally (if not more) important to the client. Providing this type of detailed information up front usually indicates to customers that the salesperson has put real thought and effort into his work.

- Salespeople must be able to work with many different types of personalities, both in their own company and among their clients. Understanding personalities, and how a personality affects a person's decision-making process, is critical to success. Sales is a relationship business, and good salespeople are selling themselves as much as they're selling their company, products, and services.

- Most clients don't have time for long-winded conversations, so good salespeople are focused when working with them. Know what points you want to make before the conversation begins, and whether that conversation can happen over the phone or if it needs to be in person.

- No one makes it through a sales career without experiencing problems, conflicts, or disappointment with a sale. Too many times, salespeople run away from a problem. Don't be one of those people! We're counting on you to help us resolve issues and move on in a positive direction. It may not be pretty, and you may not find the perfect solution, but simply being there results in two things: Your customer will have a greater appreciation for you and your company, and your problem-resolution skills will develop, making you a more valuable resource.

- Follow up and follow through with your customers. Don't wait for us to call you to tell you about problems with an order; call us and ask how everything is. Customers want to deal with people who are ready to stand behind what they sell and will actively take the reins if problems need to be fixed.

- Salespeople must have thick skins. After all, they're likely to hear "no" more than "yes" in the course of selling. You must be able to handle rejection every day. Realize, though, that we're not necessarily saying no to you as a person; rather, we're most likely saying no to your product or to the service you're offering. Moreover, this "no" may well be due more to poor timing than anything else. Unless you're working retail, selling is seldom an instant-gratification proposition; the process takes time and patience. But you should always look for a customer's need; this enables you to pinpoint a product or service that will eventually turn a long serious of *nos* into a profitable *yes*.

Q: • How Much Does Personal • Appearance Matter?

Marvin Miletsky

The Sales Perspective

↳ Although I have, for the most part, always dressed conservatively, there was a time early in my career when I thought I could get away with dressing properly—but could dispense with wearing socks. My theory was that my pants would be long enough that no one would know. And that theory held—until I absently crossed my legs during a conversation. The customers I was with said nothing, but their eyes focused on my sockless ankles told a story of distaste. My appearance had compromised the content of my presentation.

It's not just me; I've made plenty of sales calls with associates who did not look the part of salespeople. One chose to wear his earring to a meeting, while yet another was dressed in his best business-casual attire but allowed a huge gold chain to stick out of his shirt. These proved to be distractions, as will other extremes in appearance.

The bottom line: Don't let your appearance compete with your message. You want your customer to remember the discussion held in your meeting, not that shirt with the buffalo on the back or the "Mom" tattoo on your forearm. Like it or not, we're often judged more by our packaging than by the contents inside. Ladies, your makeup and jewelry should be subdued. You're attending a meeting, not a dance club; that means no three inch–diameter hoops for earrings. Gentlemen, you should be clean-shaven, and if you're wearing a tie, it should not have been used as a bib during lunch. Nails should be clean, and teeth should be bright and shiny. Shoes should be polished. Socks and hose should be without holes. Also, trying to get your 36-inch waist into a 32-inch pair of pants is not a good approach. Finally, the briefcase, planner, or computer bag you carry should be as neat and organized as the rest of you.

These may sound like basic tenets—simple common sense, unworthy of mention in a book for true sales professionals. But considering how often these rules get broken, and how important they are to your career, each one is worth reading twice. We're a visual society, and how you appear will play a big role in how you sell.

JAMES CALLANDER

THE CUSTOMER PERSPECTIVE

Like it or not, people—including clients—judge others by how they look, how they talk, and how they interact. You want your client to be able to be open-minded and engaged in your meeting, not focused on what you are wearing. If I meet with a vendor who is dressed simply and neatly, then his or her appearance is a non-issue for me. The same holds true if the vendor is overdressed. But if a vendor shows up for a sales call and appears to have slept in his or her clothes the night before, this will affect my perception of that vendor. The last thing you need is for a client to find fault in your appearance; this will almost certainly lead to a less desirable outcome overall.

Many companies have a dress code, put in place to protect the company's image and to convey a level of professionalism to clients. Obviously, if your company has such a policy, it will give you some idea what is expected and what is tolerated (although it may not cover hairstyles, facial hair, etc.).

In addition to understanding your company's dress code, you should also attempt to get a sense of any dress codes to which your clients adhere. Although many industries are moving toward business-casual attire for their day-to-day operations, not all business is conducted in this fashion. There are plenty of businesses where a coat and tie is still a requirement, not an option, for any men on site. Knowing what your client requires of its employees will protect you from overdressing or underdressing when visiting their office.

> If you're not sure whether a client has a dress code, I would always recommend overdressing; you can always remove your jacket and tie if it turns out the client is more business casual. If, however, you've worn a golf shirt to a meeting where a jacket and tie is the norm, you'll find it a bit harder to adapt.

One more thing: In addition to affecting how others feel about you, your clothing selection can affect how you feel about yourself. Dressing well can pick you up, relax you, and make you feel good. Dressing poorly can have the opposite effect: bringing your down and creating a source of worry. Dressing for success, as they say, inspires self confidence, which helps guide how you conduct yourself throughout the day. If you are confident, you can rise above a tough issue or client, and provide a level of support that is equal to if not greater than what is required.

Q: • SHOULD YOU DRESS THE SAME AS YOUR CUSTOMER—I.E., FORMAL? CASUAL?

MARVIN MILETSKY

THE SALES PERSPECTIVE

Some time ago, I made a sales trip to Hawaii—only to get the brush-off from every person I attempted to see. While I'd never met these folks in person, I knew most of them through telephone contact—and in any case, I'd made appointments to visit with them in advance. Even my best customer gave me the cold shoulder, canceling a lunch appointment and claiming a personal problem had come up. Things went so poorly that near the end of the second day, I actually considered canceling the balance of the trip and returning home. Before making my decision, however, I knocked on the door of my best customer—the one with the "personal problem"—and asked for a moment of his time. I related my two-day experience and asked if he could identify anything I had done or said that might be the cause of my treatment—and was told point-blank that my dress was totally inappropriate for the territory. My suit, my starched white shirt and a tie, and my shined shoes were completely unacceptable on the island. He told me that if I want to call on the area, I would have to become part of it. Per his advice, I promptly went out and purchased Hawaiian shirts and comfortable slacks—and was greeted like a long-lost relative for the rest of the week. Even those who had been standoffish now welcomed me with open arms.

The fact is, there will be an industry norm that should govern your dress style. But within the industry, there will be individual companies with their own slant. While you should develop your own style that is acceptable across a great cross-section, you should also do your homework before visiting with any customer. This can be as simple as asking about the company's standards of dress when calling to confirm your meeting. In most businesses, styles lean toward conservative, so don't be too flashy. And remember that "business casual" does not mean "business sloppy!" The bottom line: Make sure you're remembered for the content of your meeting—not the way you dressed for it.

For more on this issue, refer to Question #2, "How Much Does Personal Appearance Matter?"

James Callander
The Customer Perspective

⮡ As I've mentioned, your appearance is important. People make assumptions about us based first on how we look, then on how we speak, and finally how we act. First impressions are, without a doubt, the most powerful; you only get one, so make it count.

Of course, how you choose to dress is up to you—but I'd argue that you should attempt to dress in sync with your client's standards or with the standards of your own company. Use your knowledge of your client and/or your own company as a barometer to guide you in how you should dress. Doing so will help you earn your client's acceptance. I wouldn't recommend, for example, showing up at your client wearing tennis shoes. Trust me: Even if they don't say anything about it, they will notice. And when they do, their attention will be diverted from your message and focused somewhere it doesn't belong: on your selection of clothing. Remember: You don't want to draw attention by what you're wearing; you want attention by what you're offering. Anything that detracts from your message or offering will hinder your ability to be successful.

> If a sales call involves a visit to a construction site or production floor, be sure to ask in advance what safety regulations apply. In some environments, high heels and neckties aren't just inappropriate; they're dangerous.

In recent years, business attire in some industries has shifted away from the more formal dress to business casual. While business casual may well be acceptable, I suspect there will still be times when a more formal approach is appropriate—for example, if you are attending an evening event such as a trade association meeting or an award ceremony. More formal dress might also be preferable if you are calling on a client where mixed dress is common and accepted—that is, some people wear business casual while others dress more formally. A level of observation and common sense is required when attempting to determine whether you are overdressed or underdressed.

The challenge here is when you have several sales calls on any given day, each one requiring a different style of dress. Indeed, you might need to change clothes for meetings with the same *company*. I once worked with a very large public utility with several departments—seemingly each with its own dress code. People working in service centers and power plants dressed in jeans or business-casual attire, while people in other departments—like engineering, purchasing, etc.—dressed in coats and ties. Salespeople calling on the company often changed their clothes according to which department was hosting the meeting they were attending. If I were a salesperson, I'd never be caught dead wearing jeans to a sales call, but I could easily have handled the business-casual wardrobe that meetings with service-center and power-plant employees called for. And I would always have put on a coat and tie when meeting with people in engineering and purchasing. Could a salesperson have shown up at a power plant or service center with a coat and tie? Sure, but it might have made the client uncomfortable. The same might be true if he or she showed up in business casual when the right selection would be coat and tie—indeed, the client might actually become less interested in what the salesperson was there to discuss.

Prepare yourself for any dress-related eventuality by keeping a few clothing and footwear options in your vehicle.

Q: • IS THERE SUCH A THING AS 9 TO 5?
• DO VACATIONS REALLY EXIST?

MARVIN MILETSKY
THE SALES PERSPECTIVE

Part of the commitment I make to my customers is to take care of their needs. That commitment is unconditional, and it goes beyond their need for my product or service; it encompasses their need for my time, whenever that may be. Your customers will expect you to be on call at all times to provide the information and services they need—just as they themselves are perpetually on call for their own customers. You are your customers' lifeline for satisfying *their* clients, and that means making yourself available 24/7.

To a certain extent, you become your customers' employee. Their successes become yours...but so do their issues. This explains why I've received frantic calls from customers at 3:00 a.m. on a Saturday, Christmas Day, within hours of my departure for a long-awaited vacation. Unfortunately, emergencies don't punch time clocks, and they don't care whose plans they upset.

Of course, you do have the right to some free time. Sales work can be hard, time-consuming, and stressful, and it's important to give yourself a little downtime. You earn your vacation and deserve your nights and weekends off. So can you do both? Can you be there for your clients at all times and still take time for yourself? Sure. Try to anticipate your clients' needs when you're going to be away. Give them plenty of advance notice so they can plan around your vacation. Introduce them, in person, to someone within your organization whom they can talk to in your place. Get that person up to speed with your project so he or she can at least address some of the lesser issues. Don't feel threatened by the idea of sharing sensitive client info with your stand-in; your customers are *your* customers, and they won't be stolen from you. One more thing: Make it clear to your co-worker that you appreciate him or her stepping in for you, and ask that he or she keep notes or include you in all correspondence so you can be up to speed the moment you return to the real world.

Remember: No one cares about your customer the way you do. Be prepared to work at all hours, but don't be afraid to take some time for yourself. Just make sure you keep your BlackBerry at least as close as your sunscreen, just in case.

JAMES CALLANDER

THE CUSTOMER PERSPECTIVE

As a purchasing manager, I deal with multiple locations in various time zones throughout the United States. When it's the end of the business day on the east coast, it's only mid afternoon on the west coast. I need salespeople who can and want to serve me—and sometimes that means after 5 o'clock.

> Few salespeople can complete all of their tasks on a set schedule between the hours of 9 and 5. As communication methods (faxes, cell phones, e-mail, etc.) continue to evolve, salespeople are inundated with distractions and competing demands on their time. Learning to manage your time is not only key to success—it is a matter of survival.

Your customer's perception of you as the one who is available when needed gives you an advantage over your competition. The fact is, customers don't always have the luxury of waiting around for salespeople to respond to their requests for support. For this reason, the salespeople customers trust for their key needs are the ones who are always available. Your customers might think you don't care about them if they can't get hold of you; can you afford for your customer to call your competitor for help after hours?

In order to succeed in sales, you must make yourself available for opportunities before or after hours, when and where it makes sense. For example, suppose a client wants to obtain training on new products or services that might enhance their business—but bringing staff together for such training during business hours is impractical. In that case, the only option is to do the training before or after normal business hours. Even though the training must occur when you'd normally be "off the clock," you should take full advantage of such an opportunity. For one, some of those attending may well be staff who are not normally available to you, but who have influence in the decision-making process. And of course, demonstrating your flexibility to the client will increase your chances of being rewarded with the client's business in the future. Every client contact may be a new opportunity.

With respect to vacations: Everyone should enjoy their vacations. Vacations are a time when we can decompress and forget about work. But the fact is, business sometimes creeps in—especially when you've established yourself with a client and that client counts on you. Often, clients just don't have the luxury of waiting until you get back from your vacation to use your services. They must react to situations as they happen; not having options is not an option. As a purchasing agent, if I rely heavily on a salesperson for time-sensitive searches, or if I don't have any other contacts at the salesperson's company (or if the contact I *do* have doesn't return my calls), and if the situation warrants it, I will contact my salesperson even if he or she is on vacation.

If you want to limit your exposure to business calls while on vacation, I suggest making arrangements with others within your company who can help deal with your clients while you are out. Also, make it a point to touch base with your clients prior to vacation and attempt to uncover any upcoming needs that you can take care of ahead of time or arrange for others to handle—the goal being to prepare your clients, your company's support staff, and yourself for your time off.

Q: HOW IMPORTANT IS IT FOR SALESPEOPLE TO REALLY BELIEVE IN THE PRODUCT OR SERVICE THEY ARE SELLING?

MARVIN MILETSKY

THE SALES PERSPECTIVE

Imagine two people standing in front of a bowling alley, each trying to persuade passers-by to come inside and hit the lanes. One guy clearly couldn't care less. He's not into bowling; this is just a part-time job he's taken to fill gaps. In a monotone, passionless voice, he tells anyone willing to listen that they'll get to stand in shoes that a dozen other people have worn that day, pick up a heavy ball, roll it down a lane, and knock over a bunch of distant pins, only to have a machine set them up again—10 times in a row. Sounds like fun, huh? The other guy, though, is a career bowler. He's loved the sport since he was a kid. He actively pulls people in and excitedly describes the precision of lining up the ball just right, the tension as it rushes down the lane, and the exhilaration as it crashes into the pins and sends them flying into the air. Now, who do you think is going to bring in more people?

Believing in your product is fundamental to the art of salesmanship. If you don't have faith in what you're selling, you won't end up having much of anything at all. Case in point: My company used to manufacture a product that was far inferior to one manufactured by our competitor. Even so, because I was more interested in satisfying my need for an order than in meeting the needs of my customer, I made every effort to convince one client that my product was the one he should buy. No doubt my delivery was shallow and unconvincing; the net result was that I lost the order, and the customer lost a little of the faith he had in me.

That said, there are instances when believing in the thing you're selling isn't imperative. I recently attended an auction, where I observed the auctioneer barking his encouragement to the audience to up their bids. Clearly, he had no real commitment to the items he was selling; I doubt he knew much about them at all. But he correctly assumed that his customers had knowledge of the items and had already decided what they wanted to buy before they had even arrived.

The auctioneer's obligation was to the sale, not to salesmanship, and in this scenario, that works. Unfortunately, however, most salespeople are not in the same position as the auctioneer. Complete disassociation with the product they're selling can be debilitating.

JAMES CALLANDER

THE CUSTOMER PERSPECTIVE

Salespeople who don't believe in what they sell will find themselves drifting aimlessly on the Seas of What Could Have Been. Your ability to convince a customer that your product or service is something he or she needs is married to your conviction in what you are selling. After all, why should we believe in a company if its own representation doesn't appear to believe in it? Indeed, your belief in your product or service is the very thing that allows you to convince us that you can meet our needs.

All too often, however, the opposite is true. The salesperson on the other end of the line seems to be barely paying attention. He or she hesitates when asked to provide support and struggles to demonstrate even minimal interest in what he or she is selling. In contrast, energetic salespeople who make the customer feel like there is really something special about their product or service have the advantage. Their smile and confidence—in themselves and in their product—is evident, even if only through their voice on the phone.

> The sad fact is, far too many salespeople simply go through the motions—and have little to show for their efforts. They become nothing more than a quote service their customers use to establish a competitive bid. Don't allow this to happen to you! If you want to be successful, you need to be diligent in following up with your customers after you've submitted your proposal information. If you are not awarded a contract or purchase order, you must determine whether the customer's decision was based on cost or something else. This allows you to make adjustments in an attempt to win the business. The business isn't lost until the order is actually placed!

That said, believing in your product or service is not enough to win your customer over. You must understand what you are selling and be able to translate your belief in your product or service into something your customer recognizes as valuable. If, for example, you know your product or service inside and out and can provide customers with information that can save them money or help their business become more efficient, you'll get their attention.

Once you've proven you know your stuff, and the belief in what you are selling is substantiated by the quality of the product or service, a salesperson can advance the sales process by asking the customer questions geared toward identifying the areas in which he or she can utilize the offering. Don't get overexcited and ask rapid fire questions; pause between questions and allow the customer to talk. (Believe me, you will never learn anything from your customer if you do all the talking.) Your patience will pay dividends when customers give you the opportunity to provide a tailor-made solution to address their needs, enabling you to meet or exceed their expectations.

Do you believe in your product or service? You'd better, if you want to succeed. When your customers call, you want to give them more than they expect: You want to give them hope. Customers always turn to someone they can count on to deliver, someone they trust to get the job done, when the situation calls for immediate action. Failure to believe in your product or service will deny you a place on that short list of vendors. The belief in your offering, combined with product knowledge and the art of listening, will ensure success throughout your sales career.

Q: • What Is the Importance of Learning
• the Product You Are Going to Sell?

Marvin Miletsky

The Sales Perspective

↳   You wouldn't try to teach someone to drive a car if you've never taken the wheel; how can you expect to convey to your customer how great your product is if you have no knowledge of what you're selling? Trying to sell a product without understanding it will almost certainly doom you to failure. It's essential that you learn all that you can about the products, how they're used, and for what purpose.

Here are some tips for gaining insight into your products:

- If your company offers formal training in the product, make the most of it. Pay attention and take plenty of notes. Be curious. Be attentive. If something doesn't make sense to you, ask for an explanation.

- If your company does not have a formal training program (and most companies don't), seek out those within your company with more experience for guidance.

- Learn where and how to use the product yourself. Touch it. Work with it. Play with it.

- Seek out the person who prepares the product for sale, be it the shop foreman, the baker, the programmer, or the designer. Let them show you how it is made.

- Arrange to see your product in use, and whoever is using the product for his or her reaction to it. You'll find lots of end users who take pride in what they do and are more than willing to talk about their experience.

Your customers are not the expert in your product; you are. They will look to you to guide them. They will ask questions about the products, and expect you to know the answers. That said, you are not the producer or designer of the product. Don't overstep by trying to get into areas best left to company experts.

They can back you up on those more difficult questions whose answers you cannot be expected to know.

JAMES CALLANDER

THE CUSTOMER PERSPECTIVE

I realize my perspective is supposed to be the customer perspective, but I also used to work as a salesperson, and one of my experiences during that period in my career offers a perfect example to illustrate my answer to this question, so I'm going to bend the rules here by sharing it with you.

Years ago, when I was first starting out in sales with GE, I found myself constantly providing quotes for industrial pushbuttons used to start and stop large pieces of equipment. My knowledge was limited to what appeared in the GE control catalog as reference. I didn't know the right questions to ask or whether I was offering exactly what my customers needed. Realizing my shortcomings, I committed myself to learning how to build up a pushbutton from a variety of parts, allowing me to create exactly what any customer needed. In time, I was able to handle my customers' requests quickly by asking the right questions and knowing the parts required for the desired product. The benefit to my customers was clear: They had someone they knew could handle their request quickly and efficiently. As a result, we were able to significantly grow our control business for many years.

When you first start out in sales, you will usually have limited knowledge of the products or services you're attempting to sell. If your knowledge of these products and services is lacking, you'll miss things you need to know in order to get things right. You will constantly second-guess yourself as to whether what you provided was what was required. You might see opportunities to support a client with your company's offerings but lack the knowledge of those offering to convey the benefits. It's imperative that you educate yourself on your product or service offerings in order to provide value to your customers. Once you become familiar with your product or service, the burden in sales shifts to your actual selling skills.

Ask management for factory training, if available, to increase your technical comprehension—a real advantage when selling.

In addition to product knowledge, you must also have knowledge of your customer base. Your time—and that of your customer—is too valuable to be wasted on attempts to sell items the customer can't use. Study your clients. Ask yourself these questions:

- Who is my client?

- What does my client do?

- Who does my client serve?

Being familiar with your clients' business will help you determine what products or services you can offer that would benefit them. Join product knowledge and an understanding of your client base with your experience in sales to round out the package.

Your willingness to learn all you can about the product or service you are selling is the first important step in the selling cycle, and will pay dividends for years to come. Indeed, the full importance of that knowledge may not be evident until much later in your sales career. At the end of your career, when you look back on your years of selling, you will begin to appreciate how many times the training you took was used.

Q: TRUE OR FALSE: THERE'S NO SUCH THING AS A STUPID QUESTION.

MARVIN MILETSKY

THE SALES PERSPECTIVE

The answer is *true*. There is no such thing as a stupid question. What *is* stupid is having a question—no matter how dumb you think it is—and not asking it. Everything being discussed must be 100 percent clear to all involved; this protects the buyer and seller alike. Make sure you ask the "stupid" questions and encourage all others to do so as well.

I once attended a meeting that was way over my head from a technical standpoint. After it was over, I shyly asked the technical representative who was with me if he could explain what had been discussed. He looked me straight in the eye and admitted that, although he understood most of the discussion we'd had with the customer, he, too, had gotten lost at some point. I asked how he planned to handle the response that was due by the end of the week, given that he, too, didn't fully understand the discussion; he said he'd talk to various people in our office to see if they could shed some light on the subject. Wow, what an opportunity lost! We were with the very people who could have answered all our questions—the customer—and we let our egos to get in our way rather than admit that we needed help.

There will be times when interacting with a customer or co-worker that whatever he or she is saying just doesn't make any sense to you. Of course, you don't want to be seen as incompetent—which is why you may not feel comfortable asking a simple question. But if you just speak up about your confusion, you'll almost certainly find that others will chime in to voice theirs as well. Otherwise, there's a good chance you'll enter into a contract only to realize that your concept of the project differed considerably from what the client really wanted. Amazing what a simple and stupid question can prevent.

You aren't the only one who might be afraid to ask a question for fear that it's a stupid one; your customers, too, feel this anxiety. Make it a point to carefully study your customers' faces and eyes to try to determine whether they, too, are clear with everything being discussed. Don't allow them to ever feel like a question is too stupid to ask. Be ready to go back to the basics if you have to. No one knows everything, and the stupidest thing anyone can do is remain confused from fear of asking a question.

JAMES CALLANDER
THE CUSTOMER PERSPECTIVE

In my view, there are only two stupid questions: the one you don't ask, and the one you ask but don't allow me to answer.

Many times over the years, I've seen salespeople—especially less-seasoned ones—fumble asking a question, clearly nervous about whether the question will be perceived as stupid. If you're just starting out in sales, you may be more apt to hold back on questions, worried that you might be looked down on by your customer. My advice? Don't get wrapped up in whether the client will think less of you if you ask what you perceive as a stupid question. As a customer, I would rather you ask me a question and get the information you need than find out later you *didn't* ask a question that you should have asked to better understand my expectations of you and your product or service. Besides, customers don't always volunteer information, but if you ask them directly, they may provide you with information that will prove highly useful to you.

> If you ask a question and the customer answers by saying "I can't divulge that information," don't ask the question again, even if you word it differently. If you do, your customer will likely perceive you as badgering, and will begin to shut down—and once a client begins to shut down, the conversation is pretty much over. Unless you're looking for an early exit, don't persist with a line of questioning if your client has indicated he or she can't or won't answer your question.

If you do embolden yourself to ask a question, be certain you listen to the answer. All too often, in their haste to continue asking questions, salespeople break into the conversation, disrupting the client and losing any chance of obtaining information they might have gained had they allowed the client to finish. Listening—*really* listening—takes practice and discipline, but it is critical if you want to be successful at any level in sales.

Clients don't always know exactly what information you need beyond what they have provided in their initial inquiry; asking questions vastly increases your chances of uncovering useful information. For this reason, you should prepare questions before your conversation. Make it a point to avoid closed-ended questions—that is, questions requiring only a yes/no answer. These should be used for clarification purposes only. Instead, emphasize open-ended questions—that is, questions that allow the client to expound during his or her answer. You can then use the information you glean to develop follow-up questions or in subsequent conversations. This approach enables you to gather a greater amount of information; the end result is, you're in a better position to provide a solution tailored to your client's needs, thereby maximizing your chances of obtaining an order.

Q: HOW IMPORTANT IS IT TO JOKE AROUND AND HAVE A SENSE OF HUMOR WHEN ENGAGING A CLIENT?

MARVIN MILETSKY

THE SALES PERSPECTIVE

Salespeople must develop their own style of interaction with customers. We are who we are, and we can't tailor our personalities to each customer. But chances are that if you're in sales, you probably have an outgoing and friendly personality to begin with—and humor is most likely a component of that.

The use of humor has worked well for me over the years. It's an icebreaker and a door opener. Still, as with anything in life, timing is everything (deep, huh?). You should identify your counterpart's mood from the beginning before launching into some kind of stand-up routine. That bright welcoming smile and the friendly direction for you to take a seat likely indicate that you can relax a bit and inject some humor at the proper time.

That said, you should be sure to use the sense of humor you have—not one you're experimenting with. Case in point: Years ago, before I had my own office, my desk was in a bullpen area shared by everyone in the inside sales department. Naturally, considering that I'm hardly a soft-spoken individual, everyone in the area could hear me on the phone. One day, a client called me to place an order. Over the years, he and I had had gotten to know each other very well and maintained an open, friendly, and often humorous relationship. Playfully, I thanked him for his order, but told him that our factory was tired and needed a break. He'd either have to call back next week or place his order with our competitor. After some more silly back-and-forth banter, I "relented," and took his order. The next day, I received a call from one of our best, most loyal customers. It seemed he had tried to place an order that morning with one of our inside salespeople and was told in no uncertain terms that the salesperson was sorry, but our factory was too busy. Could he try elsewhere? Apparently, the inside salesperson had overheard my conversation the day before, and decided that that approach would work for him as well. Needless to say, it didn't.

The moral to my story is simple: Use the personality you were given. Don't be afraid to use humor as a tool, but be sure your timing is right and your audience accepting.

JAMES CALLANDER

THE CUSTOMER PERSPECTIVE

↳ My friend Shelby Black—whom I have come to admire over the years and for whom I have the greatest respect—is a terrific salesperson. A key tool in Shelby's selling arsenal is an extensive collection of jokes and funny stories, ready at a moment's notice. On many occasions, I've watched him launch into a string of amusing anecdotes, putting smiles on the faces of everyone within listening distance. But more importantly, I've then watched Shelby switch back to the business at hand without missing a beat. Shelby uses humor to break the ice with a customer, boosting the mood during an appointment and bringing down the client's guard, which enables him to better get across his *real* message—the value of his product.

Although not everyone has the gift of humor in abundance like Shelby, I do believe we can all use humor—or, for that matter, discussions of sports or current events—in conducting business to some degree. This approach can serve as a way to forge a bond with your client. The trick is knowing *when* to use humor. Negotiating a complex contract, for example, probably doesn't lend itself well to joking around. Before you launch into a joke or funny story, you should gauge your client's mood and calibrate your use of humor accordingly. If the client's mood is friendly and inviting, you should be able to use humor during your visit. The opposite holds true if you notice tension or if the client is fidgety. Remember, too, that no two meetings with a client are ever the same; what worked last time may not be effective the next time you meet. And you should *never* employ humor when first attempting to establish a relationship with a client; being anything but professional may hurt your chances of earning that client's business. After you've proven to that client that you can deliver and your relationship with that client takes hold, you may find opportunities to be less formal.

Even if you have established a good rapport with a customer, you should avoid overdoing the humor. Don't make it the entire basis of a sales call. Otherwise, even if both you and your client enjoy the exchange, he or she may be less inclined to meet with you in the future, believing that only more of the same is in store. Instead, use humor in moderation. A good strategy is to employ humor at the beginning or end of your conversation only—and even then allow the client to dictate the extent of it. And as always, be ready to switch from humor to your actual message at any given moment.

Q: WHICH IS A MORE POWERFUL SALES TOOL: CONFIDENCE OR HUMILITY? IS ENTHUSIASM IMPORTANT?

MARVIN MILETSKY
THE SALES PERSPECTIVE

You bet your ass enthusiasm is important! It's also contagious. It's the joy you experience being with your customer, the satisfaction you feel when *they* call *you* rather than the other way around, the smile you get from your customer upon your arrival. Enthusiasm is also confidence—the confidence in your knowledge of your product and service, and that by doing right by your customer, you are doing right by your company.

However, there's such a thing as too much confidence; some salespeople cross the line from healthy confidence and enthusiasm to just plain obnoxious—and if you cross that line, you can be certain that *no one* will want to do business with you. I remember an instance when, trying to schedule a speaker for a luncheon I was planning, I contacted an agent—essentially, the speaker's sales representative. It took a week of repeated phone calls just to get him to call me back—and when he did, his attitude was beyond confident, crossing that line into being obnoxious. Needless to say, my tolerance for this unprofessional individual quickly met its end. As there were other speakers with representatives who were professional, enthusiastic, cooperative, and accommodating, I was happy to take my business elsewhere. Just to be clear: "Obnoxious" is probably not an adjective you want clients to use when describing you.

On the other end of the spectrum is humility—also not an effective trait in sales. Yes, humility is pleasant. It has its place. But if it's part of your nature, it should be put to the rear. You're in sales. Your business card doesn't say "wishy-washy." You are a leader—the person who starts all the gears moving between your customer and your company. Being shy and humble doesn't work! Controlled enthusiasm coupled with a professional air will always trump humility.

JAMES CALLANDER
THE CUSTOMER PERSPECTIVE

┗ Confidence is your friend when you are attempting to communicate your ability to be of service to your clients. Confidence in your products and services, as well as in your company's ability to not just meet a client's needs but exceed them, is a powerful tool. You just won't make a good impression with a docile demeanor—especially if you are trying to get my business. But you should be ready to back up that confidence with real results when your client decides to offer you a piece of the pie. As for enthusiasm, by itself it is empty. You may be able to use it to gain momentum, but eventually you need something more. Enthusiasm lacks direction. But if you have both enthusiasm and confidence, then you can channel the energy into action. Most salespeople who schedule a visit with me are enthusiastic or at least appear to be, but direction, focus, and the ability to communicate are what makes them successful selling to my company.

Once a salesman I knew called on a large OEM (original equipment manufacturer) for the boating industry. The company used hundreds of products each day on its production line, which was housed in several large warehouses. The account, if he could secure it, would easily pull in $100,000 annually. After his appointment with the director of purchasing, during which the director politely reviewed the pamphlets my colleague had brought and asked a few questions— my colleague barely managed to allow the director to finish each question before he verbally pounced with his answer—he gave my colleague a tour of the main production facility. As they strolled past rows of workers assembling parts, my colleague was amazed at the variety of materials they used. As they wound their way back to the director's office, my colleague expressed a hearty interest in providing parts for their assembly, confident he could meet their needs.

Later that week, my colleague received a very large package from the director of the company. Inside was a request to quote for almost every item they purchase. The list of items topped 300 pages, with multiple items on each page. At first, he was elated! What a golden opportunity to significantly increase his sales! But after three weeks of attempting to cross over the parts they needed to ones he handled, my colleague realized he was only halfway through the list. And after four weeks, he realized he was over his head.

He set up an appointment with the director and, with his tail between his legs, he confessed that he wasn't able to provide all the parts the director had sent him to quote. Naturally, the director was disappointed. My colleague's over-confidence had set up the director—and my colleague—for a big letdown. And while my colleague could have easily walked out of that appointment with nothing to show for his efforts but defeat, the director kindly gave him an opportunity to produce a smaller package. (My colleague went on to support the company in this more limited capacity for many years.) Needless to say, my colleague never again overcommitted.

Confidence with empty promises won't give you a second chance when you are trying to establish yourself. If you can't deliver, you might as well not even attempt to gain someone's business. Confidence by itself is simply boasting—and there is little if any room for boasting in business. Temper your confidence with a dose of humility.

Q: SHOULD SALESPEOPLE BE THEMSELVES OR REFLECT THE PERSONALITY OF THE CUSTOMER?

MARVIN MILETSKY

THE SALES PERSPECTIVE

The commitment that you make to your customers is to service their needs by fulfilling your promises and satisfying your contractual obligations. It's not to present a personality that's perfectly in line with their own. Don't try to be someone you're not. Be yourself. You can't change who you are for each account, and you shouldn't bother trying. Trying to reflect your customer's persona will result in simply canceling each other out. Besides, in a world of changing client personalities, you need to be the "constant" everyone can count on.

Of course, staying true to yourself doesn't mean there isn't room for minor adjustments when dealing with various types of personalities. No two people you'll ever deal with, even within the same company, will be exactly alike. Some customers are timid, while others are outgoing and personable. Still others are aggressive or so egotistical they believe they can do no wrong. And of course everyone has habits, behaviors, mannerisms, likes, and dislikes that individualize each of them. Success in obtaining orders and building long-term relationships will stem from your understanding of the people you deal with and your ability to adjust accordingly. In each case, and for each customer, quickly assess your counterpart's personality and make a few minor modifications to your own.

There are ways to fine tune your personality without losing sight of who you are. Not interested in baseball? Then listen attentively while your customer talks excitedly about whatever team he's into. But don't do much more than listen—your client will quickly see through any attempts to pretend you're also a fan and see it as an obvious lie. If your customer is more of an introvert, then just tone down the enthusiasm a bit—without losing the outgoing personality that got you in the door in the first place. Find the balance. Adjust to your customer, but always be yourself.

James Callander
The Customer Perspective

⌐→   Your personality—who you are—is on display whenever you interact with others in your business or personal life. Right or wrong, people, clients included, will judge you based on how you act.

If you have a strong or overbearing personality, I strongly urge you to leave it at your client's door. Also, keep your emotions in check when dealing with your clients. You are there to help us make purchasing decisions; as such, you should *guide* the customer, displaying your thoughtful understanding of our needs in order to show how much better off he or she will be utilizing your company. A calm, relaxed approach is best in all communications—whether written or verbal. Just about any customer will respond better to a salesperson who can communicate reasonably and thoughtfully without losing his or her cool or becoming pushy; no client wants to be forced or pressured into making a decision.

Your client, and the atmosphere within the client's organization, should dictate your demeanor. Be observant, noting the office décor and the employees' attire. In the first few minutes of an appointment, evaluate your client's manner; this will help you chart the direction of your conversation. No two meetings will ever be the same. Even meetings with the same person can be varied; you should be aware of this and ready to act accordingly. But the goal should always be the same: Get your message heard.

You will encounter many personality types during your sales career, and you must learn to cater to each in your own way. Some customers will be more personable—open and friendly. Others will be direct and to the point. Still others will be difficult to read. When selling your products and services, you are looking to benefit from your client—but first you must find the best way to connect and communicate with us. Depending on your client's personality, you might need to be very straightforward and direct, or you might need to spend a little time socializing.

In addition to assessing your client's demeanor, take a moment to assess his or her work environment. Does it have an open layout, with cubicles? Or are there separate offices for the majority of personnel? Open offices require you to be mindful of others sitting nearby; your conversation can easily be overheard. In such situations, you must be aware both of your wording and of your volume. Monitor your conversations to ensure nothing being discussed can be overheard and misinterpreted by others. The same goes for phone calls, especially if your client uses a speakerphone. You have no idea who else might be privy to your conversation.

Q: HOW IMPORTANT IS HAVING A COLLEGE EDUCATION TO BEING A SUCCESSFUL SALESPERSON?

MARVIN MILETSKY
THE SALES PERSPECTIVE

I wish I could tell you that your formal education is a sure-fire guarantee of sales success, but I can't. A formal education has its advantages in opening doors for you, especially as you seek your first positions. The written and oral communication skills that you're likely to develop in school might give you a certain polish that will get you through the interview process, but it won't necessarily give you more of an edge when it comes to finding, dealing, servicing, and negotiating with clients.

The best lessons I've learned have come by just being out there in the trenches. They've come from the closed doors I had to pry open. They've come from sitting face to face with a potential client who's less busy listening to what I have to say and more busy making a hasty judgment about me, and finding a way to change his perception. I've had to win over the buyer who had a long-term relationship with a competitor and was not really interested in pursuing a new vendor. I've had to learn from the orders I've completely fouled up. The most painful lessons came when I've had to go back to a customer with my tail between my legs to save an account. These are the things that a life in sales will teach you how to handle, that a lecture in a classroom simply can't come close to. Work will become your classroom. Co-workers and clients will become your best teachers.

Learn what you can for as long as you can from wherever you're able. But while the thirst for knowledge is a good thing, never forget that it's your customers and your everyday interaction with them that will ultimately shape your education. Use every success and failure as a building block toward your ultimate goal of understanding how to travel down your chosen course.

Ultimately, the difference between success and failure will be the conviction in your voice and the confident look on your face—not the facts and figures up on a chalkboard. Your belief in your product tells the story. Following up and taking care of problems in a speedy and professional manner will set you apart from the other salespeople with whom you'll compete—and no diploma will help you improve these skills.

James Callander
The Customer Perspective

As a purchasing manager, I am called on by a variety of sales personnel. Among them are salespeople who have no formal education. They're typically capable in their field of expertise and provide a suitable level of support. I also receive calls from sales personnel who *do* have formal educations—and find that their sales skills are basically the same as those without a formal education. I trust some salespeople with important service needs, and others I don't—but the trust (or lack thereof) isn't based on the person's formal education. Rather, it is based on his or her ability to make good decisions, provide timely responses to my questions, follow up after the sale, and generally be effective during the sales process.

Some might argue that a college education is a requirement for being a successful salesperson. Clearly, it can be advantageous to have a college degree—not just to you, but also to your employer and your clients. This is especially true of individuals who study a specialized subject and then graduate to work within that field. For example, some types of sales might require a high degree of technical expertise, and a formal education in that particular technical area is almost a necessity.

I've noticed, though, that very few salespeople with college degrees actually end up working in a field related to their studies in college. That's not to say their formal education didn't prepare them for the job they're doing; many would argue that the simple act of acquiring a formal education better prepares people to integrate into business of any kind. The flip side of that argument, however, is the suggestion that a person can learn a lot of what he or she needs to know to succeed in while on the job and not necessarily in the classroom. This is especially true in sales.

Can you succeed without a degree or specific training? Absolutely, but the truth is that the road is much steeper and more difficult. Many companies only accept people with a college education, and those that hire people without one do so with care. But if you're willing to learn and are self-motivated, you can succeed even if you don't have a formal education. Setting goals and looking for individuals you can use as role models are essential to this process. Finding a mentor who can inspire and counsel you in your quest to become a successful salesperson is a bonus to anyone, but it is critical for someone lacking a formal education.

Is a formal education important to being a good salesperson? It might be helpful, may be a requirement for employment, and could prove essential when selling products requiring technical knowledge. Nevertheless, a highly motivated, goal-focused person is more than capable of performing well in the field of sales regardless of whether he or she holds a formal degree.

Q: CAN A PERSON TRAINED IN ONE AREA BE SUCCESSFUL IN SALES; FOR EXAMPLE, CAN A CONSTRUCTION WORKER SELL CONSTRUCTION SUPPLIES?

MARVIN MILETSKY

THE SALES PERSPECTIVE

There's really nothing in this world you can't accomplish—and that includes changing your career 180 degrees. If you're a construction worker who wants to sell construction supplies, go for it. But understand that you must learn new skills and develop a mindset that is quite different from the one you're used to. Not many people can make the transition from catcher to pitcher—and those who can typically can't do so overnight.

Imagine two people facing each other, told to look to their right. When they do, they find themselves looking in opposite directions. So it is with buyers and sellers; their viewpoints come from two totally different directions. Changing positions requires a change in viewpoint. You must recognize that you are on the other side of the table.

Your personality must go from passive to aggressive. You cannot be tentative. You must be the leader in meetings, the dynamic individual sought by others to provide the answers—and those answers must reflect your newfound responsibility: selling. You must represent your product in the most positive light possible—even if, in your past life, you liked another one better. You don't represent that other company; suggesting that product will not turn a profit for your company or you. If you venture into sales, choose a company whose products you're familiar with and have faith in.

Think about positive work experiences you had before making the transition to sales. What was it about the products you used that you liked? What was it about the salespeople who called on you that motivated you to work with them? What about them made you want to seek out their competitor? Take the best of what you experienced and apply it to your own advantage—and at the same time, remember the worst, taking care to avoid repeating others' mistakes.

Not everyone can make the transition to sales. Not everyone has the personality or inner drive. If you want to succeed, you must take the time to learn what it means to be in sales and to understand—*really* understand—what salespeople do. Don't make the mistake of underestimating the job; there is far more to selling than might meet the eye. You don't just wake up one morning and take this on; you must open your mind to a new direction, redirecting your loyalty in kind. Your background got you to this point, but you'll need a special kind of drive to take you to this new frontier.

JAMES CALLANDER

THE CUSTOMER PERSPECTIVE

Over the years, I've seen many people switch to jobs completely outside their previous work. I've even seen people join the sales ranks who were so far removed from my industry, I wondered if they were just looking for any job they could find. While some seemed unable to connect in their new role and subsequently moved on, others were quite successful.

> I'm not trying to discourage anyone from making a change to sales from a background in a different field, but I do think there is usually a connection between the businesses that provides a platform for the change.

Those who found success were able to make the transition and learn the ropes of their new field. They were eager to learn from their peers. They were motivated to develop the skills necessary to be successful. Whether you come from a similar industry, other areas of sales, or some other form of work altogether, your life experiences will help prepare you to some degree for a sales career, but life experiences alone won't make you a good salesperson; you need to apply yourself to learning all you can about your offerings, your clients, and their business.

I have a niece, Mara, who made the shift to sales from engineering. She started out in the engineering department of a company that designed prosthetic devices. She was well educated and prepared to enter this particular field right out of college. Even though she started out in engineering, and her company's sales manager wasn't sure she had the qualifications to succeed, it turned out Mara's personality was well suited for multilevel selling. She was able to bridge her knowledge of design and engineering to help her company better meet customers' needs. This ability to communicate with upper management, sales, and engineering enabled Mara to enjoy a very successful sales career. Much of Mara's success was achieved through technical selling to her clients—one area where I believe a formal education does help prepare people to sell products or services. Those with highly specialized training can effectively match the needs of their clients with the solutions available. Mara was able to bring her training and experience in the field of prosthetic engineering directly to those who could use it best: her clients.

Not everyone is suited to starting a sales career, perhaps even calling on their old business. Moving away from the perceived security associated with your current role requires a leap of faith.

Can a person trained in one area be successful in sales? Yes—provided he or she sufficiently motivated to be successful. No matter what the job description, a person must be self motivated and willing to put forth the effort required to learn and grow.

Q: Is Persistence Necessary or Annoying?

Marvin Miletsky
The Sales Perspective

Merriam Webster Dictionary defines "persistence" as "to go on stubbornly or resolutely in spite of opposition, importunity or warning to stop." By its very definition, persistence is a negative.

On the one hand, I want to tell you that whatever it takes to land an order is fair—including being persistent. But then I put myself in the place of the buyer, trying to envision my reaction to some salesperson who can't seem to accept that no means no. I'm afraid I can't say I'd be gentle with someone whose persistence made him a real pain in the ass!

Not every buyer is the same in body, mind, or spirit. Every buyer has his or her own different, distinct personality, and there is no single selling style that can be used with all. There is, however, a selling style that will almost certainly ensure failure: stubborn persistence. Look for signs from your customer that your persistence is starting to have a negative effect. The fact is that sometimes—and I hate to admit this—"no" actually does mean "no," and you'll need to be able to detect this. Otherwise, your persistence won't just hamper your ability to win over a customer in the short term; it will also affect your customer's perception of you for the future. Lose a battle, win a war.

While it's really not in a salesperson's personality to give up on any order, it's extremely important to learn how to read your customers' reactions and know when to walk away. Bring your level of persistence to the edge of where you feel you can do so safely, but know when to back off; it's the only way to ensure you'll live to present a new case to that client on some future day.

James Callander
The Customer Perspective

↳ Persistence is an important and necessary part of selling. Without persistence, many doors will stay closed, opportunities will be lost, and your confidence will sink. Put simply, the persistent salesperson is asking for business. Buyers are not just going to roll over and throw business at you; salespeople must ask for parts they know they can handle.

But there is a point at which persistence crosses the line from acceptable to annoying—and once you cross that line, you'll *never* be able to get that piece of business (unless your competitor totally muddles up the support). For example, if you get emotional or push repeatedly, there's a good chance you will cross this line. Beyond that, this line is not fixed. It is different for every person and varies depending on the situation. No salesperson can be successful if the client doesn't want to work with him or her; to be successful, salespeople must be able to assess where the line between acceptable and annoying is, and to ensure they don't cross it.

Obviously, the goal of any salesperson is to gain business, be it an order from a new client on which a relationship can be built or an increase in business from an existing relationship. If you are cold-calling a potential client in an attempt to obtain an appointment, it'll probably take a bit of persistence on your part to get past voicemail. But in following up, timing is important. You will be less annoying if you allow some time to pass between your efforts to make contact. A prospective client might not call back right away for any number of reasons; buyers are busy conducting their day-to-day business, and workloads vary from week to week. Keep the seed planted, but don't overwork the prospect. When dealing with a client you already support, you should have a better understanding of how to deal with their staff when attempting to uncover new opportunities for your business in different areas of the company.

Asking for the business is a skill that all salespeople must develop. Even if the answer is no, it is important to ask. A salesperson's persistence in asking serves to keep the subject in the forefront of the client's mind. As long as salespeople are professional and maintain control of themselves, clients shouldn't be too resistant to repeat requests.

Q: • IS IT OKAY TO STRETCH THE • TRUTH TO WIN AN ACCOUNT?

MARVIN MILETSKY

THE SALES PERSPECTIVE

What's your perspective on this question?
Let us know at PerspectivesOnSales.com.

↳ There's a major difference between stretching the truth and outright lying—and anyone who tells you that salespeople can be successful without stretching the truth a bit is, well, outright lying. And anyone who outright lies to sell *anything*—even the idea that salespeople never need to stretch the truth—will inevitably get caught in his or her own trap.

Case in point: A few years back, my organization was competing with another company—our only real competitor—for a large order for an item my company had manufactured for years. But suddenly, a third company arrived on the scene. Their sales manager bid for the work that we knew should be ours, telling the customer that although his company had never made the item before, their manufacturing department had created samples that had passed independent laboratory testing and were ready to be produced. He also offered much faster delivery at a substantially lower cost. The customer bought this guy's story, got what they wanted faster, and saved a bundle of cash. All was well with their world...until the bottom dropped out. It turned out the sales manager from the other company had outright lied. His company had neither produced nor tested any of these units. His scheme was to obtain the order first and then produce the product. Ultimately, the product they produced failed miserably. The buyer won the resulting court case, and we supplied our product as a replacement—and at a higher price than our original quote.

In the end, these bold sorts of lies will come back to haunt you more often than not. Salespeople live and die by their reputation, and nothing will tear down a reputation faster than getting caught in a lie. That being said, there will be times when a little manipulation of the truth is unavoidable. In a perfect world—one with no competition—it'd be great to tell the customer the truth at all times and let the chips fall where they may. But the world's not perfect. Competition does exist, and if the customer's decision comes down to some minor point, then stretching the truth is just a necessary part of sales survival.

Some people may argue that a lie is a lie, no matter how you look at it—that "stretching the truth" is merely a euphemism. But anyone who's read Dante's *Inferno* knows that hell has a lot of levels, and not all sins are equal. The difference between stretching the truth and outright lying is that stretching the truth retains some level of honesty, and can be explained away rather easily in the event you are questioned. For example, suppose a potential customer has already indicated that he's satisfied with your price, but he's concerned that you won't be able to deliver on time. He needs a sample in two weeks, and you know it probably won't be done in less than three; so, you tell your client that you're confident you can ship product in two weeks to obtain the order. If you end up shipping it late, it'd be fairly easy to provide a rational excuse to cover yourself—after all, you only have to buy yourself a little extra time. Besides, a good stretch of the truth can even serve as motivation: Tell the factory that story, and it's very possible they may speed things up and find a way to make good on your promise.

Of course, while embellishing the truth can be justified, a good salesperson knows when not to do it. The previous delivery scenario, for instance, becomes a much different story if the product is needed before Christmas for a holiday sale, but the delivery can't possibly arrive until after the new year.

Your need to stretch the truth will diminish over time as relationships with customers mature. You'll know their timelines and sensibilities, and be better able to anticipate their needs—allowing you to rely on pure honesty more often. But there will always be situations that force you to stretch the truth. Find the line between embellishment and lying, and use it judiciously.

JAMES CALLANDER
THE CUSTOMER PERSPECTIVE

I do not recommend stretching the truth to win an order or to attempt to impress a client. The relationship between the salesperson and the client is important, and must be managed carefully. Your customer relies on you to provide accurate information; your failure to do so jeopardizes that relationship. The fact is, your client has any number of choices when it comes to filling a need, of which you're only one.

Suppose a customer comes to you with a request that's both time sensitive and important to the purchasing agent and his organization. Your proposal quotes a price that is slightly higher than that of your competitor—but you've stretched the truth with respect to how quickly you can deliver the product, promising a lead time that is much faster than your competition's. The customer chooses to contract with you, paying more to receive the product in the specified timeframe.

You may think you are taking a calculated risk when you fudge the delivery time, but you have no control over how long it will take for your proposal to go through your client's purchasing organization. Any delays on this front will start a domino effect, making it that much more difficult for you to meet your client's deadline. And when the product doesn't show up when you said it would, the customer is going to hold you accountable for the delay. Not only will the amount of time you spend expediting, communicating your findings, and ultimately paying for premium freight cost you more in the long run, your customer will see through your excuses and possibly remove you from consideration for future sales opportunities.

From the customer's point of view, the success of any transaction is measured in direct dollars as well as in time lost in the event issues arise as a result of a purchase. If a customer's purchasing decision was based on truthful information, then those engaged in the decision-making process will bear the ill effect of a poor purchasing decision. If, however, the decision to procure a product or service from you or your company was based on information given in an untruthful or misleading manner, then you, too, will also be affected. Not only will any dividends connected to the sale be eroded, but your ability to conduct future business with the customer will disappear as well. You simply cannot afford for your image to take a hit by less-than-truthful comments or statements.

Besides, even without stretching the truth, issues will arise from missed deadlines, pricing errors, shipping delays, or damages. It happens—and you'll have to deal with the fallout. When you do, you'll want your client to trust you to resolve the issue quickly, honestly, and professionally. How can we trust if we've been lied to?

I recommend that you ground yourself in truth. Never put yourself in a position that raises a moral or ethical question. If you don't base your dealings on truthfulness, your chances of establishing and maintaining a solid customer base will be greatly reduced—if not eliminated completely. Is it okay to stretch the truth to win a sale? No! Wouldn't you rather be a person your customers trust—the one customers want to have handling their requests? I know that's the kind of salesperson that I want to work with.

Q: • Should Salespeople Sell • or Solve Problems?

MARVIN MILETSKY

THE SALES PERSPECTIVE

↳ If your product line is such that repeat orders just keep coming in without requiring any effort on your part—problem-solving or otherwise—then you're probably selling a commodity to a client whose needs are simple. In such cases, the need for problem solving is minimal—as is the need for your sales expertise. If a client needs an item in your regular product line—i.e., a standard item that requires no special effort to produce—he or she can easily visit your company's Web site to view your online catalog. It's written in plain English with lots of photos and drawings, clearly stated item numbers, and a precise index, making it easy for any client to find what he or she needs, with no help from you.

People who sell but don't get involved with problem solving are not salespeople; they're merely order takers whose positions become more tenuous as modern technology develops. Think about it: Many of these people could actually be replaced by answering machines *now*. Can you imagine what the future will bring? Try to balance selling with problem solving to provide more value for your clients and differentiate yourself from your competitors.

Determine what they're having problems with: Were they unable to obtain an item from a competitor? Did a vendor let them down by not delivering on time? Do they require samples or prototypes so they can further develop their own product line? Do they need 10 units of something that requires a minimum order quantity of 50? Do they need only $100 worth of goods, but your minimum billing is $500? And on and on and on.

Just know that solving many of these problems might take some imagination on your part. Don't be afraid to be creative. In the case where my company required a minimum order of $500 but the order was for only $100, I entered the order for the minimum amount required, but added instructions to ship only the first part, worth $100, right away and to ship the balance at a later date.

Then, as soon as the initial shipment went, I cancelled the balance. (Note to my current employer: Please do not read the previous advice. Note to all others: Read and learn.)

Problem solving has always opened doors with both new and existing customers for me. Anyone can take an order; it takes a salesperson to develop one. I find that if I can solve someone's problem, the orders start coming in—provided I actively solicit those orders after coming to someone's aid. The reward for your willingness to tackle the tough challenges comes in the form of steady business. (Well, usually. Once, after calling several of my competitors, a non-customer called me with a severe emergency. After I solved his very difficult problem, he thanked me, and promised to call us in the future—not to do business, but for help with his next emergency. I really had to educate him about what we wanted in return for our help: an opportunity.)

Throughout this book, we'll be discussing an important part of salesmanship: the art of listening. You have a wonderful opportunity to put your listening skills to work when your customer shares with you a problem that he or she sees on the horizon. (Remember, I'm talking about the *possibility* of a problem—not the reality of one.) Try to get as much information as you can—the time frame in which they might require goods or services and especially when they will know if there really is a requirement. Contact your office to inform them and set up a plan of action so that your company can react immediately to any problem-solving opportunity. In the case of customers with whom you've had experience, you can take a chance and produce product in advance of their instructions to do so. Chances are that even if the problem does not come to pass, you'll be able to use the product elsewhere, or your customer will need it at some time in the future. A customer once remarked how speedy we were at handling their emergencies; the truth was that unless we started at the first hint of the occurrence, we could not have come close to meeting their requirements. We always acted on instinct, and it always paid off.

JAMES CALLANDER
THE CUSTOMER PERSPECTIVE

Clients often have problems that need solving. Some are simple—for example, a client might need a light bulb replaced. Others are more complicated —for example, a client might need to obtain spec-grade materials for a construction project. Either way, clients are going to look to their vendors for solutions.

In some cases, the contact at the client's company will be a buyer, not the person who will actually use the product, service, or solution; because these buyers typically aren't qualified to determine the solution to the problem at hand, they rely on their vendors to bring their knowledge and expertise into the equation.

Solving problems is intertwined within the selling process—so much so that often, it's difficult to tell the two apart. Indeed, they are often two sides to the same coin. That is, salespeople often solve problems for their clients in an attempt to garner additional business. After all, as a client, if I tap you to help me solve a problem, it means I trust you enough to allow you to be of support—which bodes will for future transactions.

Even the strategies used to sell and solve problems can be similar. For example, just as a salesperson can sell from a reactive position—that is, simply responding to inquiries from customers—so, too, can you solve problems reactively—that is, waiting for clients to contact you for help. And just as salespeople can sell proactively—making sales calls, which requires preparation, conveying a message, finding a niche, and pinpointing a solution—so, too, can salespeople proactively solve their clients' problems by contacting clients and uncovering issues through active discussion.

When you are in problem-solving mode, you are generally in constant contact with your client.

Either way, the salesperson's goal should be the same: to fully understand the client's situation through artful listening and by asking questions that enable the client to offer new details, thereby further clarifying your understanding of the situation. Salespeople must draw out from the client background information on the issue at hand that may not be included in a standard inquiry. Your listening skills are your best friend in these situations; soak up as much information as you can!

Uncovering a problem through normal sales activities—during a regular sales call or visit—rather than waiting for a call from the customer can really help a salesperson improve his or her position with a client—especially if the salesperson can plot a course going forward that the client can work with.

Let's face it, you can't always be the hero. Sometimes, you just won't be able to solve a problem for a client. But even if you weren't able to help, if you applied yourself, you will still have made inroads with your client. Your client will remember your efforts, and will almost certainly attempt to employ your services some other time.

If a salesperson is faced with a problem that's outside his or her expertise, that salesperson should tap into others within his or her company (or companies he or she represents) for help. That said, salespeople should take care to ensure that the client doesn't become overwhelmed by multiple contacts attempting to solve the problem. The resulting confusion may well do more harm than good.

Q: DOES IT MATTER IF THE SALESPERSON IS NOT THE MOST POLISHED SPEAKER OR ELOQUENT WRITER?

MARVIN MILETSKY

THE SALES PERSPECTIVE

Not too long ago, a young man who was just embarking on his sales career joined my company. Armed with some basic skills, and having served a short apprenticeship in inside sales, he thought he was ready for the big leagues—person to person, on the road. Before we allowed that, however, we monitored his conversations with customers on the phone—during which he told one customer that his automobile registration was out of date and that an officer had almost *compounded* his car the night before. Told another customer that he had a wonderful system for retrieving files that involved keeping them all in the *argyles*. Told still another client that there were just some people who walked on *hollowed* ground. (Really, I couldn't make these up.) Not surprisingly, his career in sales didn't amount to very much.

The harsh reality is that it's practically impossible to succeed in sales (or any career, really) without having mastered the ability to speak and write eloquently. For some people, these are natural talents that seemingly come easy. For the rest of us, the good news is that speaking and writing well are skills that we can, in fact, learn—through a combination of formal education, real life, and on-the-job training. Help yourself help yourself. Speaking and writing well are prerequisites. Take the time to improve these skills by whatever means necessary.

JAMES CALLANDER

THE CUSTOMER PERSPECTIVE

Eloquence in both speaking and writing can provide salespeople with an advantage when dealing with clients. Fortunately, I believe both skills can be learned.

With respect to writing well, being able to do so is critical when it comes to communicating the benefits of your offering to a client. By providing clear information, you enhance the client's understanding, enabling him or her to evaluate your proposal more thoroughly.

Of course, if your customer operates in one of any number of industries or markets that employ various rules or regulations to guide how business is conducted, you will be required to conform to those rules and regulations when communicating with him or her. Similarly, many companies utilize standard forms for quotations or proposals that require you to fill in specific information only; the most writing you would need to do beyond that is a cover letter or an e-mail. In both cases, the style of writing required is easily understood and to the point. Areas where writing well *is* important include "scope of work" documents. In these, you must be able to communicate exactly what is and isn't in your proposal. As such, your wording is vital. Your ability to deliver clear, well-written materials substantially reduces the chances of issues arising later on, and increases your chances of obtaining yet more business from the client down the road.

Spend a little time preparing a letter or detailed proposal instead of waiting to the last minute and rushing through the prep work. Doing so will greatly increase your odds of success.

Speaking well—one on one or in front of a group—is also a very important skill, one that everyone must master to some degree in conducting business. Speaking in front of a group does take some getting used to, although it does become easier the more you do it. Speaking one on one—for example, sitting down with a client to go over a proposal (a very important task)—is typically less threatening than speaking to a group.

Becoming effective at public speaking requires a bit of practice, which you can do in front of a mirror. Alternatively, consider joining a group such as Toastmasters to develop these skills; it provides a wonderful avenue for anyone wanting to improve their public-speaking skills.

Regardless of your audience, you will find that the more you know about the subject at hand, the easier it will be for you to speak about that subject. In any case, you must choose your words carefully when presenting a proposal or making other types of sales calls. Make it a practice to take time to prepare, including having questions selected and phrased appropriately so your client can respond with greater detail.

It's not uncommon for newer salespeople to feel nervous or shy when speaking, which decreases their ability to communicate effectively. Take heart: Time will take care of the jitters. They may not go away, but they'll become more manageable.

Q: • How Much Does Brand • Matter in Making a Sale?

Marvin Miletsky
The Sales Perspective

When I shop for an appliance, my eyes are drawn first to the brand names that I'm familiar with. Although I might quickly look over the off-brand product that the salesperson swears is the exact same as that offered by the name brand —and at half the price—I really can't say I even *consider* buying brands I don't recognize. I am comfortable with the brand's reputation and its longevity in the industry. So why, then, would I expect anyone I am soliciting to be any less loyal to a brand that he or she is comfortable with?

Of course brand makes a difference! A familiar and accepted brand sets the standard to which all challengers aspire. Chances are, the brand or brands you are competing with are "king of the hill." They come with a pre-existing acceptance from your customer. After all, customers' time is typically at a premium; if they can make their jobs easier by simply purchasing an accepted brand, why wouldn't they?

Well, actually, there are a number of reasons. If you're approaching clients from the unenviable position of being a lesser-known or smaller brand, then it's up to you, as a salesperson, to convince prospective clients to take a risk and give you a shot. Here are a few tips:

- Typically, the price of your proposed product will be the door opener. To determine a price that your client will find attractive, do some research about the pricing of the lead brand. (If your company has tried to persuade any other clients to switch to your version of this product before, then this information may already be available to you.) If you do business with one of your prospect's competitors, you may be able to get an idea on appropriate pricing by examining that account.

- Provide samples. Make sure these are hand delivered and that they get into the proper person's hands. Often, the purchasing agent must get approval from someone else in order to make a substitution and buy from another vendor; make sure you know who's actually got to be impressed and that you include him or her in your meeting.

- Arrange to do a presentation of your product in front of your customer. Bring an expert with you to demonstrate, discuss, and field the tough questions if there's any chance you won't know every answer yourself.

- Bring the power of senior management and, if possible, a member of your executive staff with you to show your company's commitment.

- Put your money where your mouth is. Guarantee a successful experience with your product, and promise to provide the client with the original brand if he or she is not happy with yours. (Make sure that you can do what you claim.)

Except for one time in my sales career, I have never had the pleasure of walking into a customer as a representative of the preferred brand. (I admit, it was great to be able to simply ask what their delivery requirements were and how many they wanted and leave with an order in hand.) I have spent a lifetime competing against the big names. Well-established and trusted brands will always be among your biggest competitors. They should be respected, feared, and admired—but they can be defeated. Just like building Rome, though, it's not going to happen in a day. You might need to temper that resolve with a little bit of patience.

JAMES CALLANDER

THE CUSTOMER PERSPECTIVE

Do you have a brand preference with cars, soda, or toothpaste? Sure, some may say it doesn't matter, but everyone has preferences when it comes to products they use in their personal lives—and the same holds true in business.

Clients often develop an affinity for one brand over another; the preferred brand is the one they choose by default when they need to repurchase. Their preference might be based on many different factors:

- **The salesperson:** If the salesperson who handles the brand has proved competent in terms of both pricing and service, and if the client has come to trust what the salesperson is offering, then the client will continue to do business with that salesperson.

- **Staff acceptance:** If the client's staff prefers the product or service, the buyer will likely continue to purchase that brand.

- **Customer acceptance:** In some cases, clients may be told by their customers what to buy.

- **Lack of knowledge about other options:** I've known people who make a decision based on brand because they've never seen a competitor's product. In other words, the product they use is comfortable.

> Always attempt to uncover why a client fails to purchase a product from you. If the reason is brand, try asking why the client is locked into using a different brand.

If you sell your client's brand of choice, you are in a good position. You won't have to sell the product or service in the normal sense; you just need to support the client's needs through servicing the account. The client's satisfaction is based on the brand, on the cost associated with his or her selection, on your company, and on you. Even if you inherit such an account, you can operate in maintenance mode.

> Even if clients prefer your brand, you should never let your guard down. Your competition is looking for ways to unseat you; they want to provide a solution that would allow them to take business from you. Because of your client's preference, you do have some breathing room—but that doesn't mean you havr the luxury of sitting on your duff and counting your money. Stay hungry, and keep looking for opportunities to provide your clients with new items that might one day become their brand of choice.

If your clients prefer a different brand, can you persuade them to make the shift to a brand you are offering? Absolutely. Often your offering will be similar to that of a competitor, but with a few unique features. If you know your product or service and how these unique features can benefit your client, you can plant a seed in your client's mind that may grow. Timing can play a part in your ability to establish a new direction for your client. Normally, you'll be attempting to displace a competitor and their offering, which is a huge win. If you manage to engage a prospect in an area he has recently been challenged by, either because of your competitor's abilities or the product or service provided, the client's interest will be piqued by your efforts to offer up a different solution.

> When I'm buying, I usually give a manufacturer's name and part number along with a simple description. If I'm open or able to use a different brand, I'll make it "or equal." Now the challenge is in my vendor's hands to identify an equal. The salesperson should also offer information about additional benefits from the "equal" brand he or she is offering.

Q: DOES BECOMING A SPEAKER OR AUTHOR IN YOUR INDUSTRY IMPROVE YOUR ABILITY TO SELL?

MARVIN MILETSKY

THE SALES PERSPECTIVE

The vast majority of salespeople will never be published or speak in front of any audience short of a group gathering. But although it is not a requirement for a salesperson to become a writer or speaker—not everyone is suited to it— if you have the resolve and talent to become one, the benefits can be widespread. By becoming a speaker or author in your industry, customers and competitors alike will view you as the authority in your field. You will be the one customers and new prospects seek out for answers to their problems. After all, who better to ask than the teacher?

> Your writing need not be solely on the subject of the products that your company produces. You can broaden your horizons and become respected for your knowledge in a cross-section of industry topics. This also gives credence to the presumption of your expertise in your own field.

There are lots of ways to become an author, speaker, or both:

- Participate in your local or national industry trade organization meetings, volunteering to speak on a subject that you are familiar with.
- Arrange to speak at a trade show.
- If your trade organization has its own newsletter, become part of its staff.
- Write an article for a trade magazine.
- Write a letter to the editor regarding a topic covered in a recent issue.

If you don't feel quite ready to try these ideas, start small. If your company produces a company newsletter, write an article for it, and share it with your customers; let them see your name on the byline. Or if your company comes out with a new product or innovation, invite a select group of customers to a meeting of introduction. Leading the meeting, serving as host, and taking the opportunity to speak to the group will bring credibility to you in the eyes of your customers.

> Trade shows, industry groups, and publications that serve your industry usually limit your ability to mention your company's specific products or benefits. After all, their purpose is to serve their members by providing information, not advertising. But the credit you will be given as the speaker or author can include a description of your background and where you work. In this way, you can get your name, and your company's, in front of your audience.

Whether you become a speaker, author, or both, doing so can be a strong tool in attracting new customers and keeping the ones you have. That said, I do have one major cautionary note: Before you consider speaking or writing, you'd better make sure you know what you're talking or writing about. Make sure your facts are dead-nuts accurate and that you can support any of your claims. Anything short of that will put you in the same class as a politician.

JAMES CALLANDER
THE CUSTOMER PERSPECTIVE

If you become a speaker within your industry, that is a great accomplishment. The same holds true if you are fortunate enough to become an author. But I don't believe either achievement is significantly important to your sales career or advancement with your clients. There are many other areas—major areas—that matter more to your future in sales. Cultivating new business and maintaining the business you currently have will keep you occupied for many years.

While becoming a speaker or author might occur if you develop your level of expertise to the degree required to speak or write on the industry you serve, opportunities to advise your clients, co-workers, and others will happen regularly throughout your career. For example, I'm frequently asked by clients and co-workers about fluctuations in the price of copper. Because my industry, the electrical industry, uses a lot of copper products, I monitor the daily up and down movement of copper pricing on the market. The price of copper affects our buying habits, which can improve or hurt our projects' bottom line. Without this information, we would be unable to make good buying decisions when the need arises. By answering questions like these, you'll find opportunities to provide support for your clients and influence their perception of you—much more than you would by speaking before an audience or writing a book.

Serving as an author or speaker within your industry will have little to do with your success in sales. You may aspire to be one or both—which is great—but in doing so, you must keep your efforts in supporting your clients front and center. Focus your attention on improving your relationship with each client. Grow your business through persistence, always looking for ways to help your clients meet the challenges they face each day. Your success in sales can then be the catalyst for speaking engagements and book deals.

Q: • WHAT IS CUSTOMER SERVICE
• AND DOES IT MATTER?

MARVIN MILETSKY

THE SALES PERSPECTIVE

↳ Customer service is an inherent part of the commitment you make to develop a positive relationship with your clients. It's listening to their complaints and understanding that their position on a matter is important to them; they deserve to have that position heard. Regardless of how you see it, their position is absolutely right in their eyes, and that's the position you must address.

It's critical that you field all complaints with professionalism and understanding so that in the end, no matter what the outcome, your customers feel you've helped them to the best of your ability. You're looking for a win-win, where both of you come out of a situation feeling victorious. Even if you fail to totally satisfy the customer's needs, that customer can still walk away knowing you've done everything in your power to make things right—a small victory in itself. In a partnership between a vendor and a client, both parties have to come away feeling like they've won a little something. It cannot possibly be a one-sided. Have you ever heard the sound of one hand clapping?

A key aspect of customer service is managing your customers' expectations. One of the first things I recommend you do with a customer to ensure good service is to clearly point out and articulate the terms of any sale for your products or services at some time during your negotiation. Even if the terms of doing business seem obvious to you, don't assume that everyone else will feel the same way. For example, if you're selling dairy products to a market, you might feel like they can't reasonably expect you to be willing to accept a return of the product after its expiration date, but they might assume that any milk that wasn't sold could be credited—that your company would bear the cost of the failure of the product to sell. Rather than take the chance that someone may have a different view, I would opt to discuss what seems like the obvious.

There will be times when you've cautioned your customers of the terms, but they still come back and ask if there's something you can do to help them. Try not to turn a deaf ear to this request. Perhaps there's something creative you can do to ease the loss and help them recover—for example, offering a discount on an upcoming order if they are willing to increase the amount or commit to more items in the future. Whatever it is, you've tried to partner with them to create business; don't abandon them in a negative situation.

And speaking about negatives, an important aspect of customer service is calling to alert them to a missed delivery schedule before they have to call you to inquire where their items are. It's also following up to see that their order was everything they required and in line with what they expected after a delivery is made. Communicate with your customers. Let them know that you care and that each experience is another building block toward the relationship you're trying to build.

The way I see it, rather than concentrating your efforts on why you *can't* do something for a customer, your customer-service philosophy should be to come up with solutions to their problems that will satisfy them and at the same time not negatively affect your own bottom line. But don't think you can come up with a one-approach-fits-all menu; it's just not going to happen. Customer service is always a work in progress. You'll develop your own strategies by combining the lessons you've learned during your sales career with those new ones that are right around the corner. The true measure of success is in the relationships you establish and keep.

JAMES CALLANDER

THE CUSTOMER PERSPECTIVE

I've been a customer all my life, and so have you. And I'm guessing like me, you're very disappointed in what many companies today call "customer service." All too often, I find companies that haven't a clue what it means to serve. While they may make money (presumably in spite of themselves), they could do so much better.

For example, take a pet peeve of mine: voicemail. Sure, voicemail is a fantastic tool. Thanks to voicemail, we can leave detailed messages to assist those on the receiving end to act prior to calling us back. But frequently, salespeople (and others) hide behind their voicemail, opting not to pick up their phones even though they could answer. Of course, I realize that staffing is always an issue for companies, and that salespeople's workloads have increased. But the fact is, I'm not afforded unlimited time to respond and support my colleagues when they submit requests for assistance. I have deadlines, and if I fail to meet them, I may well disrupt work that needs to occur down the line. Poor customer service is the main reason I switch vendors, even more so than cost. If my attempts to work with a vendor become difficult due to that vendor's inability to communicate—or any other reason—I'll have to seek an alternate avenue for support.

Customer service is not a buzzword to be handed out like business cards. It's the heart and soul of any business. It's a way of life. Why? Because you influence your clients' buying decisions. Through your efforts, business flows to your company. This requires that you and everyone in your organization live up to your clients' expectations. The backbone of any company is the people who are employed there; your ability to serve your clients is directly affected by the support you receive from others in your company (so much so that many companies tie bonuses not just to your effectiveness, measured by the amount of revenue and profit you bring to the company in a given year, but to how well the company or office in which you work does as a whole—meaning that even if you are on budget, if the office isn't doing well as a whole, you will be penalized). They determine how successful the company will be and ultimately how successful you will be. The minute your client begins having problems with you or your support staff, the damage can be severe, impairing your ability to serve the client effectively or possibly even dissolving your working relationship.

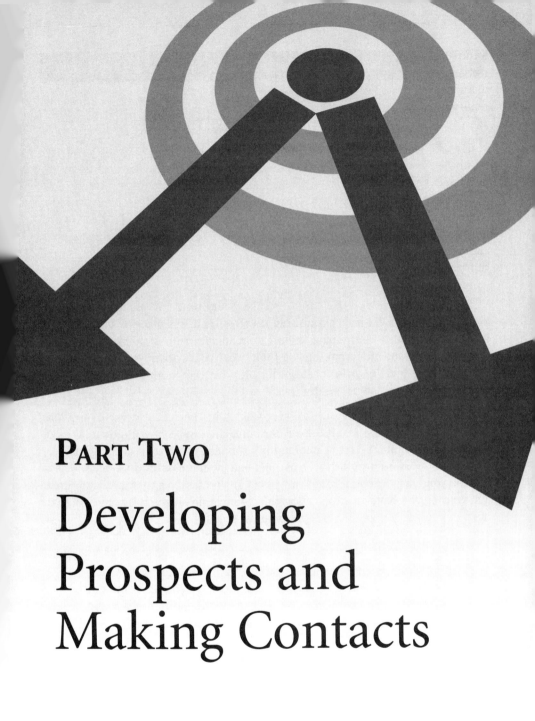

PART TWO
Developing Prospects and Making Contacts

Q: • WHAT KINDS OF RESULTS DO
• YOU EXPECT FROM YOUR SALES CALL?

JAMES CALLANDER
THE CUSTOMER PERSPECTIVE

↳ You should ask yourself this question every time you make a sales call—and know the answer *before* you show up at your client's place of business. Not planning your visit beforehand invites a broad spectrum of topics to enter the conversation—and they may not be topics that will garner you business. And without some level of prioritization during your visit, your client might wonder why you are there in the first place.

Obviously, you want the result of your visit to be the continuation of the sales process. Clarifying the results of a recent bid, showing a new product, and discussing improvements in your company's service are ways to achieve that. Do you simply want to provide information about some new product or service, or are you following up on a recent proposal? If you said yes to either, then great! That means you have an expectation for the meeting—which is something you need so you can gauge whether you were successful.

Hopefully, you are measuring the results of your actions to ensure you are doing enough to support your client's needs. Start your day by planning what you want to achieve by the end of the day and determining what actions will be required to do that, and then put that plan into action. Then, on the next morning, review your day to see how successful you were at achieving your goals. The more you use this method, the better you will become at achieving results—and results are what all salespeople need to be successful!

Good salespeople approach each visit with one goal being to book the *next* meeting. After all, you're working toward building a lasting relationship with your client—and you can't do that if you aren't in front of him or her on a regular basis. To achieve this, pay careful attention to what the client says during *this* meeting. Often, clients give information that doesn't seem important at the time but, once reviewed, provides you the opening to visit again at a later date. Sometimes, during the course of the discussion, the client will ask a question for which you don't have an immediate answer—offering you yet another opening to schedule additional meetings. And depending on the urgency of the question, there may even be times when you *do* have an answer but withhold it, enabling you to immediately schedule a follow-up visit to provide the details the client is requesting.

Generally, when I schedule a visit from a vendor, it's because we have a specific piece of business to discuss. The appointment can take varying lengths of time depending on the depth of our discussion or what other issues I'm dealing with that day. I've had appointments that should have taken 15 minutes last more than an hour; likewise, when another urgent matter required my attention, I've had to cut important meetings short. Either way, I'm interested in the subject we agreed to discuss during the visit—and no matter what may happen when you and I meet, I'm going to make sure this information is discussed.

MARVIN MILETSKY
THE SALES PERSPECTIVE

Did you ever play a team sport, but not as a starter—just waiting on the bench for your chance to get in the game? "Hey coach! Put me in! I know I can deliver if you'll just give me a shot!" A sales call is similar. You have confidence in your abilities, your product, and your company. But to make a sale, you have to be given an opportunity—and an opportunity is exactly what you should expect to get out of your meeting.

Depending on the level of the meeting, your opportunities will differ:

■ The initial meeting is the one that sets the stage for all the future ones. It's the one you worked so hard to get—and the one that will leave that lasting impression for both you and your target. Your expectation should be to come out of that meeting with a general understanding of your customer's requirements and how they do business. If you manage to leave a door open for a next meeting or a reason to follow up, then your goals for this meeting have been met.

■ In the second meeting, you'll be able to start identifying specific requirements and gain a better understanding of their business. Your expectation should be to leave with the knowledge that you've gotten their interest and that they want you to deliver a formal presentation or product demonstration in the near future.

- The presentation meeting is where you prove the worth of the statements you've made about your product and its ability to solve your client's problems. Be prepared to defend your position; often, there will be at least one participant who tries to demonstrate his or her own knowledge rather than listening to you. You should come out of this meeting confident that you have defended your product in front of the nay-sayers. Expect to leave with an understanding of who the ultimate decision-maker is and whether your product or company has been qualified—or what remains to be done to meet your client's standards. It's not unreasonable to also expect to learn when your customer would actually like a price and the materials required.

See Question #61, "Can a Pitch or Presentation Be Cookie-Cutter? Or Does It Need to Be Completely Customized for Each Prospect?" and Question #62, "Can a Salesperson Recover from a Bad Presentation?" for discussions of presentation techniques.

- If there's a follow-up meeting required to address open issues not covered in your presentation, your expectation should be to come out of that meeting with acceptance of your product.

- At long last, you've been asked to provide a pricing proposal, and they've accepted your offer to personally hand-deliver it. Although expecting a commitment on this call is the desired result, it's probably a reach—but your observation of their body language, handshake, and attitude should give you an indication of where this negotiation is going.

Even if you develop your own set of expectations as you approach a meeting, keep in mind that you must come out with more than you went in with. That is, you should leave with some information you can use to take this negotiation to its conclusion: the sale.

Q: • How Important Is It for You to Understand a Customer's Business?

James Callander

The Customer Perspective

Knowing what your clients do is fundamental to understanding what you can offer them. Without some knowledge of your client's business, you have no way to determine how they might use your products or services. You are shooting blind, and your only hope for success is to magically hit some target. I doubt you have the time or energy to use trial and error as a method for finding the opening you need; learn the basics about your clients, and then focus your efforts on areas you can support if given the chance.

You shouldn't limit yourself to simply learning what your client does, however. You should also research other aspects of their business, such as the following:

- **Who your client does business with.** This knowledge can help you secure business. The next time you're in a client's waiting room before an appointment, take the time to look at the publications your client has laid out. These publications often focus on the market your client serves. (It's not a bad idea to lift one of the subscription cards so you can get your own copies.) The articles they contain can provide a glimpse into your client's business, and may provide information you can use on return visits. This will highlight your growing understanding of their business.

- **Who your client's competitors are.** This knowledge may provide you with a new source of business if you can establish a relationship with the competitor. The aforementioned publications might contain information about your client's competitors.

- **Who's who in your client's organization.** If you don't know the key personnel in your client's organization and what their roles are, you limit your ability to sell to your clients. With the key personnel identified, you can make additional appointments within the company. Those added appointments can provide a wealth of information that may help you be more effective.

If you don't know the roles these individuals play, you risk missing an order; this typically happens when pricing and availability are equal with your competitors' but you didn't communicate with all the right people. The one person you missed could be the decision maker—which is not always the buyer.

- ■ **Who is competing with you for your client's business.** You may have more competition at one client than you realize. If so, you'll want to find out who you are competing with. This may lead you to reassess whether you have a real chance to be successful. There is nothing worse than a client who uses you as a quote service.

- ■ **Your client's payment practices.** Learning how your client handles payments is vital to maintaining a good working relationship. Obviously, you want clients who pay their bills and do so on time. Knowing your client's payment practices up front up can save you a lot of headaches later on. For example, if a potential client expects payment terms outside your company's normal practice—perhaps extending payment to 60 or 90 days—you should know this before you land a big order. If a client's account is put on hold due to lack of payment, you won't be able to sell anything to them until they resolve the problem. Inevitably, you'll be pulled into the fray—meaning you'll have to spend God knows how much time attempting to help fix the problem for both sides. Your credit department may be able to provide some information—perhaps even a full-blown credit report.

MARVIN MILETSKY

THE SALES PERSPECTIVE

My knee-jerk reaction after reading this question was to say that in certain categories—for example, if you were peddling paper or setting up retirement packages—knowledge of your customer's business is not required. But then I got to thinking, even if you're selling paper, knowing how your customer uses it could enable you to better serve their needs. For example, you might discover that they are sometimes required to prepare formal presentations to impress their customers—meaning they'll appreciate you showing them that special paper you sell that's thicker than they're used to or that holds the ink better when drawings or photos are printed on it. You may also have other products, such as presentation folders, that you can add to their shopping list. And even if you're simply setting up retirement packages for a client, knowing your target's business might allow you to find at least one stock fund among the thousands available that will be of special interest to the people you are looking to impress.

My philosophy, if you haven't figured it out by now, is to try to become my clients' partner and to pinpoint their needs by understanding their business. I don't want to be just a component supplier; I want to be a problem solver. I once had a customer who packaged a fastener that we manufactured as part of their resale product. My knowledge of his business and product enabled me to introduce a better item to him, which he subsequently included in his package to replace the original one. As a matter of fact, the item was so much better than the old one—and than any items offered by my competition—that my customer touted its inclusion in their advertising of their own product. You've got to learn as much as you can about their business in order to place your best product in their hands.

A great way to learn about a company's business is to pick up one of their catalogs and look through it; another is to try to meet one of their salespeople directly. It's quite possible that the buyer or purchasing agent is not terribly familiar with what their company does, so you might have to seek out others. And don't be afraid to ask questions; most salespeople answering them will do so with the same pride that you have when talking about your company and products. Pay careful attention to them, as they could be the key to your learning where you can better fit in to their company's future. (We've discussed how to meet these people in other areas of the book.)

Remember: You're not a rote salesperson. You're a professional who makes things happen, with the goal of making your customer as comfortable with you as possible. What better way than to speak the same language—the language of his company's business?

Q: Should Like Title Call on Like Title?

James Callander
The Customer Perspective

↳ Your client base has various business structures, and you must understand each one in order to be successful. For example, a smaller company won't have many layers of management. Odds are that you'll be able to successfully manage your contacts within this type of organization on your own (unless, as discussed in the preceding question, they present you with a request that is beyond your expertise). Larger clients may have multiple layers of management—possibly spread across multiple locations—that can influence decisions affecting your sales. In these types of companies, identifying all the players and their roles is more difficult. When dealing with clients of this sort, you must constantly evaluate the client's personnel and the roles they play, looking for changes that may make the difference in winning or losing an order.

When it becomes difficult to identify the key players within your client's organization or you don't have access to them, you need to enlist senior members of your company. Odds are, the client's president will be more open to meeting with a vice president or president of your company than with you. They share a level of responsibility and leadership that permits them to see a broader picture of the business at hand.

The same holds true for people within your organization who hold other titles. For example, engineering is especially detail oriented. The people in a company's engineering department need a vendor's engineering or product-development staff to assist them in understanding designs, capabilities, and issues surrounding a product or service. When they have access to like title, they can quickly work through complex information and move to a conclusion. They speak the same language.

Financial management is another area where like titles can provide influence. A finance manager at your company can communicate effectively with your client's controller or manager to review payment terms, options, and changes that may be needed to support your client's interest. When well-managed, this can help produce more opportunities and fewer repetitive transactions and keep your client paying on time.

Where does this fit into the sales equation? You are not an island unto yourself. Your clients are looking to you for quality service at all levels. You can use others in your organization to bring a total business solution to each of your clients. Be aware, however, that when you allow others to provide support, you must still manage both sides of the situation, making sure your client is satisfied with the information he or she is receiving and that your company feels it is benefiting from the effort being put forth.

MARVIN MILETSKY

THE SALES PERSPECTIVE

If you're in the diplomatic corps, then, well, let's face it: You probably have no reason to be reading this book. But for the sake of argument, let's say you are—and as such, you understand the importance of like titles negotiating with like titles. Ain't politics great?

Well, we're not in politics. We're in sales. We don't sell to titles; we sell to people.

Chances are you might not even know the title of the person you're calling on until you're actually in his or her presence. And even then, after the Exchange of the Cards ceremony, you may look to see the name but skim right by the title. Who cares?! You've just met someone who's giving you an opportunity to introduce both your product and yourself in an effort to get them interested in doing business. Once you've sold the prospect with your confidence and ease, you'll both be the same, on even terms: human beings. Titles shouldn't mean a thing.

That said, I have on occasion made use of titled individuals in my company. Once, we were being considered for an order that was pivotal to my prospect's success with their customer. They could not afford any mistakes with product, quality, or delivery schedule. Their usual vendor had stumbled on the previous order, leaving the door slightly ajar for us. I knew that I'd be pitching to the highest-ranking individuals in the company; to avoid a mismatch of power, I set aside my ego and asked the president of my organization to accompany me to the meeting. His attendance confirmed our commitment to the project, as did his verbal assurances; we landed the order and a long-term relationship developed. Normally, though, the person you are should sell to the person they are. Don't be intimidated by anything—least of all a title.

Q: • Are Personal Referrals
• the Best Way to Achieve Sales?

James Callander
The Customer Perspective

Personally, I've never found the need to provide personal referrals while doing business—and as a client, I don't believe I've ever had a vendor attempt to solicit a personal referral from me, either. (Not that I wouldn't, in certain instances, fulfill such a request, but it definitely would not be the norm; the notion that I would require or somehow benefit from having a vendor's personal referral eludes me.) For me, it comes down to this: Listing your accomplishments to a prospective client may make you feel more important, but I doubt your client will see things the same why. My guess is it will come across as boasting. And because you of course want to avoid creating a negative perception of yourself on the part of the client, you should be very careful about flaunting referrals—unless the client specifically requests you do so.

I have, however, used personal experience gained working with other clients to support my efforts to develop a solution for a new client. This experience, which will be invaluable during your sales career, can make the impossible situation possible for a client who is at his or her wits' end trying to resolve a problem. I even use my experiences as a salesperson in the electrical industry on the other side of the table, as a buyer. With it, I'm better able to gauge how vendors are being utilized and their level of support for our business and apply their own capabilities to improve the service they offer us. Having this insight allows me to educate them on what they can do better. Sometimes I feel like I'm doing their job for them, but I'd rather help them help me than struggle to meet my needs supporting my project teams.

I do sometimes use referrals when dealing with vendors as a way to inform them that I've dealt with others in their organization before. I've even had sales managers or branch managers contact their respective counterparts in another part of the country—for example, to give them the opportunity to prepare for a new job site we're starting up, or to familiarize their sales staff with us so when we start calling for service, they don't stumble when coming out of the blocks. This has been a very effective strategy for me and my company.

That said, when selling, I highly recommend you stick with the basics. Sell yourself through your conviction and your understanding of the products and services you offer. Know your client and their staff. Use the art of listening to gather information and gain perspective of the client needs, and then offer the appropriate product or service to meet those needs. Build the vendor-client relationship by backing up your efforts with service that meets or exceeds their expectations. As for personal references, offer them only when your client requests them.

MARVIN MILETSKY

THE SALES PERSPECTIVE

 Never underestimate the power of a referral. Personal referrals can vastly improve your chances of identifying prospective clients—and quickly. Salespeople spend lots of time and effort seeking out the right companies to contact to generate new business and identifying the person within those companies to target with their sales effort. What a head start you'll have if you've obtained this information from a contact you already have or, even better, if that target contacts you because of a referral! Getting a referral—an endorsement of you and your work—from an existing client can put you miles ahead in your quest for new business.

Don't be afraid to tell your new prospect who you were referred by. The fact that someone has referred you indicates that person's satisfaction with your work.

Although some referrals will be unsolicited, there are ways to generate them on your own behalf. Here are some tactics to consider:

- Ask your existing customers to refer you to other people they know in their company or industry who might benefit from your services.

- Ask your existing customers to refer you to their customers. For example, suppose you're in the lighting-fixture business and you provide lighting fixtures and lamps to a customer during a construction project. After the project is complete and your customer moves on to the next one, *his* customer—the one who moves into the completed structure—may require service in the future: for example, replacement bulbs or perhaps even new fixtures. Get that referral, and seek that customer out.

- Ask contacts who are changing positions or moving to a new company to refer you to their replacement.

- If you are meeting an individual who is new to the client's company, ask that person to refer you to his or her replacement at his or her last place of employment. (Be careful, though—he or she might not have left on good terms, which could reflect badly on you if you are referred by that person.)

- Ask friends, acquaintances, or other people you encounter in life if they have contacts you might be able to use in your business.

No one lives in a vacuum; we are all exposed to a great cross section of people from different walks of life. A casual conversation can lead to just the piece of information you've been seeking.

Q: • DOES COLD-CALLING, EITHER OVER • THE PHONE OR IN PERSON, WORK?

JAMES CALLANDER

THE CUSTOMER PERSPECTIVE

Cold-calling is one of the toughest aspects of sales because of the high rejection rate. It's no wonder salespeople tend to procrastinate in this area more than any other; fear of rejection inevitably creates a formidable mental block. But cold-calling can yield sales opportunities—*if* you apply yourself.

> As I've mentioned, salespeople must grow thick skins. Rejection is just part of the business. Do not take negative responses personally; they are not about you.

Preparation is just as important in cold-calling as it would be if you were heading to an established client's office for an appointment. Showing up at a prospective client's business without knowing who the buyer is or, for that matter, what the company does is a lousy plan. For cold-calling to have any chance at being successful, there has to be a real potential for establishing a relationship. Indiscriminately handing out business cards at every office in a business park will only fill up the recycle bins.

> Cold-calling by phone is much the same as doing so in person. Although you can potentially reach more prospective clients in a shorter period of time, the results will turn out the same if you don't understand who you are calling.

When cold-calling, whether in person or via phone, I recommend you keep a few points in mind:

- Know something about the company you are targeting, including what the company does.

- Determine who the appropriate people to contact at the business are.

- Determine what you can offer this prospect. If you have multiple items to offer, narrow them down to one or two to avoid overwhelming the prospect.

- Determine what your message to the prospect will be based on your narrowed down list. This message should be focused—narrow in scope and focused on a perceived benefit—and one you can communicate quickly if given the opportunity.

Although using this approach does not guarantee that prospects will respond positively to your efforts, it increases the likelihood that they will. At the very least, the odds that you will get an opportunity to sit down with a prospect will be better than if you just make call after call with no discernible purpose.

One more thing: Chances are you will make a bigger impact by doing buddy cold calls—that is, making cold calls in person accompanied by another individual, such as your manager, another salesperson, or a sales representative from a company you represent. By feeding off of each other's energy and comments, you'll find that the two of you will be better able to convey a message to the prospect than you would as individuals—and also enjoy a shared sense of accomplishment when you get past the front door. Sometimes you won't make it past the receptionist, but by working together you can sometimes identify the proper contacts within or something else about the company you didn't already know. I don't know why, but sometimes, working alone versus making cold calls together is like night and day!

If the person you are working with is a rep for one of the companies you represent, making buddy calls will have the added benefit of providing you with insight into what is important to them when establishing a new account, as well as the opportunity to develop a rapport with the person that may prove beneficial in the future. Making buddy calls with your sales manager can be a little more challenging, however; the fact that he or she will be looking to critique your efforts might make you nervous.

MARVIN MILETSKY
THE SALES PERSPECTIVE

Read any number of books or articles or ask your contemporaries, and you'll find any number of differing opinions about the value of cold-calling, be it in person or over the telephone.

Let's start with cold-calling by phone. You might be thinking, flat out, how much confidence can you possibly have in a practice that the Federal government has outlawed on behalf of private citizens, calling it intrusive and an invasion of their privacy? Logically, you would think something that is so annoying to the majority of the population has no place in your business efforts. Perhaps that may be the case in some instances, but in my experience, cold-calling has proven to be a valuable way to identify possible leads and eventually become successful in adding them to my list of customers. I'm a great believer in the use of a telephone for communicating in general and especially when it comes to making cold calls.

Cold-calling by phone offers one obvious benefit: efficiency. Just picking up a phone and dialing a number can result in a great economy of your time. When using this method, however, you should be prepared. Make sure you've got a tough outer shell because for every successful contact you make, there might be dozens more who will try to get you off their phone by any means possible, from politely stating they're not interested to questioning your personal hygiene to screaming at you for interrupting their day. At the beginning of my career, until I had a steady stream of customers, I made lots of cold calls. Naturally, the more calls I made, the more I was rejected—but I also managed to produce lots of positive leads. Look, it's a numbers game. The more calls you make, the more successful you're going to be. I've never outgrown my faith in this method of acquiring new clients; I continue to use it to this day. I have reaped some handsome rewards as a result of these contacts.

That same tough outer shell you need for cold-calling by phone will also serve you well when cold-calling in person; showing up on someone's doorstep and expecting to be greeted with open arms is a bit of a reach. But that doesn't mean cold-calling in person can't be a great way to turn a prospect into a customer. To make the best use of my time, I often keep a list of potential targets with me; then, if the opportunity arises while I am near one, I just pop in and take my chances. The worst they can say is no; all I will have lost is a little time (and perhaps taken a little hit to my ego). As with cold-calling by phone, in the beginning of my career I attempted more in-person cold calls than I do now, but I never tire of using this method to expand my horizons and supplement my other efforts.

There are several ways to identify candidates who might be receptive to your unsolicited approach:

- Consider purchasing a list from a legitimate provider. Many companies on the Internet sell lists of names of companies in your target business community, complete with addresses, telephone numbers, and other contact information.

- Seek referrals (refer to Question #23, "Are Personal Referrals the Best Way to Achieve Sales?").

- Industry magazines and guides often present some wonderful hints about who's doing the business that you're seeking to support.

- Be a student of your existing customers' business. Understand the industry they serve. Find where their advertising is targeted. Finally, try to determine who their competitors are; these competitors should become the target of your cold calls.

- Using the Internet is a great way to pinpoint targets. Use those keywords and search away. Think of it as a detective story with you as the investigator, sifting through all the clues to identify viable targets.

- Look at old records in your company to try to identify customers who once were active but haven't been lately. Although this is not truly a "cold call" in theory, the fact that you are contacting these people after a prolonged absence makes it similar. As an added bonus, there is every possibility that your company name and product will be readily recognizable to the target, which might provide you with a head start.

With your list of strong targets in hand, do some homework. Understand what business your target is in and consider what his or her needs might be. Then determine what your company has to offer that can meet those needs, is new or improved, is more readily available, or costs less. The last thing you want to do is approach a target and ask what they need from you; remember, you contacted them. You should be able to tell them what you can offer them that will prove useful. (In this day and age, with the Internet, it should be rather easy to at least get some basic information so that you can best determine where your company's products might satisfy their needs.) Also, once you've made that initial contact, don't waste the opportunity that's been given to you: Speak in a confident manner and get right to the point. Imagine there's an alarm clock that is ticking and about to go off. Don't give in to your desire to engage in small talk; get to your point. Your purpose in this first meeting, be it on the phone or in person, is to open a door and set up an opportunity to advance to the next step, which is a confirmed appointment at some future date. In cold-calling, success should be defined as a positive experience with a prospective company or person that will lead to further conversation in the future. Put another way, your cold call has been a success if there's a follow up to be done. If that's the case—if, for example, your target has asked for a catalog, a brochure, or even a sample—make sure to fill their request in a speedy fashion.

Before continuing your efforts to add more clients by cold-calling, make sure that those you have been successful in contacting are taken care of. If you promise a sample or brochure and do not produce, the long-term effect could be disastrous.

If the contact's business is nearby, take the opportunity to hand-deliver the sample or literature, setting an appointment with your prospect beforehand. He or she is probably too busy to see you for an in-depth meeting or presentation, but will likely have a few minutes to shake your hand and accept your delivery. When delivering materials to a new contact after a cold call, never leave them with the receptionist or other disinterested party. I have my doubts that these items actually get to the right people. I also recommend against sending these items by mail or delivery service. Inevitably, the materials will find their way to a pile that has been put aside for some other day. I once sent a sample to a customer who was located quite a distance from me. When I was in his area later that year, I met with him—and noticed my sample lying in a corner of his office, unopened. One more thing: Don't send direct mail to the company with no person indicated in the address line; send it to targeted people within the organization. Unless a specific person is named, odds are it will never reach anyone of authority. You are forced to rely on whomever handles the company's mail to direct your correspondence to the right person, and the easiest thing for that person to do is to simply discard it.

Q: • SHOULD YOU SHOW UP
• WITHOUT AN APPOINTMENT?

JAMES CALLANDER
THE CUSTOMER PERSPECTIVE

↳ There are times when you will be able to show up at a client's place of business without an appointment and be seen—for example, if you are responding to the client's urgent request for literature or a sample. In this situation you most certainly can—and should—make the effort to call on the client with or without an appointment. Whether you get the chance to sit down and discuss what you have brought, however, depends entirely on the client. Don't expect an audience with buyers or others that involves more than providing details to support your visit. And unless specifically asked to comment or discuss other business, you should limit your visit to the business at hand.

Cold-calling is another situation where you might drop in without an appointment. Be aware, though, that your efforts to actually see a buyer will more than likely be thwarted by the receptionist. But as I mentioned earlier, even if you don't get the opportunity to really see anyone, you can still gather information that may prove useful in follow-up phone calls to gain access. This is perfectly acceptable in prospecting as long as you've done your homework on who the prospect is and what the prospect does.

In general, though, showing up at a client's office without an appointment probably isn't a great idea. I certainly would advise you to avoid making it a habit. Let's say you visit my business unexpectedly because you're in the neighborhood. The fact is, I may already be dealing with more issues than I have time for—meaning that there's a good chance I won't have time to visit with you. And that means you've lost precious time out of your day—time you can never get back. Poor planning on your part costs you more than just a missed visit; it takes time out of your day that you could have spent in more productive ways.

Even if I *do* take the time to visit with you, you can bet I will be distracted by events already underway—and if I'm distracted, you can be certain you won't have my full, undivided attention. Even if you have prepared for the visit and decided what you want to discuss or present, I may not be able to be fully engage in the conversation—a situation that will be exacerbated by the inevitable disruptions from co-workers or phone calls. As you can see, this type of visit probably won't be very productive.

All this is to say that in my view, effective sales calls require planning, preparation, and an actual appointment with your client. When your client agrees to see you, he or she is making time that otherwise might be filled with someone else or working on other tasks. The client is more apt to hold his or her phone calls and keep others issues at bay. The uninterrupted appointment is the best method for a meaningful meeting.

MARVIN MILETSKY

THE SALES PERSPECTIVE

Not every industry requires that a salesman call in advance for an appointment to see a prospect or client. Actually, many are open to people just stopping by to discuss or show their products. I have one friend whose products are sold directly to independent food markets; he stops in to discuss them, provide sales assistance, and give advice on implementing special offers to their customers to attract sales. Another friend represents a dozen different toy manufacturers with a customer base of local toy and gift shops, which he visits on a regular basis. And who hasn't sat in a doctor's waiting room, waiting for an appointment, and witnessed a pharmaceutical salesperson drop in to try to see the doctor?

I've focused on industrial sales with a product line that has included both commodity items and those that are highly specialized and target a limited audience. The commodity items lend themselves to being shown to wholesale distributors, where it's common to just arrive at the location and discuss them with both the inside salespeople and the buyers. They're usually more than happy to see me and take some time to review whatever I'm trying to peddle. Attracting buyers for the other items involve is tougher. These products have a more limited audience and, in the case of what I sell, must be reviewed by a professional eye. They must be proven to the customer and usually require in-depth information and review, with the ultimate sale being made after many factors have been addressed.

You'll have to determine whether it's acceptable to show up without appointments in your industry. And even if it is acceptable, you'll need to determine when the best time to visit will be. Tremendous frustration and wasted time can result from entering premises when your target is not there, is tied up with his or her own customers, is on the telephone, or cannot devote the necessary time and attention for any of dozens of other reasons. What is your target client's slowest time of day? Is it first thing in the morning or late in the afternoon? Are they less consumed in the minutes leading up to lunch than they are at other times? Determine when a visit from you will be most welcome.

Even if it's acceptable to pop in at a client's, there can be a real benefit to making appointments in advance, the most important being the optimization of your valuable time. It's especially important when your travels take you far from your home base. In these instances, it's imperative that you make an effort to set up and confirm meetings ahead of time. I usually set up a certain number of appointments with my most important customers and then compile a list of alternates that I can take a chance on just stopping by. If you're in an industry where no appointments are required, try to make them anyway. And even if your customers tell you to just stop by whenever, you may find that if you actually make an appointment, they'll give you more time. They may also provide a private area to meet, meaning there are fewer interruptions.

After making contact with a prospect, whether by telephone or direct mail, your best bet is to visit them in person, usually after the lead has been qualified. Often, however, your target will sidestep your request to visit. Showing up without an appointment might be just the trick to start a discussion.

Even the toughest prospects have been known to take a few moments to see you. If you're so lucky, realize that your prospect's day was probably pretty full before you decided to show up and add to it—meaning that if you actually get through, you must make the most of the time you're given. Don't expect to be given enough time to make a presentation, so don't even bother. Get to your point, have your business card and any literature ready to hand out, and let your prospect get back to work. Even if your prospect only comes out, shakes your hand, and tells you to call for an appointment, you've achieved your main goal: to meet the person and break the ice. It also means that your next call to the person won't be a cold call; it will be as a follow-up to your brief encounter, which has more punch. And regardless of the extent of contact, be sincerely appreciative of the time your prospect gives you.

If you drove three hours out of your way in the hopes you would be able to see a prospect, keep it to yourself. Come up with some excuse for being in their area—even just "I was nearby and thought I'd give seeing you a try!"

Q: • WHEN IS BREAKING • AN APPOINTMENT OKAY?

JAMES CALLANDER
THE CUSTOMER PERSPECTIVE

You've busted your hump to get an appointment to showcase your wares —and now you need to cancel. Maybe your kid got sick. Maybe you were involved in a car accident. Things happen; it comes with the territory.

I want to emphasize, however, the difference between *needing* to cancel and *wanting* to cancel. Want involves a desire driven by the individual; need is an obligation driven by other circumstances. The bottom line: Want has no place in breaking an appointment.

> Those in sales enjoy a certain level of latitude. There are no set hours; you can start as early and work as late as you like. These flexible hours are not to be taken advantage of; they're to be utilized to do what is required. It's up to you and you alone to use your time wisely. Sure, there will be days when you get up late or finish early—but don't slip into the habit. If you do, that behavior will eventually seep into your sales calls, and you'll find excuses to break appointments that, let's face it, you could make. Once this happens, it's game over. Your sales numbers will reflect your lack of effort, and management will notice.

If you do have a legitimate reason to break an appointment, you can typically call your client and cancel without issue. Most clients will understand. Depending on the circumstances, you might not need to cancel the appointment outright; you may be able push it back an hour or two if that works for the client. If you do in fact need to cancel, however, you should ask to schedule another appointment as soon as possible to make up the one you are missing.

In any case, never allow yourself the liberty of canceling an appointment simply because you want to. Appointments should be broken only if you are faced with something that requires your immediate attention.

MARVIN MILETSKY

THE SALES PERSPECTIVE

I once made an appointment with an existing customer to give a little sales presentation before some new people on their staff—and cancelled. Twice. Both times for arbitrary reasons. It took me *six months* to set up a new presentation date. You've worked hard to get an audience with a customer. Don't blow it by canceling! Put yourself in your customer's place: How tolerant would you be if a salesperson canceled on you—especially one from a company you don't currently partner with?

Short of a family emergency, there is no reason to cancel an appointment—especially at the last minute. (By the way, the family emergency must be a real one. Don't try to put one over on your contact.) Of course, things happen that are out of your control—but your schedule should be set in stone. If a real emergency arises, attempt to find a co-worker to fill in for you. Perhaps your boss or someone else in an executive position can go in your stead. In short, do everything in your power to keep the appointment—even if you can't be there yourself.

If you are forced to cancel, make the call yourself. If your contact was important enough for you to seek him or her out, then that person is important enough to be contacted by you directly in the event of a cancellation—and as far in advance as you can (although, admittedly, the timing of emergencies is out of your hands). Don't make up excuses you think will satisfy the customer; be as open and honest as you can be. If you've managed to enlist a replacement, it is you who should call to advise your contact of this change—and it is you who must follow up after the meeting to see how it went and to handle the after work.

Q: • WHAT IS THE VALUE OF • ATTENDING TRADE SHOWS?

What's your perspective on this question?
Let us know at PerspectivesOnSales.com.

JAMES CALLANDER
THE CUSTOMER PERSPECTIVE

↳ Local, state, regional, and national trade shows attract companies in every market imaginable, bringing together manufacturers, distributors, potential clients, and current clients to showcase products and services. If you are in sales or looking to become a salesperson, it's really not a question of *if* you will attend a trade show; it's a question of *when*.

The open flow of information at a trade show provides participating companies a setting in which they can interact with potential customers, who themselves typically attend trade shows to look for new or initiative products they can use. The mix of potential clients—who might range from the president of a company down to the maintenance guy—represents a broad spectrum of potential customers, affording vendors more opportunities to attract new business. If vendors are successful, they will uncover new prospects, leading to increased sales.

The challenge facing any business that places a booth in a trade show is how to drive floor traffic to their area, thereby increasing their chances of finding prospects who are interested in a visit or more details. To this end, many companies set up extravagant displays that are lit up like Las Vegas. But the best booths are the ones that create an open and friendly atmosphere. Customers will be drawn toward any booth—even if it consists of a simple table—with salespeople looking directly at them and greeting them with a smile before inviting them to peruse their offerings. These booths are constantly busy.

If you are tapped to staff your company's booth at a trade show, you should make the most of the opportunity. The extent to which you benefit from the trade show depends on how you conduct yourself during the event. There is nothing worse than a booth manned by disinterested and uninvolved salespeople. Many people visiting a trade show will walk right by if you don't encourage them to come over to view your booth. Unless you attempt to connect with people who are walking the floor, you simply won't have a successful show; this might prompt your company to decide that the value of the show wasn't worth the cost and to reduce or eliminate their involvement in the future. You are there to promote your company's products and services, and that requires you to put forth some effort to bring customers to your booth. As mentioned, making eye contact, offering a friendly smile, and extending a hand to shake are key.

If, at a trade show, a potential customer asks you a question that you just can't answer, either involve a co-worker who is more familiar with the topic or attempt to gather the prospect's contact information so you can follow up at a later date. The objective is to provide the potential customer with information he or she can use; whether or not it becomes a sale or reference, you've done your part.

MARVIN MILETSKY

THE SALES PERSPECTIVE

Whether it's a local show and you spend only a day or a national one that requires a longer stay, the value derived by your attendance can be immense (and by "value" I mean "increased sales"). Where else do so many things go on in such a short period of time—and all under one roof?

Due to industry changes and the advent of the Internet as a tool to disseminate information, the number of trade shows organized each year has decreased, as has their frequency. Take advantage of the ones that have survived. That said, even though there are fewer shows, you can't attend every one. Choose the ones you want to attend carefully.

To make the absolute most of your trade-show experience, keep these points in mind:

- **Establish attendance goals and objectives:** Before your trip, sit down with team members and make a detailed list of the kinds of technologies, products, and services you want to see, demo, and learn more about. Once the list is complete, prioritize the items in the list, noting the things you most want to see or learn about.

- **Familiarize yourself with the show offerings:** Prior to the show, study the product categories being displayed on the show floor. A list of product categories is usually made available on the trade show's Web site or in brochures or other literature about the show.

- **Dare to compare:** Make a list all of the exhibiting companies that will be showcasing the technologies and products you want to explore. Spend some time thinking about the ones you most want to meet with.

- **Communicate:** Contact exhibiting companies that are most relevant to your attendance goals to set up on-site meetings and appointments in advance. That way, you can be certain to meet with the proper representatives from the exhibiting companies and can ensure that your time spent together is tailored to address your specific needs.

- **Make reservations:** Make your hotel, travel, and dinner plans in advance. These shows often have high attendance—meaning the best places sell out fast.

- **Schedule visits with customers:** Make appointments well in advance with customers you wish to meet. Remember, your competition is also vying for their time.

- **Map it:** An exhibition hall is like a mini-city. Use the online and printed floor plans like you would a city map to plan your journey around the show floor. Get a good idea in advance of where the booths you most want to visit are located, how large the various exhibits are, and who's next to whom.

- **Educate:** In addition to visiting exhibitors, make sure to attend some of the many seminars and technical sessions taking place at the show for insight into the future of the industry and to obtain additional technical knowledge. In addition to being exposed to new products, you'll get a sense of what products have yet to be developed for your market—information your company may be able to use to design its own offering. And inevitably, what you learn in these sessions will strengthen your sales presentations. Make sure you know when these sessions are scheduled.

- **Take a break:** Don't forget to include breaks and lunch in your daily schedule; you will need plenty of food and water to fuel your body at the show.

- **Carry lots of business cards:** In addition, bring some sort of case in which you can stash all the business cards you collect. Finally, bringing a pad and pen is a must. Take tons of notes, and jot down information about any follow-ups that are required.

Using the back of a business card you just received to jot down what follow up is required is not the recommended technique. As mentioned, it's best to note this information using a pad and pen or even one of those new gadgets that allows you to write your notes on a pad and then have them automatically transcribed on your computer. I can't tell you the number of times I've jotted down notes on a card, attempting to fit two paragraphs of information in a tiny space, only to have no idea later what the abbreviations I so cleverly used actually mean. And of course, the number of cards that survive is inevitably much fewer than the number I actually gathered. Plus, although I always mean to put the cards together and transfer the information into a computer-readable file, it rarely happens. So what I'm trying to say, in my long-winded way, is that you should jot down your notes in a notebook or on a pad, and if you're in the habit of transferring your notes or information on a business card into your computer, do it as quickly as you can.

- **Dress comfortably:** Dress for comfort, but adhere to the traditional style of your industry. Also, comfortable shoes are a must. The convention floors are usually very hard.

- **See what your competitors are up to:** Help yourself to their literature. Observe who is visiting their booths. Try to get their names (everyone wears a badge at these shows) and perhaps attempt to meet them yourself.

If you're toying with the idea of seeking new employment, trade shows represent a great opportunity to meet your competitors and learn a little more about their business. You can also visit booths of other companies that are not direct competitors but have product lines that, given your experience, you can easily adapt to. Be careful not to look too obvious as you put out feelers, however; you never know who is watching.

- **Be present:** If your company is exhibiting, be at the booth for your share of the time—and when you're there, act like the professional you are. Dress appropriately. Get off your phone. Don't get caught sitting and reading your newspaper; remain standing. If you get tired, get some relief.

- **Seek out new business:** A displaying company might be a good candidate for one of your products. Get the names of the company's buyers so you can follow up when you get back to the office.

- **Skip the "goodies":** Don't be tempted by all those silly premiums. They'll only weigh you down. After all, how many stress balls and pens can you possibly need? And do you *really* need another bag advertising someone else's company? Sure, the candy and the sticky-pads and the yo-yos are all great for the scavenger hunt you were planning, but you should try to focus on your real reason for attending the conference in the first place.

- **Limit your literature intake:** You cannot imagine how heavy this can get at the end of the day. Take only the information that is most important to you; as for the rest, see if it can be sent to you through the mail.

- **Follow up:** Follow up on what you saw and who you met as soon as you return to your office. Putting it off until some future date does not work; that date never comes.

It's entirely possible you'll run into someone you know already from a customer or client. While it's great to share a moment or even some time with that person, be very careful about discussing any sensitive issues such as upcoming projects or requirements. There are lots of ears all over who just might hear some information you would not want to get out. I've actually eavesdropped on several discussions that gave me valuable information I would not otherwise have obtained. If you run into a former associate, remember: That person is no longer your ally. He or she is the competition. Exchange pleasantries, ask how the family is doing, but discuss nothing about your company or its business. Any information you provide could come back and bite you in the ass.

Q: • ARE TRADE ASSOCIATIONS A • GOOD WAY TO MEET PEOPLE?

JAMES CALLANDER
THE CUSTOMER PERSPECTIVE

Trade associations provide yet another avenue to meet people inside your industry or trade. Indeed, their entire reason for being is to enable members to network with others, as well as to provide resources for their members and sponsor community activities and events to promote their industry or trade.

The type of trade association you choose to join depends on your motivation. Are you looking to learn more about your own industry? If so, you might choose an association that relates directly to your product or service. Such an association will allow you to network with people within your field—perhaps more experienced salespeople from whom you can learn. If, however, your goal is to learn more about your customers' industry, then you should find out which trade associations your existing customers belong to and then join up yourself. Doing so can help you learn more about your customers' industry, get more time with your customers without asking them to set aside additional meeting time, and gain introduction to potential new customers. Regardless of your motivation, if you do decide to join a trade association, I recommend you first take time to research associations that are active in your area to determine which ones best match your interests.

> Many associations require members to pay dues. These are typically minimum investments meant to help fund meetings, speakers, food, and promotional materials. Most associations allow interested parties to attend one or two meetings before making a decision to join.

Often, trade association meetings are preceded by a social hour. For example, if the meeting starts at 7:00 p.m., the social hour might start at 6:00 p.m. While it might be tempting to blow this social hour off, mingling with other members is a great way to make connections. You'll likely find that people are open about who they are, where they work, and what they do for their company—which can be very instructive. Don't, however, corner some poor soul and hit him or her with a barrage of questions; more than likely, that person will run and hide from that point on. Instead, attempt to connect with other members by finding common interests. Find subjects that allow you to relate to them on a personal level. Maybe you share an interest in the local college football team. Or maybe you both enjoy the same recreational activities. No matter what you find in common, the goal is to find opportunities to really connect with the people you are talking to—even if they don't represent a direct path to a sales opportunity.

Membership in a trade organization is not a one-way street. That is, you're not the only one there seeking to benefit from your membership. Always remember that other members have their own reasons for being involved in the association.

When networking at a trade-association event, the objective is to build relationships, *not* to sell your company or product. In fact, you should keep any selling —apart from selling yourself as a resource—to the bare minimum. If an opportunity arises, you can always follow up the next day with a phone call or visit to discuss it in more detail. Be aware, too, that if you are looking for a quick profit through your association membership, you will surely be disappointed. You should participate in any trade association with an eye toward long-range benefits. The opportunities of membership in one of these associations are not measured in days or months, but in years. Think in terms of distance—you're running a marathon, not a sprint.

MARVIN MILETSKY

THE SALES PERSPECTIVE

Well, here's a question to answer a question: Where can you find people from every segment of your industry in one area at one time? The answer: at a trade-association meeting.

I've worked in the electrical industry for most of my career and have consistently attended meetings of my local trade association. These meetings draw people from every segment of the industry:

- Purchasing agents

- Designers

- Engineers

- Salespeople

- Owners

- Operators

- Maintenance people

- Consultants

- Inside office personnel

- Teachers

- Students

- Representatives

- Manufacturing people

- Inspectors

- Government agencies

- Media personnel

- Field personnel

Your industry will be different, but an equally diverse group will be members of the trade organizations in your business community.

The benefits of participating in your local trade association are endless. Imagine the contacts you can make and the education you can obtain! At a trade-association meeting, you can learn from actual users about what problems they encounter. In one meeting, I received a complaint about one of my products—the information from my fellow association member was used to improve the product and ensure its continued use. You'll also find out about new projects before they become public. And that new purchasing agent you've been trying to get an appointment with might just be in attendance.

When you attend an association meeting, the idea is to build up contacts and network—basically to set yourself to present your company and its products to these contacts privately, at some other time. An association meeting is not the platform for making a sale or taking care of any specific piece of business. There's nothing more distasteful than sitting at a meal and being pitched to. Nobody comes to an event like this to hear your sales pitch; keep any specific business issues in your pocket until you can arrange a time to get together. One last piece of advice: As I mentioned in my answer to the preceding question, be aware that there are ears all around you. Be careful about what specific information you discuss and with whom. Remember that old "loose lips" adage!

Q: How Do You Make the Most Out of a Product Demonstration Meeting?

James Callander
The Customer Perspective

↳ Giving a product demonstration to a group, be it large or small, can represent a huge opportunity for a salesperson—as long as the group is interested in your product or service or has real sales potential. A mandatory meeting that employees are forced to attend might not have the same effect as a meeting whose audience *wants* to be in attendance.

Your audience—which should consist of people who might actually use or benefit from the use of the product or service as well as anyone involved in the decision-making process—must be engaged throughout the event if you are to enjoy the fruits of your labor. To ensure that happens, keep these points in mind:

- Preparing for a product demonstration is vital. Gather any samples, catalogs, or other promotional materials you will need, and be certain you know the specific message you want your presentation to convey. Consider the importance of your client's time and, more importantly, of their staff's time and prepare your presentation accordingly.

- When presenting, your energy level must be high, but not out of control. Maintain eye contact with audience members to keep them engaged.

- Project your voice to the back of the room so all participants can hear you. Don't drone on with your voice at the same volume and pitch; use voice inflection to keep your audience's interest.

- Use open-ended questions to involve the group in a quick discussion. For example, you might ask "Can anyone tell me the benefit of using this type of product?" The question should reveal whether the audience has an understanding of the product or service, knows how it can benefit the user, and whether anyone in the group has experience using a similar product. The answers offer you a way to dig deeper into the product or move on to additional information in a different area.

- It may be that some members of your audience don't completely understand the application of your product or service. For this reason, you'll want to take the time to explain the features and benefits associated with using the product or service. This gives the group an opportunity to assess whether they can utilize the product or service in their business.

- Stay on message, and don't linger too long on any one area of your presentation. Avoid over-communicating or become long winded. Make your time with your audience count by staying focused. If your audience becomes restless and they start shifting in their seats, you'll know you're not presenting the information quickly enough.

- If you and your client have agreed on a time frame for your demonstration, make sure you finish prior to the end of the allotted time. This will allow time for a question-and-answer period after your meeting. Use a clock on the wall, a watch, or even your cell phone to keep track of time during your presentation.

- Provide catalogs and cut sheets as supplements only, not as the main attraction of the meeting. This product information should enhance the experience of those participating in the meeting, not define it.

- If you have samples, bring them. Your audience will appreciate an opportunity to actually see your product and hold it in their hands.

- Don't worry if you mess up part of your demonstration. Odds are, no one in the audience has ever heard the presentation before—meaning they won't know if you mess up or forget part of your message.

- Pass a sheet around so that each person in the group can sign his or her name. A record of the attendees can be useful when following up with the client.

MARVIN MILETSKY
THE SALES PERSPECTIVE

It's amazing how much time we devote to the things we like—and how little to things we need. Case in point: Attending a product-demonstration meeting can be of tremendous value to customer, but because it's not a sporting event or a movie, it is not looked upon with great anticipation.

Part of the problem, of course, is that attending a presentation that is not delivered well can be as boring as watching paint dry. In my earlier days, before I'd had a chance to master this art, I stuttered through my share of presentations.

During several meetings, I came close to putting *myself* to sleep, not to mention my audience. (Observation: Putting people to sleep during a presentation is not a good thing—unless said presentation is designed to promote sleep aids.)

To ensure that both your audience and you benefit from the presentation, keep the following points in mind:

- **Prepare:** Make sure that you know what your audience expects from your presentation and take the time to rehearse what you are going to talk about.

- **Set up beforehand:** You're not going to be able to command much of your audience's time, so use it well. Don't waste it by attempting to set up your presentation after the audience has filed in. Arrive in advance and give yourself sufficient time to set up any displays. That overhead projector must be in place when the people arrive.

- **Offer refreshments:** If you provide coffee or refreshments, lay them out ahead of time. Try to encourage everyone to partake when they first arrive so they do not interrupt the meeting.

- **Turn off your cell phone:** You can't tell people to turn off their cell phones; that would be rude. But at the same time, you want to make sure no one's phone goes off during your presentation. I usually take mine out of my pocket and turn it off in front of the group; I might even mention that I don't want to be disturbed during the meeting. Some people *do* take the hint.

- **Circulate a sign-in sheet among the attendees before you begin**: Don't just tear out a piece of paper from a notepad and use that as the sign-in sheet; instead, have the sheet professionally printed beforehand. At a minimum, the sheet should ask for names, telephone numbers, and e-mail addresses, but can include space for attendees to provide any other information that might be useful to you.

- **Use your time wisely:** Once everyone is in place, start the meeting. Get on course quickly and stay there.

- **Be animated:** Start the meeting with a smile and exude all the energy you possess.

- **Keep your audience's attention:** Make sure your voice carries to the back of the room. Look out into the audience and speak directly to one person at a time. Seek out those who are taking an interest (they'll be out there and easy to spot) and look right into their eyes.

- **Tailor your talk**: Chances are, the people in your audience have varying levels of expertise in the area of your presentation. It's difficult to talk on all levels, though, so determine the level of expertise of the largest contingent and speak to them.

■ **Accept that some people aren't interested:** Not everyone will have the same interest level—meaning that there's a good chance that at least some members of your audience won't be fully awake through the whole meeting. You will spot some closing eyes, especially in morning meetings. Don't be dismayed. Look past these people.

■ **Be conversational:** The most successful presentations are those that are conversational in style. Encourage audience participation in the form of questions and comments.

■ **Stick to what you know:** If you find yourself getting into areas that you are not qualified to discuss, don't go too deep. And don't think that you must have answers to every question on the spot. Field the questions, write them down, and get them into the hands of someone qualified to respond. Disappoint the wise-asses in the audience who are just waiting to trip you up by not going beyond your qualifications; let them know that you will find the answer and get back to them.

■ **Control the meeting:** Make sure the group will not be so large that you cannot control the presentation. If others from your office have joined you for the presentation—perhaps someone from a technical department or a senior executive—keep in mind that the customer is yours. *You* are the one who set up this meeting, and it is yours to control. In the event side conversations develop between members of your team and the individuals in the audience, you must tactfully curb them. Find a way to get—and keep—everyone on track.

To head off a situation in which your presentation is derailed by a co-worker, speak to your team in advance. Let them know they can talk with individuals in the audience after the meeting.

■ **Follow up:** Don't let your efforts in putting on the meeting go to waste. Remember the names of those who were especially interested. Personally thank them at the end. Have your business cards handy. Send any literature or samples you promised immediately upon your return to your office. Get the answers to those who asked questions you couldn't answer. Call to follow up. Set up personal appointments with any prospects. Sorry to nag, but it's all in the follow-up from here; most of your work will come *after* the presentation. Never forget the number-one reason you called everyone together: to provide an avenue to increase your sales.

Q: HOW MUCH TIME SHOULD YOU ALLOW FOR A MEETING AND HOW LONG SHOULD IT TAKE?

JAMES CALLANDER

THE CUSTOMER PERSPECTIVE

In general, you should allow for no more than one hour, although how much time you actually need may vary. If the meeting is one-on-one, then you might not need a whole hour. And if you are meeting with a group of people, you may need the full hour, but don't expect the meeting to last longer than that (unless it's a training class; these can be longer, depending on the topic). Of course, if you've made contact with multiple people at a company, then you might spend more than one hour there because you'll be attending multiple appointments.

More important than the visit's duration is its quality. First and foremost, showing up unprepared to discuss a specific business item, be it one-on-one or in front of a group, will not help you grow your business or your relationship with your client. Get your message clear in your mind and identify what needs to happen for this meeting to be considered a success. Second, especially if you are meeting one-on-one with a customer, observe his or her demeanor carefully. If he or she seems warm and inviting, make an attempt to socialize for a moment. This can assist you in connecting with your customer, which in turn progresses your relationship. (Be ready, though, to shift to your message at a moment's notice.) If, however, your client is more intent on getting down to business, you'll want to launch right into your message. Prompt presentation of the essentials also allows time for you to ask your client whether other groups or people in the office might be able to employ your services. Of course, there are no guarantees you'll have the chance to ask questions such as these or that the person will provide the information you're asking for; if this happens, you'll want to conclude your visit promptly, thanking your customer for his or her time. Before you go, however, look for a reason to schedule another appointment. Use a request made or a question asked by the client or an observation made by you during the meeting to open the door for the next meeting.

The same points apply if you are meeting with a group. You must still arrive with your message and expectations clear in your mind, and you must assess the demeanor of the group to determine how to proceed. In addition, though, you must be prepared in the event various members of the group want to discuss different things and allow for the exchange of ideas from different directions. This is a good problem to have—that is, any of those present who are active in a meeting (i.e., asking questions) are obviously very interested, which is a good thing (in most meetings, people can't wait to get out of them)—*if* you can manage to stay focused. You'll also want to allocate sufficient time for the group to ask questions and comment on the material presented. In addition to enabling them to more fully understand your presentation, this can offer you tremendous insight on the client's staff and provide an opportunity for you to offer support.

So how do you determine whether to dive right into your message (which you are of course ready to deliver at any moment) or to enjoy a few minutes of socializing? Body language is one way:

- If your client is sitting with arms and legs crossed, then he or she will more than likely want to get right into the discussion. Additionally, he or she may be a bit more close-minded about whatever it is you want to convey and require more convincing on your part.

- If your customer is relaxed in his or her chair, you can expect him or her to be more friendly and inviting, as well as more open to taking a few minutes to be social. In this case, you don't need to cut right to the chase; take the opportunity to probe your client a bit in an off-topic discussion. But be mindful of the time so you don't overstay your welcome.

- If the person you are visiting is leaning forward in his or her chair with his or her arms resting on a desk, that person is very interested in you and, more importantly, the reason for your visit. (Note that most people don't start an appointment in this position, but move to it based on their interest.) In this case, in addition to conveying your message, you may also be able to discuss items *not* related to your visit—most notably, who else in the customer's office might find it beneficial to meet with you. Additionally, in this situation, you should be able to ask probing questions to confirm the client's interest.

Another way to assess how quickly you should get to the meat of your message is by assessing your client's attitude. Is the person smiling? Is he or she frowning?

- If your client is smiling, you should be able to take a few minutes for social conversation before getting to the point.

- If your client is frowning, you can bet that person has something on his or her mind. Regardless of whether the person is frowning because of you or is preoccupied with another issue, you can reasonably assume that the meeting will be short. In this case, you'll need to get right into the reason for your visit.

- If your client seems visibly upset, I doubt anything you say or do will be effective. In this scenario, it might actually be best to attempt to reschedule.

Of course, not all sales calls will relate to a specific item of business. You might have more than one reason to visit. Whether you are able to delve into these additional areas depends to a large extent on your client's willingness to allow the meeting to continue. If my day is full of tasks and appointments, I may simply not be able to deviate from my schedule. If I'm taking calls or allowing others to interrupt your visit, you can bet my time is extremely short or other pressing issues are a priority for my day, distracting me from your visit. If this is the case, get your message across right then and there.

Managing your time—and guarding that of your clients—is tremendously important to becoming successful in sales. Spending too much time at any one client can negatively affect business in other areas. By keeping your sales calls to one hour or less per call, you can make more calls per day, increasing your opportunities to grow your business.

MARVIN MILETSKY
THE SALES PERSPECTIVE

More often than not, it's safe to assume that no one really wants to attend a sales presentation. So if you've set up a meeting with a customer—prospective or existing—try to keep that in mind. Make sure to respect the time that's been granted you. Don't do what I did once when presenting to a group of potential clients: Before getting to the heart of the meeting, I broke the ice with some small talk about the big game that had been played the day before. Before I knew it, an in-depth and lengthy discussion ensued, with all the Monday morning quarterbacks in the room putting their own two cents in—until the main person I had come to target got up, politely explained that our meeting had run past the time he had budgeted for, apologized for the fact that he had another pressing meeting to attend, thanked me for coming, and left. (He did mention that he thought his team would do better the following Sunday.) My meeting was over before it really ever got off the ground; without my main focus in attendance, its continuation was an effort in futility.

You're not the social director on a cruise ship, and these people are not your pals. They represent your future paychecks. Your success is not measured in the time you spend with them, but in the sales that are produced as a result of the presentation you've made. Take control of the meeting right from the outset and keep your focus on the reason you're there. Understand, too, that you might be talking to a medium to large audience, with not all in attendance as interested as you are in what is being said or shown.

So how do you control a meeting? Here's some advice for running meetings, based on some of my experiences:

- Introduce yourself with a warm smile and let your audience know how much you appreciate their attendance.

- As you get ready to start, while shuffling papers or arranging samples or literature, make some off-the-cuff remark in a conversational tone—but nothing that will cause a debate or an in-depth discussion to break out. The weather and traffic problems are safe; there really can't be much disagreement on either.

- Continue the conversation while adjusting your papers, business cards, or literature. This should happen as people are entering the room, before they've settled down into their seats. The idea is to stall until everyone is in the room; it's very difficult to start a presentation while people are still filing in. It disrupts the continuity of the presentation, and inevitably you'll lose the attention of those who were already seated when you try to bring the late arrivals up to speed. After everyone has seen and heard your human side, pick the moment to start your presentation.

- In the beginning of the meeting, try not to get into individual conversations with people. Leave that for after the meeting or some later date during a follow-up visit.

- During the presentation, it's as important to sell yourself as it is your product or service. Relax, talk to the participants—but don't lecture them. State what brought you there in the first place; identify the need they have that you have come to satisfy.

- With the foundation set, go straight to your solution. Hit them with the grabber. Show your product or the new innovation that will meet their needs. Share how your company can help them tackle their problems. Don't be another me-too vendor or the low-price-on-the-street type. You are a salesperson; you've got to have something exciting to say about your product, services, or company that will give them reason to see you again—and you've got to get it out fast! Otherwise, you'll lose them to boredom.

- After you've succeeded in making your point(s), field any questions, listen to any comments, and give them the freedom to end the meeting at their convenience. Before they do, however, thank them all for their attention and make sure you all understand what the next step should be.

One more piece of advice, based on another of one of my early blunders: Take care to avoid damaging the meeting space. I once gave a presentation in a conference room that had a beautiful mahogany table. I had brought more than a dozen samples of industrial products made of various metals to show, so I set them out on the table. After the meeting, which went great, I noticed that my samples had scratched the table. I felt really terrible. There wasn't much I could do about it, although I did apologize to the contact who arranged the meeting and I offered to pay for any repairs. It was an innocent mistake, but one that really threatened the success of the meeting. These days, I carry around a little piece of carpeting to set samples on.

If you keep these points in mind, your audience will know what to expect from you at the next meeting. And when that meeting occurs, those initial barriers will have been broken, and a more relaxed atmosphere can start to present itself. But please, no discussions of politics, sports, or religion. It's all about the sale!

Q: HOW SHOULD YOU IDENTIFY THE ACTUAL DECISION MAKER AND ALL PLAYERS WITHIN THE COMPANY?

JAMES CALLANDER
THE CUSTOMER PERSPECTIVE

It's critical that salespeople develop a complete understanding of their client, staff, and how they all fit together. Failing to grasp who the players at a company are and their roles can have a negative impact on your sales. You simply cannot serve your clients well if you don't know who the players are.

As a salesperson, you will encounter people in three different roles:

- **The buyer:** The buyer is the person responsible for developing the inquiry and processing the order after the final decision has been made. The person who plays the role of buyer may also play one or both other roles, depending on the type of inquiry; small-dollar orders requiring quick turnaround will generally fall in this category.

- **The decision-maker:** This person reviews all the available details, including vendor proposals, internal issues, overall requirements, and comments from those people who might influence the decision based on their unique understanding of the company's situation or needs. The decision-maker then decides how to proceed. The decision-maker has the final say on what, where, and when to buy. Decision-makers tend to handle large-dollar orders, high-risk transactions, or scheduling issues.

- **The influencer:** This is someone who gives advice or provides comments to convey the action required by the staff. He or she might be a department head or the actual user of the product or service. The influencer's role can affect your ability to make the sale positively or negatively, depending on his or her understanding of the application the product will be used for. With the support of an influencer, you'll not only be able to make a sale, you'll be able to cultivate a commitment on the part of the client for continued use of the product or service. To achieve a higher level of success, you'd be wise to identify these people within your client's organization. Once you do, you should attempt to secure appointments with him or her, much as you would the buyer. One approach might be to offer technical support through documentation and/or samples.

If you spend all your time attempting to cultivate your relationship with the buyer, you're going to miss out on additional business that might have come your way. Your ability to gain access to the other key players starts with an understanding of your client, their organization, their buying practices, and their acceptance of you and your company. Ask the buyer, "Once you have all the proposals, does the decision rest with you?" If the answer is no, find out who else is involved and attempt to meet with them. As an added benefit, asking this question should guide you in identifying the steps of your client's purchasing process.

Once you determine who the players are in your client's organization, you should develop a database of contacts at each client. This increases your ability to sell and provide solutions that meet or exceed the client's expectations.

Marvin Miletsky
The Sales Perspective

⮔ In many areas of sales, purchase decisions are made based only on price and delivery, with no outside influence on the buyer from anyone else in the company. In these cases, the decision-maker is right before your eyes, and is the only one whose needs must be satisfied in order to complete your sale. This is the person you'll be interfacing with in the future, and your relationship will be built upon the value and service you provide (along with that personality of yours, which will make all the difference).

For products or services that require a more in-depth qualification process, a common method of gaining approval or acceptance is making a presentation in front of a larger group composed of the buyer's support personnel. While making your presentation, you might find one person who shows more interest and asks the most important questions. This person might be one to take note of and follow up with in the future, as he or she might have a positive influence on the buyer. That said, don't make the mistake of going around the purchasing agent, ignoring him or her and aiming your efforts at the person you've identified as the one with the most influence.

> You should be aware that a silent chess game is going on here; as you are assessing the prospect, so, too, is the prospect assessing you. Show your strong personality, and that you control business on your end. Your customer wants to deal with a decision-maker, just as you do.

Your follow-up presentation and subsequent meetings will include technical representatives. Walk a fine line here. The person who signs the order is the purchasing agent, so you don't want to count him or her out. But the one with the most *influence* will be the technical person, so make sure you *sell* to that person. Don't favor one over the other, however, as doing so may result in a power struggle between the two—which may well lead to your elimination by either or both.

Q: • HOW IMPORTANT IS
• IT TO REMEMBER NAMES?

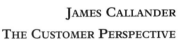

JAMES CALLANDER

THE CUSTOMER PERSPECTIVE

A person's name is one of the most personal and significant things about him or her. First names are often given to honor relatives and last names can represent ethnic heritage. Remembering a person's name tells that person that he or she has significance to you. But while names are important, there is nothing unusual about having trouble remembering them. If you have trouble remembering names, make it a point to try any of several techniques for improving name recognition. One technique is to repeatedly work the person's name into your initial conversations until his or her name is well established in your memory. Another technique involves associating images or catchphrases with a person's name.

But simply remembering a person's name is not enough; correctly pronouncing it is equally important. My last name, Callander, is often mispronounced. I tell people it is pronounced the same was as "calendar," like what you put on the wall; it's just not spelled that way. If your client's name is more complicated than Smith or Jones, be sure you are pronouncing it correctly. It's far better to ask your client to repeat his or her name or ask whether you are pronouncing it correctly than to repeatedly mispronounce it. If a client's name is derived from a language you don't speak, try to find someone who does speak the language to help you improve your pronunciation.

Of course, just as you may have trouble remembering names, so, too, might your customers. Clients are often distracted and may not have had interaction with you lately; your name may have escaped their memory. They'll appreciate your making it easy for them to remember your name by handing out your business card on second and third meetings.

The bottom line? Names are important, and your ability to remember them may not just engender the goodwill of your clients, it may give you some advantage over your competition. Conversely, *not* remembering or mispronouncing a client's name can be a source of irritation and diminish the impact of your message.

That said, your ability to remember names pales in comparison to the importance of you having product knowledge, being reliable and prompt, and providing thorough responses to requests.

MARVIN MILETSKY

THE SALES PERSPECTIVE

I wish I had the ability to remember names, but I've accepted the fact that there are certain things that will always escape me. The truth is, not remembering someone's name has never been a show-stopper for me. I really can't remember a situation where not recalling a name has proven disastrous to my efforts. (Of course, I'm not going to be as easy on myself if I've met someone on several occasions and still can't recall his or her name; I do make an extra effort to ensure that this does not occur.)

All that being said, I do have a few tricks that may help you in this department. Most notably, when I attend a meeting or give a presentation, I make sure to be the last to get the sign-in sheet. If I can't manage that, I'll go so far as to make up some excuse to get it back after everyone's signed it, like I may have accidentally put down a wrong e-mail address. Once the sheet is full, I look it over and make a chart that shows where each person is sitting. That way, I can identify people during or after the meeting, which gives me a better chance at remembering their names later on.

You'll probably find that this name-recognition problem will be at its worst when attending a function or meeting, such as a trade show, where you are meeting any number of people from many different companies at the same time. I have a hard enough time remembering someone's name at his or her office; but take that person out of his or her environment, and his or her name will absolutely escape me—even if I saw him or her the day before!

If remembering names is important to you, Google a phrase like "name memory" or something similar; no doubt you'll get hundreds of thousands of hits. But I've always gotten away with a simple (if embarrassing) "Uh, excuse me, but I seem to have forgotten you name." Works all the time!

Q: • WHEN DO YOU BRING • TECHNICAL SUPPORT WITH YOU?

JAMES CALLANDER
THE CUSTOMER PERSPECTIVE

When you involve others in a sales call depends on your expertise and experience with your products and services. When a client makes a request, consider what you do know about the issue raised; then assess whether you are able to provide the solution yourself. If a client's request goes beyond your knowledge and abilities, you'll want to look to others whose knowledge can benefit the client.

When you realize help is needed—either to provide a clearer understanding of the client's need or to propose a solution (usually based on pricing, timing, the capabilities of the product or service, or some combination of the three) that meets or exceeds the client's expectations—you should immediately solicit others to assist you.

Be aware, however, that bringing others into play to deal with a client inquiry does have its pitfalls—most notably that this third party may lack the skills to deal directly with clients. They are at an even greater disadvantage because they are typically not involved with the client's company or co-workers. You must protect them—and yourself—by giving them the game plan up front. Spend some time before your meeting with the client discussing what your expectations are of them, what they are to talk about, what they are *not* to talk about, and who you will be meeting. If you fail to do so, you are asking for trouble. For example, the main topic might not receive the required level of emphasis and thus your proposal will suffer. Or comments by the person you've brought in may be taken out of context by the client, causing him or her to shut down or even end the meeting. If this happens, you, the salesperson, are forced to launch into damage control with the client instead of securing an order from a satisfied customer.

But things aren't all bad when you bring others with you on a call. Let's talk about the plus side. Serving your client entails more than just taking orders and counting the money. Your client is looking to you for help; to provide this help, you have more resources available than you probably use—including technical resources. There are co-workers and manufacturer representatives who covering every product or service you handle, and many of these people can be of tremendous help to your clients. I've had vendors bring in reps from a manufacturer they carry to discuss a new product line that could save my company time and money; these manufacturer reps inevitably provide specific information about products new to the market that might benefit my business.

Often, everyone can benefit when a salesperson brings in a manufacturing rep. The client learns about products or services that might benefit their business; the salesperson increases the likelihood of a sale now or in the future, and the rep has an opportunity to show his or her product. As an added benefit, the rep is able to determine that you, the salesperson, have good rapport with me, the buyer, and can be counted on to sell the rep's products or services.

MARVIN MILETSKY

THE SALES PERSPECTIVE

Congratulations! Your initial presentation made them want more. Your immediate goal has been fulfilled! You've made it to the second step: the follow-up meeting.

This meeting will be different from the first one—more intense and focused—as you have defined the product or service your customer is seeking. That means your answers will likely need to be more specific. Your overall product knowledge and your basic familiarity with how it's put together were enough to get you to this point. But now it's time to bring out the heavy ammunition: technical support. Bring them out at your earliest opportunity and use them like you would a tool, because they're exactly that: a tool that you will use to get closer to the finish line, the sale. (By the way, I'm not demeaning anyone by calling him or her a tool; when you come right down to it, you're also a tool being used to make the sale. I guess we're all tools to some degree....)

Discuss beforehand what you expect of your tech by way of answers—the depth of information discussed and the amount of time that should be spent.

(I once had a tech get so carried away with his product presentation that he—honest to God—showed the customer a way to bypass the product we were there to sell.) Make it perfectly clear that you won't answer technical questions, and he is to stay away from commercial ones—i.e., about price or delivery—no matter how simple they appear.

Once you're with the customer, remember that *you* are in charge of the meeting, not the tech. The tech's talent is in the knowledge of the product; yours is in the communication with the customer. Control your technical backup, making eye contact when you need him or her to speed up or stop. (Once, when asked by the customer whether our product met the spec, the engineer I'd brought with me pulled out a 50-page military specification to review with my customer. The question was whether the product *met* the spec, not what was *in* the spec. A simple "Yes" would have sufficed.) Many times, techs get so deep into their presentation that they lose the audience. A polite interruption is better than losing your prospect; the tech will get over it, and your customer will thank you later.

Play nice with the tech; he or she can be the best tool in your arsenal. Make sure to share with the tech the results of the meeting. Thank the tech for his or her support and keep that person informed of the progress you make with this effort. If you get the order, let the tech share the celebration; after all, he or she played a vital part in the success. Take the tech to lunch. Become a team.

Q: • How Do You Approach Multiple • Contacts in the Same Company?

James Callander
The Customer Perspective

↳ Everything starts with the first contact—the person through whom you first formed your relationship with the company. This person should be the base from which you branch out in the organization. Use this person to get referrals within the company; other personnel will likely be more receptive to meeting with you if you are introduced by a colleague than they would if you requested a meeting cold. After you've established multiple contacts within your client's organization, you'll want to target specific individuals with information they might find useful. You can also use each new contact as a springboard to reach additional personnel at the client.

> Take your time establishing yourself with multiple staff members. Expectations by various members of your client's staff may pull you in several different directions. If you are not prepared for this, you could wind up being disappointed—or worse, disappointing your client.

Providing training or a product demonstration is another way to make additional contacts within your client's organization; depending on your clientele, you may have opportunities to do this once or twice a year. Your presentation should go beyond being a dog and pony show and allow for a broad appeal, with the objective being to gain preference by those staff members who are ultimately responsible for determining whether your offering will meet their needs.

> Ask those attending your training or demonstration to write their names on a sign-in sheet at the start This can help you identify who you might be able to contact in the future. Ask them to print their names rather than signing it; many signatures are difficult to read.

Even as you build relationships with other personnel in the company, your first contact—the buyer—will likely remain your main contact. You must never lose sight of this individual in any of your dealings with other staff members. Make it a point to regularly communicate to him or her any discussions you've had with others in the office (or in other offices if more than one location is involved); this information can play a pivotal role for you when talking to the buyer.

Note that your targeting of multiple contacts in a company doesn't just help you; it also helps the buyer—which is why buyers will likely appreciate your efforts to work with other members of the staff. When other staff members are able to provide comments and participate in the selection process, not only are additional opportunities often revealed to the salesperson, but the buyer's job is made easier. And seasoned buyers know that vendors who are fully engaged with their clients' staff tend to have relationships beyond price. These engaged vendors recognize issues even before any actual problems surface, they communicate their findings, and they outline how they are going to handle the situation. Simply put, your involvement with other members of their organization gives buyers confidence in their vendors.

The challenge of dealing with multiple contacts at a single company is always keeping your facts straight—which is why you should take good notes when you interact with them. These notes will help guide your next visit or conversation whether you're providing them with information or they're providing you with feedback.

MARVIN MILETSKY

THE SALES PERSPECTIVE

Here's an example of how *not* to approach multiple contacts at the same company: A long-time friend with whom I had done tons of business accepted a position at a company where I had yet to have any success. Thinking my orders from his new company were all but guaranteed, I made an appointment to see him, and when I arrived I was greeted like a long-lost brother in front of his new co-workers and staff. Naturally, I enjoyed the reception, and I did all the right things with my contact: a long lunch and laughing it up in his office for a while. The problem? I basically ignored everyone else I came in contact with during my visit, including the people I was trying to break through to. You can guess what happened when my contact didn't last the month: I was *not* greeted with open arms when I made my next call. Rather, I felt as if I was being punished for my gross lack of judgment on a previous visit. And you know what? I couldn't blame them in the least. The moral of the story: You'd better be nice to the people you meet on the way up, 'cause they're the same ones you'll be seeing on the way down.

Just because you've identified and are dealing with the decision-maker doesn't mean there aren't others who influence that person. If the decision-maker is good at what he or she does, odds are that person takes a team approach and includes colleagues in his or her considerations. It could be a simple observation by one of that person's co-workers that you appear to be capable of filling an order or easy to work with, or a remark that's passed on by a clerk about how nice you are, that's the tiebreaker between you and your competitor. That said, use some caution here. You can't play it up too much with others in the hopes of having them intercede on your behalf. It might look staged or contrived and could work against you. Be yourself! Just keep in mind that you need all the help you can get to be successful—and you can never really predict where the next helping hand might come from.

I've often been in situations where I realized that it would be in my best interest to meet additional personnel at a client's office and wracked my brain trying to figure out a way to do so, only to discover that I needed only to ask my main contact to introduce them to me. Don't ever discount the obvious; the best approach might be right under your nose. But of course, there've been plenty of times when things didn't just fall into my lap and I was forced to be creative. For example, once, en route to the men's room, I purposely made a "wrong turn," which led me right into the office of a person I wanted to see. Feigning ignorance, I apologized for my mistake, asked for some help finding the facilities, and added "By the way, what do you do for the company?" as we were walking along. After hearing his reply, I responded with "You're kidding! Wow! I've got a product that might be of interest to you. Perhaps I could have your card so I can make a future appointment? Or better yet, do you have a few moments now?" A new contact was born.

Thinking up creative ways to make contacts within an organization is something you'll do throughout your sales career. You'll also give plenty of thought as to how to approach these multiple contacts within a group. Make it your business to treat each and every contact as if he or she were the decision maker and *the* most important person to the success of your business effort. Be a good listener and respond to everyone with the information they require in a speedy and professional manner. A cardinal rule is to treat each person in any group the same, never showing favoritism to one over the others, and never trying to impress others with how well I might know one individual. I know my relationship with that person; I don't need to broadcast it to everyone else.

I've been lucky over the years to have been invited into clients' premises and given free rein to visit any number of people within. I've always considered this a privilege, not a right, and have viewed it as a sign of the trust they have in me. I keep their trust by always remembering that this site is not *my* office, it's theirs. I never barge in on people, I don't use my cell phone, and I don't interfere with the normal flow of their business. You're going to insinuate yourself the same way into your clients' facilities; never abuse this privilege.

Q: • CAN YOU ASK A PROSPECT • WHOM THEY COMPETE WITH?

JAMES CALLANDER

THE CUSTOMER PERSPECTIVE

Selling to your client requires you to know more than just your own products and services. You also need to know who your client is, including the various personnel involved. You should know who your clients customers are and what they do. You should know who *your* competitors are with respect to your client. And you should also attempt to learn who your client's competitors are. Your client might have several competitors, depending on the market they are in. A single location could be competing for business locally, regionally, or possibly nationally.

So what is the importance of having this information? There are two main reasons:

■ **You may be able to use the information to cultivate a new client:** The client's competitors may offer you another avenue in sales if you are able to call on them. Adding a competitor's account to your customer base potentially doubles your chances of securing an order when the two companies are competing for the same piece of business. Working with two or more companies that compete against each other also places you in a resource position for these companies. They may want to contact you for information on inquiries you might have seen or work for which they are interested in receiving a proposal from you.

> If you are calling on two or more clients that are competitors, you must manage these relationships well. Any perceived favoritism for one or both can have serious repercussions.

- **It may give you a better understanding of your client's business:** Knowing who your client's competitors are can help you in your efforts to support your client. Especially if a competitor becomes a thorn in *your* side, you may find yourself working more closely with your client to assist them in securing a piece of business they want. Ideally, their trust for you will deepen, and they'll quickly see that working with you is the best way for them to succeed.

There are many ways to find out who your client's competitors are. One is to ask your client directly for the information. They may not give you a full picture of who they compete with, however. Another resource might be your client's own customers; they may tell you which companies, other than your client, they use for services. Yet another resource may be the companies you represent. They will probably know who is using their products and whether they would be a competitor to any of your clients. Regardless of how you get it, it's good information to have, and it may be helpful in future dealings with your client.

MARVIN MILETSKY
THE SALES PERSPECTIVE

Yes, by asking a prospect who they compete with you run the risk of raising suspicion about your future loyalty. Lots of companies don't like their suppliers to support their competition. But the way I see it, they don't pay you not to, so wherever you have to go to seek orders is fair game.

When I approach a prospect, I'm not just a salesperson; I'm a detective. I want to know every bit of information I can about them—including their competition. This information can be used immediately or referred to at some later date. Like a spare tire, it's great to have when you need it!

I've mentioned already that you should take as little of your prospect's time as possible during an initial meeting; your primary function there is to introduce your company and its products and to stir up interest. You won't want to waste time during that meeting by asking questions that will take them away from their main focus. But as your relationship grows, opportunities will arise for you to obtain the answers you want. Be patient. The information will find its way to you—though possibly not from the buyer, whose knowledge of the business side of the company is usually limited.

Often, the company I provide a proposal to is bidding against others to obtain their own orders. But just because they lose *their* order doesn't mean I have to lose one, too. For example, suppose you're in the packaging business, and you've given a proposal to your client. Your client, in turn, proposes a product to his customer, including your product as part of the bid. If your client loses his bid to another company, there's nothing wrong with asking who that company is; with that information in hand, you can then try to offer your packaging to them. I know it sounds cold-hearted, but you don't get paid for good effort or coming in second. You were loyal during the bid process, but you need to convert the proposal into business to save your own ass—even if it's a long shot, you must try.

In trying to obtain this information, be as subtle as you can. An "off the cuff"/ "by the way"–type question is always the best approach. If the opportunity does not present itself, however, don't ask. Your number-one goal is to service those who are in front of you at the moment; they must believe that you would put no one else before them.

Q: CAN YOU IDENTIFY TO WHOM YOUR CUSTOMER IS PROVIDING MATERIALS, AND IS IT RIGHT TO TARGET HIS INTERNAL CUSTOMER?

JAMES CALLANDER
THE CUSTOMER PERSPECTIVE

The answer to this question depends on the industry your client is in. The construction industry, for example, has a vast client base that includes residential, commercial, industrial, utility, and others. In some cases it would be acceptable to sell within the client base; in others there would be no benefit to attempting to establish a relationship.

In any case, targeting your client's customer base has both a downside and an upside, for both you and your client. The downside is that your client may reasonably conclude you are interfering with their business by calling on their customer. The fact that, in doing so, you are causing no problems between them is no consolation to the client; their perception of wrongdoing on your part is all that's needed for your relationship to sour.

The upside is that your products or services may become the preferred one by those companies supporting your client. For instance, say you sell for a company that calls on distributors that sell to end users in a given market. If you call exclusively on the distributors, how well you do ultimately depends on how well the distributors perform their sales functions. Sure, your ability to support the distributor helps increase your sales, but the distributor controls how successful you'll be from year to year. And if they also work with your competition, you may lose business due to price, availability, or other factors.

If, however, in addition to calling on the distributor you also call on the actual end user, you can potentially persuade that end user to purchase your product or service rather that that offered by your competitor from the distributor. As end-user demand for your product increases, the distributor will inevitably begin to focus further on your products or services, further escalating your sales and increasing market share, enabling you to nurture your business at each distributor.

All that being said, you shouldn't spread yourself so thin that you cannot manage the clients you already have. Managing those clients effectively is critical to your success. If you don't, the erosion of support needed to maintain or increase sales begins. Do not give your competitors the opening they need to dislodge you.

MARVIN MILETSKY

THE SALES PERSPECTIVE

Selling is like putting together a gigantic puzzle. You've got to look at every piece from every angle to make them all fit together. Identifying who your customer is providing materials to is an important piece of the puzzle. Always be in information-gathering mode when you're in contact with your customer. Trade some of your information for some of his or hers. Ask what other departments in his or her company could profit by the use of your product or service.

Be aware, however, that your direct contact might not appreciate your efforts to cut him or her out of the loop—but sometimes you gotta do what you gotta do to advance your cause. So identify and target—just do it with care. Here are a few points to keep in mind:

- A facility tour can be extremely valuable in learning where your products are used and who exactly uses them. Greet each person you meet on the tour with a handshake and a smile, and be sure to give out your business card. If you can, ask these people some questions or, if you sense that politics may be an issue, let people know they can get more information about your company by asking the person who's showing you around. In any case, keep your pad handy and write down the names of anyone you meet so you can contact them directly in the near future. Having met you already, they should be far more receptive to your phone call.

- If, during a presentation to a group, you notice one person who takes more of an interest in what you're saying than the others, he's your guy! Get to know him. Befriend him. Put your salesman's hat on as you help to solve his problems, and enlist his aid in guiding you within his organization.

- Many companies employ departments dedicated to planning and/or estimating. Often independent of purchasing, these departments can be a wonderful source of information that will help in your sales effort. Work with them to position your products in the right place for their future projects. It's especially important to follow these projects as time passes to see if they have been successful; if so, make sure the purchaser is aware of your efforts and support during the planning or estimating stage. It's not thanks you're seeking—it's an order!

- Making the acquaintance of a salesperson in your target company could prove valuable, as they're usually more than willing to talk with you and share some of the frustrations they encounter in trying to market their finished product. In this way, you may be able to learn more about how the company uses your product and who else you can contact to generate orders. It's easier than you might think to find these salespeople; often, a simple phone call to the sales department will produce the necessary name and contact information. Alternatively, try attending a trade show where the company is displaying; some key salespeople might be manning the booth.

Use your ingenuity to make contact with the buyer's internal customer. Once, I was attempting to sell products to a construction company for use by their field personnel. I couldn't get past their uncooperative purchasing agent, so I went directly to a project site and generated enough interest that the field personnel insisted the PA call me. Similarly, a salesman who was attempting to sell products to *my* company actually stopped by at break-time and got into a discussion with some of our factory people about a product he wanted to introduce. Our PA wasn't too happy about it, but the guy did make the sale. Remember, all's fair in love and sales!

Q: • Is Your Prospect a One-Time Deal?
Q: • How Do You Treat Them?

James Callander
The Customer Perspective

↳ I have several transactions each year with one-time-only vendors to meet my co-workers' needs. The majority of these vendors specialize in a particular service or product that I will need only once. I treat them exactly as I do vendors we use daily, with one exception: I don't have a working relationship with them beyond the one order. I keep their contact information in case another opportunity to use their services arises; if I threw that information away, I would have to go through the whole process of identifying a vendor on the off chance I ever needed them again. And some of these vendors are thoughtful enough to contact me later in the year to see whether we might need additional services anytime soon; when they do, I always attempt to have a short conversation with them or reply to their e-mail. But usually, once they've delivered that one time, we part ways.

As you are prospecting, you are generally not focused on the one-shot order. More than likely, you are attempting to expand your business by providing a continued service for the prospect; any prospect you are attempting to develop is more likely to either become a client or not a client at all than becoming a one-time customer. Your effort is focused on obtaining this goal. That said, the one-time customer is nothing to shy away from. Even if a customer represents only a one-time opportunity, you should provide your services as if they are the most important client you have. The main reason is simple: Your next prospect might just be a referral from that one-time customer.

MARVIN MILETSKY

THE SALES PERSPECTIVE

↳ Unless you're selling caskets to people for their own personal use, I really can't imagine thinking of any prospect as a one-time deal. Even if a one-time opportunity with a company were to present itself, it wouldn't necessarily hold true that the person you're dealing with in that company won't move to a new company in the future. In that case, you could easily restart your relationship. The lesson: Keep in touch with these contacts as you would a regular customer. Make sure they're up to date on your company and products. They might not be on your "A" list of people to see, but you really cannot afford to assume they'll have no relevance in the future.

I've never considered any customer to be a one-time-only prospect, and never treat them as such. Sure, there will be times when the likelihood of obtaining a repeat order appears remote; even so, you must serve the client in the same way you would a repeat customer. Your main focus throughout your selling career will be relationship-building that brings repeat business. While it may not seem like there will be future opportunities with a customer, consider how often people change jobs in the business world. Your satisfying a person's one-time need at his or her old company may be just the reason he or she calls you at his or her new one. Also, a satisfied one-time customer may well provide you with information on other prospects, not to mention recommending you to their colleagues in other companies.

Treat the one-time customer as you would any of your steady customers. The worst thing that will happen is that the client will have a good experience with you, and nothing further will develop. I do have have one word of caution, however: Make sure you or your accounting department ensures that payment of your invoices will be guaranteed. I've had experiences where one-time customers have not paid according to agreed-on terms, their attitude being that as they don't need us anymore, their failure to pay can't hurt their business. How short-sighted of them! The fact is, many *have* had occasion to return to us for service or a question about their original purchase. You can imagine the level of cooperation they received....

Q: • DOES PROMOTIONAL MATERIAL • HAVE AN INFLUENCE?

JAMES CALLANDER

THE CUSTOMER PERSPECTIVE

↳ I receive a truckload of promotional materials each year. People say that this type of advertising is cost effective and that people do respond to the mailings, but at the end of the week, when I shred the large pile of materials I've received, I'm not sure they're right.

That said, there are certain types of promotional materials that I do find useful: those that give me an opportunity to try a product or service free of charge for a period of time. I can provide these items to the relevant people in my company and, using their feedback, I can better assess the effectiveness of the product or service and, more importantly, the level of acceptance by those who might benefit from its use. If you have these types of promotional materials available to you, you'll want to offer them to clients whenever possible, whether they're prospects or existing clients. After placing the item with a client, you should make yourself available to answer any questions they may have after trying the product; in addition to helping your client, following up in this way also enables you to provide feedback on the product or service to your company.

The promotional materials that I find to be *ineffective* for generating interest are the flyers salespeople leave that simply promote a product. Typically, there's no discussion or follow-up by the salesperson to determine whether we in fact might have a use for the items mentioned in the flyer. Flyers and other promotional literature accompanied by samples are more interesting. Being able to see and touch the item gives perspective that printed literature can't provide. Now, use samples and promotional materials along with a group meeting, and you will have a much better chance at actually making something happen.

In general, promotional materials that are client-specific will be more successful than promotional materials that use a broad approach—for example, covering an industry or market-focused slant.

I'd like to see the development of promotional materials that allow for more interaction, such as Webcasts. We use Webcasts at my work to highlight saving plans, health-care benefits, and so on, but I don't see many vendors embracing this type of media to promote specific products or services. When a salesperson supports a client that has more than one office or branch, pulling together personnel from multiple locations in order to promote a product or service can be tricky; Webcasts offer a great way to overcome this problem. With Webcasts, you can add value to your company's offerings and attract a larger audience at your client's location—and by extension differentiate yourself from the competition.

MARVIN MILETSKY
THE SALES PERSPECTIVE

↳ I really can't answer this question without first clarifying that there are two separate and very distinct types of promotional materials:

- **Literature:** You know, brochures, catalogs, flyers, and so on.
- **Premiums or handouts:** This includes the inevitable keychains, pens, pencils, mugs, and so on.

Literature is invaluable and must be included in your toolbox. It backs up the claims you make about the product or service you're trying to sell. Don't get caught short without enough brochures or catalogs to give to each individual you see on a call.

> Not a piece of literature gets into the hands of my customers without my business card being permanently attached in a very prominent position. Make sure you do the same. Don't worry if they already have your card; this piece of literature must permanently be associated with you. You can always buy more cards if you run out.

Let your inside backup know that you must be informed of any inquiries for literature that come in. Use your own judgment as to whether you want it sent or hand-delivered. Hand-delivery is always your best bet—provided you can get there. If not, use the fastest method to get it into your prospect's hands. Just consider what *you* do with stuff you get through the mail compared to when it's handed to you personally; you always pay more attention to the hand-delivered item. In any case, maintain a list of people who've received literature through the mail. Call them to confirm their receipt. Tell them you'll be in the area on a certain date and that you want to stop in to talk. Don't ask if they want you to come in; tell them when you are coming. This removes their option to decline.

In addition to using the professionally printed brochures developed by great marketing minds who've tested each and every photograph, product shot, and paragraph before going to press, spend some time to make your own homemade brochures. Before I see a potential client, I use a digital camera to take some product and application shots that are unique to their needs. It shows a more human side to our company, gives the prospect personalized information, and underscores my own understanding of their specific issues. In my experience, these less-professional efforts have garnered more interest and positive comments than the far more expensive—but somewhat stand-offish—materials I get from the marketing department.

As far as premiums, or handouts, go, I've never been a fan of giving junk to my customers. I can't really remember when giving a keychain, pen, pencil, ruler, calendar, or mug produced an excited reaction. Still, there are some creative ways to give very inexpensive premiums to have your name remembered. Once, we included a roll of LifeSavers candies in each package of an industrial product we shipped. A label attached with our logo told the recipient to "Enjoy your next break on us." The cost of the LifeSavers was insignificant compared to the attention we got and the reorders they brought.

Don't hand out "one size fits all" premiums. Try to give premiums that will be of value to the recipient. Instead of passing out a couple hundred rulers, get a few golf shirts made. Put your company logo in an inconspicuous place—say, on the sleeve. Your customer is more likely to wear this than a shirt with your logo in the center of the chest. He knows who he got it from; he doesn't need to be a human billboard for your company.

Premiums offer wonderful opportunities to bring your sense of humor into play, as I did with a prospect who had promised to place an order in a few days. He requested a dozen of my company logo hats for his fellow employees; I told him I'd send the hats after he placed the order. We wound up stalemated, with him telling me with a laugh, "No hats, no order." To resolve the impasse, I charitably offered to send half the hats before the order was placed and the balance upon its receipt—only by "half the hats," I meant, literally, half the hats. That is, I cut them in half. I sent the first batch of half-hats to the customer. When he got them, he called, laughing, to place his order, at which point I of course made good on my word and sent the second half. Today, 10 years later, he still has those half hats on his desk.

Q: Do Samples Help Open Doors?

James Callander

The Customer Perspective

Samples don't just play a major role in opening doors, they're a huge part of gaining business and locking clients into continuous use of your product. Being able to actually see and use a sample in a real-life situation helps establish acceptance of the product by your client. You can never hand out too many samples to your clients at all levels and departments in their businesses.

Sales is all about recommending products and services to your clients, be they prospects or customers you've done business with for some time, that will help them solve a problem or that they have never seen before—and offering samples is an inexpensive way to do that. Vendors frequently bring me samples of new products they want the people in my company to try. I then decide who in my company would be able to determine whether using the sample in our work is practical. Many times, the feedback from my co-workers is positive. They like the product and would use it—indeed, may even request it (the ultimate achievement for any salesperson)—in the future. This makes my job easier as I'm attempting to fill their requisitions; I now have another option I know my co-workers can use.

> I have samples in my office that are two years old. They serve as a constant reminder of what I might be able to use one day. They are a constant calling card, similar to a business card, in that they remind me of the vendor who brought me the sample.

After you've left samples with a client, schedule a follow-up meeting in a couple of weeks to get their feedback. This follow-up meeting should be short and should focus on the client's use of the sample. Likes and dislikes should be noted; note, too, any comments from individuals who were given the chance to make use of the samples. (You'll want to touch base with these individuals on future visits to your client.) This gives you the option to suggest alternatives or rectify any misunderstandings the client might have that are preventing them from accepting the product.

If your client loves the product—maybe it resolves a problem the client had or exceeds their expectations—your reward is a satisfied customer who will use the new product for as long as they maintain a need for it. Another benefit is the trust your client will bestow on you now that you've recommended a product that met their needs. Given your success this time around, what client wouldn't come to again when faced with a new problem? Now the only obstacles are pricing and availability. Bringing me a sample of a product that isn't fully developed or has insufficient inventories will do you more harm than good; you might want to hold off showing samples of new products if the availability is suspect.

MARVIN MILETSKY

THE SALES PERSPECTIVE

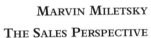 In the right circumstance and when given to the proper parties, samples are a wonderful way to open doors and, going a little further, could even turn out to be the means by which you seal your deal. Just keep in mind that the samples in different industries will have a different cost to you and effect on your customer. Be sure to protect your interests in all circumstances. For example, if you're providing a sample of a design you might have for a new addition for a building, you've got to be careful not to hand over so much that the client can go forward without you.

A sample might serve as reinforcement for your claims about your product and its suitability for the buyer. It also confirms your confidence in the merchandise. Notice, however, that I'm talking samples—not necessarily *free* samples. There's a cost associated with every sample you hand out, which should be recovered in the form of actual dollars or information. The smile you receive from the little old lady you helped cross the street is all the payback you need for that deed; providing a sample to a potential client requires a whole lot more. Remember your Latin (or Hannibal Lecter in *The Silence of the Lambs*): It's *quid pro quo*.

When deciding whether to give out a sample, consider whether the cost of the sample is proportionate to the expected return. For example, if you were selling drapes to a consumer, you could afford to give a sample swatch of material. If, however, you were targeting a department store, then the sample you provide would be a complete set of drapes. The same would apply if you were selling sinks.

You probably wouldn't be able to recover the cost of the sample by giving one unit to a homeowner who might need two, but providing a sample to a plumbing-supply distributor will likely yield a handsome return.

Your cost recovery does not necessarily have to come in the form of monetary remuneration. Payback could come in the form of a customer providing you with feedback on the product. In that scenario, make sure the customer is aware of this expectation. Have formal paperwork drawn up to this effect to ship with the sample, and include a packing slip that should be signed as evidence of their receipt. If possible, hand-deliver the item and paperwork or arrange to visit with your customer shortly after the item and paperwork arrive.

Another payback scenario might involve your customer agreeing to test the sample. If you go this route, make sure *you*—not the customer—pick a date that is not too far in the future for the delivery and/or installation. This gives you control over the implementation. Then follow up on the phone or in person to make sure the unit is being tested or used. You may have to do a bit of prodding; customers will rarely feel a sense of urgency to test your sample.

Here are a few other points to consider when handing out samples:

- When deciding whether to provide a sample, don't be afraid to ask your client what he or she expects to gain from its receipt and use. Can you count on him or her to place an order based on the results?

- Make sure that you know your price is in line with that of other similar products on the market. You don't want to hand out a sample only to be priced out.

- Timing plays a role. Providing a sample for a foreseen need in the distant future might be less effective than waiting until the need or purchase date draws closer.

- Make sure your sample lands in the hands of the right people. Use the purchasing agent as the conduit to get the sample into his or her company, but make sure the decision-makers and qualifiers are in the loop.

- If the product requires installation, have it installed by someone trained to do so. For example, satellite TV dishes must be installed on the highest part of a building and fixed at a precise angle to obtain the signal. If such a dish is being set up as a sample for trial, the satellite company can't rely on someone who is unfamiliar with this type of installation to put it in place; their own installer should do the job. It's the only way to guarantee that a product will have its best shot at success.

There may be times when a sample actually solves a problem for a customer and remains in their possession permanently. I once worked for a company that manufactured an industrial hanger capable of supporting a massive amount of weight in a very confined area. Our customer, a transit agency, wanted to test the unit to ensure it would do what we claimed. This was a double-edged sword, because if the unit worked, they would hardly want to dismantle it and return it. To resolve this, we proposed that they order the unit and pay for it in full with the agreement that if it did not satisfy their needs, they could return it for full credit. Having put money on the table, the customer had more than a passing interest in ensuring that the unit was tested and used. And of course, customers might well order additional units in the future if the one you provide meets their needs; in our case, the transit agency paid for our hanger, used it, and ordered several more later on.

If the sample you provide doesn't meet the buyer's requirements, you're entitled to know what aspect of the sample fell short and if there's something that can be done to make the unit acceptable. You also have a right to ask whose unit *did* satisfy them so you'll have a better idea about the competing product in the future. And if the unit fails to operate in a manner consistent with your claims, it's imperative that you dissect the failure within your company and return to your prospect with a full report to ensure that the failure of one item doesn't compromise the relationship you're trying to build.

Then there's a whole world of sales where giving out samples is a standard operating style, such as with commodity items or food products. There are advantages to handing out samples to consumers for their trial. How often have you gone to a football game or supermarket to find a promotion going on where samples of products are being provided for your taste or use? These are usually given along with discount coupons that can be redeemed for a purchase of the product at a local vendor. Even in the world of industrial sales, I've seen many companies give what they call "counter days" at wholesale outlets where many users come by during the course of the day. A salesman stays in attendance for a long period of time and provides samples of his product to be tried and used in an effort to expose as many people to the product as possible. These handouts are usually inexpensive items that can be tried in small amounts, so the cost of the sample can be recovered by a purchase that is usually in larger quantities. For example, if you were handed a sample of the latest and greatest paper clip, one that revolutionizes the paper clip industry, you might try one or two, but your eventual purchase will be in the hundreds if not thousands of pieces. And how many times have you been handed a sample sip of a new juice in the supermarket that has satisfied your taste buds enough to entice you to purchase the item? Try walking through a department store fragrance aisle without being squirted with a barrage of different products that are supposed to make you irresistible to the opposite sex. Although I've always questioned who really would like to smell like any of the aromas they spray, it seems to work and reinforce the endorsement advertising seen in magazines, direct mail, and on television. A small sample of aromatic mist, possibly coupled with name and endorsement recognition, is enough to entice you to part with your money and complete a purchase.

Q: • SHOULD DIRTY LAUNDRY BE • DISCUSSED ABOUT YOUR COMPANY?

JAMES CALLANDER
THE CUSTOMER PERSPECTIVE

Although negative discussions about your company's personnel, your client's organization, or even a competitor will almost certainly present themselves, you should be apprehensive about participating in them. Likewise, you should remove yourself from any conflicts that occur during meetings at a client's place of business, which can occur when various staff or departments have different internal agendas.

If you are caught in the crossfire of a conflict at your client's office, hopefully it will be over a minor issue and will quickly blow over. Until that happens, you should avoid interjecting your opinion or comments. Guard your opinions even after the conflict has been resolved and your regular discussion continues, even if your client wants to bring up the conflict again. You don't want to be seen as taking sides, which might lead to someone on the client's staff being alienated from you.

If the conflict is more intense or emotionally charged, it might be best for you to excuse yourself from the client's office—especially if you sense that your presence is making your client feel embarrassed. You can always reschedule your visit. (Chances are, your client may appreciate the gesture, leading to a more fruitful relationship in the future.) If you are not able to excuse yourself, ask your client to explain what happened when the situation clears up in order to determine whether you should reschedule or whether you might indeed be the source of the issue. It's doubtful that your presence was the source of the issue, but if it was, you definitely want to know—and why.

In any case, throughout your sales career, you will no doubt be exposed to many situations in which you must tread carefully to avoid jeopardizing your relationship with your client, which includes keeping a lid on conversations or situations you witnessed while visiting a client. How you handle these situations—and yourself—is paramount. Any discussion of an individual's behavior or demeanor during the course of a business visit should be of the positive variety only. Do not allow gossip to be your downfall. It's better to let things pass without comment and move on to the business at hand.

The same goes for issues in your company that may be known by your client. You may need to acknowledge any internal strife, but you shouldn't present information to your client that might affect his or her opinion of you or your company. If the issue relates to business, such as how an order was handled, you can provide details on how you and your company are correcting the situation so it doesn't happen again. The last thing you want to do if something goes wrong is tell a client how bad your company is.

MARVIN MILETSKY

THE SALES PERSPECTIVE

- "The head of our quality-control department is a drunk."
- "Our CFO served his prison sentence with real class."
- "I swear, the receptionist could bring down the whole company with what she knows."
- "It's a damned good thing we have product-liability insurance!"

Honestly? Sometimes honesty isn't the best policy. Even if the head of quality control really *is* a drunk and your CFO has more than a little bit in common with Martha Stewart, you really are kidding yourself if you think you can sell a product or service without selling your company behind it. Prospects make judgments not only on the products produced but on the company that turns them out.

The people within your organization are as important as the products or services you're turning out. When talking to customers, you speak as highly of your co-workers as you would members of your own family (assuming you speak highly of your family, of course). You must describe your staff as the absolute best group of people you've ever had the pleasure of working with. In fact, when making presentations touting a product that will save the day for a prospect, I've actually made it a point to highlight the various talents of the staff behind our offerings. I've talked about Charlie, the manager of production, in the most positive ways possible, noting that his knowledge of his work and his sense of responsibility to get products out in a timely professional manner is a source of great pride in our company. And all that is basically true. But what the customer *doesn't* need to know is that Charlie is actually the most miserable s.o.b. on the planet. *I* know that—but my customer doesn't need to.

As you attempt to gain business from a prospect, you can rest assured that at the same time, they are trying to determine whether your company can be a trusted resource. A smart purchaser will try to delve a little deeper into a potential vendor. If he or she asks questions regarding personnel issues within your company, just remember that you're not dealing with a friend; you're dealing with a business partner. Too much information is *too much information*! If you have nothing good to say, say nothing.

Q: • ARE THERE PEOPLE YOU ARE JUST • NOT GOING TO DO BUSINESS WITH?

JAMES CALLANDER

THE CUSTOMER PERSPECTIVE

⮑ I'm not worried about you finding people who won't do business with you. You'll encounter plenty of them throughout your sales career. For whatever reason—maybe they're not wild about your product, or perhaps they simply don't connect with you—you will simply never earn their business.

But what about the opposite—people you won't do business with? Inevitably, you will at some point wind up at a crossroads with a client, requiring you to make an important decision about the future of your relationship and business. The decision can and will affect your future both with the client in question and as a whole in your total client base. Sometimes, the decision will be made for you due to circumstances beyond your control—for example, if your financial department halts the acceptance of any new orders from a client due to unpaid invoices. While this decision might be permanent, it's more likely temporary— but if you find yourself working with a client who constantly falls behind on their payments, you need to determine whether that client is really worth the aggravation.

Other times, you may simply be unable to tolerate a client's attitude. Admittedly, as a purchasing agent, when I'm facing critical deadlines and am under the gun to deliver necessary materials to my co-workers, I need my vendors to handle my inquiries promptly and completely—and as a result of this urgency, some attitude might slip into my conversations. I seldom find it necessary to raise the volume of our discussions, but it does happen. But there are clients for whom loud, aggressive conversations are the norm. They will try to intimidate and bully you into responding to their requests. This type of person is constantly riding you to improve your pricing, get quicker deliveries, etc. And even if you meet or exceed their expectations, their tone doesn't change. It's like you can't please them, no matter what you do! Some salespeople work well under these conditions, but if you are not one of those people, you may be faced with the tough decision as to whether you really need this client. Some salespeople have the luxury of walking away, knowing they have plenty of other clients to make up the difference in sales. But even if that's not the case, walking away from a client can simply be a matter of survival.

On another note, suppose you are attempting to develop a new client through cold-calling or trying to increase your business with an existing account. If, even in the face of your substantial effort, there isn't any noticeable movement, you must set in place a plan to pull away. Indeed, this is as important to your success as making a sale. If you are using valuable time to cultivate business, you are by definition taking time away from generating sales. This time could be redistributed among those who already support you.

Are there people you are just not going to do business with? The answer is yes! Whether it's due to a lack of client response or a client whose personality is one you can't deal with, you should shift your efforts to a more comfortable and reliable source of business.

MARVIN MILETSKY

THE SALES PERSPECTIVE

Can you believe that anyone wouldn't come knocking down my door in an effort to give me an order? After all, I've got all this charm and charisma; it just beckons people to seek me out. It really shouldn't matter what I'm selling!

Well, I've had to believe it, and you'll have to, too. You're going to come across lots of different personality types and lots of situations that will result in your inability to do business. There's an expression about cutting your losses and moving on, and the earlier you recognize the signs, the faster you can go forward.

There's a simple truth about some people with whom you're going to interface, either in business or social situations: For some unknown reason, they might not be comfortable with you, and at the same time, you're not really taken with them. You meet them and, for some unknown reason, there's just something between you that's uncomfortable. Unfair as this may be, I've actually seen people from a distance and instantly disliked them. Inevitably, you'll run into someone here or there at some point in your sales career who just rubs you the wrong way or vice versa; chances are, you will not be able to business with this person.

Other situations will present themselves where the reality is that the products or services you are selling do not offer any advantage or price benefit to a prospect. Or maybe your prospect has already identified vendors who satisfy their needs and don't want to add another me-too vendor to his or her list. Case in point:

Very early in my sales career, I sold corrugated cardboard boxes. There was one company in particular that I wanted to add to my client roster. I visited the account several times, but they never placed an order. Finally, out of frustration, I asked the buyer why I hadn't been able to get as much as a trial order from them; he responded that although my pricing was competitive and the products met their needs, the only time they could ever consider my company would be in the case of a dire emergency, as their main source for boxes was the owner's cousin.

In situations like these, there comes a point when you just have to walk away. Notice I said "walk," not "run." Give yourself plenty of time to work the account before you throw in the towel. Ultimately, though, your success in sales is not measured in the number of calls you make but in the amount of sales you do. If a prospect just isn't receptive, write this one off and live to sell another day. But be careful here: Don't burn your bridges behind you. You can never predict when your paths might cross again, and under what circumstances.

Q: • HOW DOES MULTIMEDIA HELP • TO DEVELOP NEW PROSPECTS?

JAMES CALLANDER
THE CUSTOMER PERSPECTIVE

⮡ Historically, those in the sales profession have relied heavily on the print medium—mailers, magazine ads, fax messages, fliers, etc.—to maintain their client's attention. But print advertising directed to the prospect doesn't always achieve the desired effect—even if the advertisement is for a product or service you know they use. (Fax messages in particular are DOA—dead on arrival, typically tossed in the trash minutes after they arrive. That medium is simply not an acceptable tool for prospecting.) These days, we can communicate information to current and potential clients using Web links, pictures, scanned documents, audio, video, and so on.

Bundled e-mail promotions involving messages that contain links that recipients can click to visit a company's Web site are believed to target a specific audience that ensures a better response rate. In my view, however, promotional e-mails are not effective unless the prospect has opted in—that is, requested to receive information from your company. In the case of those prospects who haven't, these types of advertisements typically end up in a junk folder or are blocked by the prospect's IT department. And even those prospects who *do* receive and open an e-mail message from your company are unlikely to respond. As for the people who respond: They'll quickly lose interest if your e-mail simply urges them to check your Web site; instead, it should provide links specifically to the page containing the information to which the e-mail message refers.

To keep the attention of prospects who visit your Web site—whether from an e-mail message, an Internet search, or some other method—you must ensure that information on the site is easy to find. As a purchasing manager, I search vendor Web sites daily for documentation needed for clarifications or technical support—and often, the information I need is buried under layers of screens. When this happens, I want to turn to the vendor's catalog and search the old-fashioned way: using an index. Search engines on Web sites should be the workhorse that serves any clients looking for information. If the search feature is powerful, then many normally unanswered requests can yield a result that enables the client to narrow their search and hopefully find the exact item they are looking for more quickly. Also, consider adding videos to your site that enable clients to see your products in action. This can be a key way to interest a client in an actual live demonstration.

In my view, multimedia is not a primary tool in the selling cycle, but rather a secondary tool to enhance your client's experience with you and your company. I still say your best bet for prospecting is an old-school phone call or in-person cold call. Your goal is to get an audience with someone who can use your product or service. So work your prospects in person or over the phone, then follow up with e-mails, literature, or Web site information once you have been accepted.

MARVIN MILETSKY
THE SALES PERSPECTIVE

I did write an answer to this question, and it was pretty good, but since multimedia tools have been a huge part of my son Jason's own sales efforts (he's CEO and creative director of his own marketing firm, PFS Marketwyse), he pretty much forced his way in here to provide a guest perspective. So without further ado....

GUEST PERSPECTIVE: JASON I. MILETSKY

Let me start by framing the approach I'll take in my answer. The definition of "multimedia" has been so broadened over the years that it's come to mean different things to different people. For some, multimedia literally means the use of more than one marketing medium. For others, it's strictly limited to interactive presentations made on CD- or DVD-ROM. But more often, and more generally, multimedia relates to the use of a computer or Internet-based tools to communicate a message, so I'll give my answer with this in mind.

Multimedia options can open salespeople up to incredible opportunities for prospecting and presenting. Using multimedia, salespeople can stay in touch in ways that could hardly be imagined not too long ago. Used correctly, it can make sales efforts easier and widen overall reach, allowing a single salesperson to expose himself, his company, and his product and services to a far larger universe of potential clients.

The number of multimedia weapons salespeople can include in their arsenal is truly staggering; it would be impossible for me to go into each and every one of them in just a couple of pages. But the following list cites some of my favorites, specifically related to prospecting:

- **E-mail blasts:** You know how to send an e-mail to one person. You know how to CC multiple people on that same e-mail or BCC them if you want to share your correspondence with one or more people, private from everyone else receiving the message. E-mail blasts work much the same way as BCCs, but far more powerfully. Using a third-party program or Web-based service—I like iContact (www.icontact.com)—salespeople can upload and organize lists of contacts into as many categories as they'd like (by company, industry, company size, region, etc.) and then write, schedule, and send e-mails to any number of contacts without them seeing each other's e-mail address. You may be thinking, big deal, right? Doesn't sound much different from BCCing people. The big deal is that e-mail blasts can do two things that regular e-mail can't. First, it allows for e-mail to be sent using HTML code—the standard code used to build Web sites. That means when recipients open your e-mail, they won't just see written copy; they'll see a graphically designed and laid-out page that looks like a Web page, a newsletter, or anything you'd like to design, with links back to one or more pages of your company's site. This can be a major help in getting prospects' attention and conveying your message. Second, e-mail blasts are completely trackable. That is, you can see who's opening them and who's clicking through to your site. If you can track your blasts over time, you can see who regularly opens your blasts and clicks through to your site—in other words, those showing active interest. Give those people a call!

- **Animated introductory or overview presentations:** Using any number of programs, presentations that introduce your company, demonstrate a product or service, or provide an overview of the benefits your company can provide can be built and saved on CD-ROMs or DVD-ROMs. These presentations can include links, downloads, animations, video, voiceovers, photographs, and more to get a message across and engage a prospect. Hand these out at trade shows, through direct mail, in brochures—whatever it takes to get them into people's hands.

- **Corporate blogging:** Blogging is something that the company you work for needs to be on board with before you do it, but it can be a big benefit in reaching new prospects. In fact, it allows prospects to find you. Blogging isn't strictly limited to individuals chronicling their family vacations or political pundits fighting for a cause; corporate blogging is gaining momentum, and salespeople can use their own unique blogs to discuss their thoughts about things that are going on in their company or industry. These blogs can help establish you as an expert. And if you tag (that is, use keywords to describe the content) each blog post, your blog may find its way into the browser window of potential clients.

- **Social networking:** As with blogging, many people don't understand the benefits that social networking can provide to salespeople. For example, you may have a Facebook page that you use to stay in touch with friends and family, but with 90 million people using Facebook, there are plenty of users in a position to make purchasing decisions. Start a fan page for your company and ask co-workers, clients, and vendors to sign up. This will give you access to those people and their networks. LinkedIn is another popular social-networking site, geared specifically to helping business people increase their connections, seek out help, and develop prospects. It's well worth the time to learn how to leverage these sites to expand your network.

- **Webinars:** Webinars are basically online seminars. You, as the presenter, upload your materials (such as PowerPoint decks), switch on the camera (if you want to appear on video), and make your presentation. Your audience never has to leave their desks; they simply log on and watch you without having to kill the day traveling to a single seminar location. It's quick, convenient, and easy for everyone involved. Online chats allow people to ask public or private questions; as the moderator, you can keep a copy of all attendees and their contact information for future sales or marketing efforts.

All these—and other—tools can be great resources for salespeople, but practically none of them can be used without at least a little technical knowledge. Chances are you're going to have to find someone with moderate development skills to help you take advantage of multimedia in your sales efforts.

One last point I want to make that I firmly believe applies to all multimedia tools, including those that didn't make it onto my list: Nothing will replace the need for creativity and a solid message. The biggest drawback of most multimedia tools is that they make it too easy for salespeople to get so caught up in the sparkle of animation, funky transitions, and catchy sound effects that they forget all about the content. Multimedia can be an amazing tool for reaching people, but it becomes pointless if the bells and whistles are used to gloss over the fact that there's no real message. Use the tools at your disposal to push quality information—not to replace it.

Q: • CAN YOU AND SHOULD YOU TAKE
  • ADVANTAGE OF AN UNTRAINED BUYER?

JAMES CALLANDER
THE CUSTOMER PERSPECTIVE

⤶ If you haven't already, you will inevitably come across a so called "untrained buyer"—someone new on the job and still attempting to get up to speed. The question then is whether to cash in your future with the client by taking advantage of him or her now or to manage the situation to improve the chances of a long-term business relationship with this person. I think we both know the right course of action.

While you might think this green buyer represents a golden opportunity to push ahead with new business—and it may perhaps turn into a good situation for both parties—for the sake of longevity, you should make every effort to avoid taking advantage of him or her. Actions to the contrary will provide only limited benefits—and those benefits will be short-lived. Once that person becomes more capable, he or she will have a better understanding of past dealings with you—and if that person determines that those dealings involved deceit on your part, I seriously doubt you will ever overcome the ill will that results. Keep in mind, too, that new employees are usually overseen by upper management or department heads. This fact alone should be enough to scare you off of taking advantage of the new employee; if I were to find out that a salesperson was taking advantage of one of my subordinates, I can promise you he or she would experience an early exit from the big show. If that's not enough to straighten you out, consider the blow to the untrained buyer's confidence that would result from your actions.

A person in a new position is looking for guidance and acceptance from his or her managers, co-workers, and, yes, vendors. Your experience dealing with the new employee's company or industry enables you to offer support while that person becomes acquainted with his or her new environment. Use this opportunity to teach and encourage this person. Your future is and will be tied to some degree to how successful this untrained buyer can become. As the buyer settles into his or her role and becomes more competent, he or she will establish a base of trusted vendors to turn to for steady and reliable support—and you want to be on that list. If you invest time in helping a new employee, you will likely be rewarded with a business relationship anchored by trust and respect.

MARVIN MILETSKY

THE SALES PERSPECTIVE

↳ While you might win a battle by taking advantage of a person's inexperience, winning the war will be far more difficult. Sure, you might enjoy higher profits for one order—but the minute that untrained buyer gets up to speed, that person will know they've been had.

Everything you do to develop and maintain accounts should be founded in building long-term relationships. You're not in it for the quick kill and then on to something else; you are in it for the long run. And trust is the foundation upon which all relationships are built. Violating an untrained buyer's trust by taking advantage of him or her will make it nearly impossible to foster a solid relationship over the long haul.

Instead of taking advantage of an untrained buyer, turn the buyer's lack of experience into an advantage for *both* of you. Take him or her under your wing. If the buyer's weakness relates to product knowledge, share yours. Field all questions the buyer may have—no matter how basic or complex—answering those that you are qualified to handle using language the buyer can understand and passing the rest on to your technical staff. Go that extra step to make the buyer comfortable enough to rely on you in the future. Become the go-to guy, and the orders will follow. Be careful, however, to avoid sacrificing *your* needs in the process. It is *not* your responsibility to inform the buyer about other products or companies, and you should not do so. Don't shoot yourself in the foot.

Having gained the trust of your client, you might be tempted to take advantage with respect to pricing. In a word: Don't. Make a fair profit, but do not go beyond fair. It will be difficult (if not impossible) to explain yourself when you get caught—and you *will* get caught!

Q: • ARE CONSUMER REBATE PROGRAMS • VALUABLE IN MOVING MERCHANDISE?

JAMES CALLANDER

THE CUSTOMER PERSPECTIVE

↳ Rebate programs, generally geared toward increasing volume either by attracting new customers or encouraging existing ones to buy more, have gotten a bad reputation in years past. Either the paperwork required was too time-consuming or the rebates were never paid, leaving a bad taste in customers' mouths. Some company's bookkeeping policies may even make rebates unworkable. In more challenging economic times, however, individuals and businesses look for every means possible to save money. Even those who previously ignored rebate programs may consider them now.

If a vendor can offer me a savings opportunity, such as a rebate, I am inclined to consider it, provided it involves no additional burden on me or my accounts payable personnel. The rebate has to represent a real savings, not just a merchandising gimmick. Otherwise, I will simply seek out quantity discounts or some other savings opportunity.

> The credit-card industry, for example, provides some good consumer-rebate programs. Whether the offer is for sky miles, points towards hotel stays, or even merchandise, there seems to be a program for everyone.

Rebates are typically not paid until after the product or services are paid for, giving the company issuing the rebate temporary use of that capital. This, in addition to driving sales, makes them an attractive marketing tool for many. Unless you own your company, you may have little choice as to whether a rebate program is part of your sales strategy. If it is, it's critical that you, as the salesperson, make every effort to understand the benefits to the client, how the program works, and the documentation required, and that you monitor the use of the program for both your company and your client. Also, be aware that programs that are rushed to the market and introduced poorly will be less effective in enticing clients to participate, as the vendor sales force will generally be ill-prepared to answer questions and promote the program's features. As with any other task associated with sales, you must develop a solid plan prior to rolling out your company's program. Which clients would benefit from its use? Why would the client benefit? The shotgun approach of blasting a large group of clients in the hopes you will get a "hit" is less effective than a focused approach targeting specific clients.

MARVIN MILETSKY
THE SALES PERSPECTIVE

↳ The answer to this question is a bit outside my purview, but I know a guy who's an expert in this area: Jack Benrubi, VP of Business Development at Advertising Checking Bureau (ACB). One of the powerhouses of trade marketing, ACB specializes in consumer-rebate, incentive, and consumer-loyalty programs, serving more than 40 percent of all Fortune 500 companies.

GUEST PERSPECTIVE: JACK BENRUBI

Manufacturers implement consumer rebates for different reasons, such as the selling off of inventory and the continued selling of successful products as well as those products that sell poorly. In good economic times, manufacturers run rebates every quarter or twice a year. In poor economic times, manufacturers may run rebates continuously throughout the year.

According to industry surveys, manufacturers favor running cash rebates, fully branded debit cards, and store credit cards. And according to those same industry surveys, consumers prefer to purchase products that offer a rebate over products that don't. This is especially true in today's economy. In today's economic climate, where financial institutions are failing, home mortgages are defaulting, and the retail market is plummeting, consumer rebate programs are increasing. Companies are implementing consumer rebate programs more than in any other period in our history. While the result of these programs is not an increase in sales, companies running consumer rebate programs are maintaining the sales they'd see in normal economic cycles.

> As of mid-2008, 40 percent of rebates offered were cash rebates; 30 percent were debit cards; 20 percent were store credit cards; and 10 percent were free product.

Consumer rebates confront manufacturers with several challenges. To implement a consumer rebate, you need to consider the following:

- When should the rebate be launched?

- To which products from the product list should the rebate apply?

- How much should the rebate be worth? To figure this out, you must determine what range, in terms of the dollar amount, will more likely convince the consumer to buy the product. You must also consider profit margins, redemption rates, lost checks, etc.

- Based on analytical and statistical assumptions, how many rebates will be redeemed and how many rebates will be lost or discarded by the consumer? Generally, for a $20 rebate, the redemption rate is about 30 percent; of that 30 percent, roughly 5 percent of checks issued will not be cashed for various reasons.

- Should the rebate be in the form of cash, a store gift card, free product, or a fully branded debit card?

In addition to consumer rebates, there are instant rebates. With an instant rebate, consumers receive their rebates at the time of purchase. They need not send in any documentation and then wait to receive their rebate by mail. Not surprisingly, most consumers prefer this type of rebate; so, too, do retailers. Why? Because at the end of each month, the retailer receives a certain percentage for every instant rebate cashed in by consumers. So the consumer benefits by receiving dollars off at the time of purchase, and the retailer benefits by receiving a credit on their monthly purchase from the manufacturer.

Another marketing tool used by manufacturers to move inventory is spiff programs. Spiff programs, which many companies use, are incentives geared toward retail salespeople. If a consumer is led to a particular product by a retail salesperson, you can bet there is a spiff on that particular product. The way it typically works is, the manufacturer attaches a dollar amount to a product—say, $20. Then, when a retail salesperson sells the product, he or she receives $20 from the manufacturer, usually in the form of a check or fully branded reloadable debit cards. In some cases, rather than attaching a dollar amount to the product, manufacturers set up a points program. Each product in the program is assigned a given number of points; low–profit-margin products are typically given a low point value, with high-selling products given a high point value. As retail salespeople sell product, they accumulate points, which can be redeemed for merchandise in a catalog such as jackets, cameras, T-shirts, cell phones, etc. Some companies have even expanded their offerings to include purchases from online firms such as Amazon.com. (Note that these types of points programs are decreasing in popularity, as salespeople generally prefer to receive cash.)

Many retailers do not allow their salespeople to receive spiff payments. Large retailers such as Lowe's, Home Depot, Best Buy, Wal-Mart, etc. ask that companies send spiff payments directly to corporate headquarters with each check clearly indicating the salesperson receiving the reward. The retailer then has the option of using the funds toward their bottom-line profit or in some other way rewarding the salesperson.

In terms of the type of reward, companies prefer checks for consumer rebates and fully branded reloadable debit cards for spiffs. In a debit card, the company's logo and product illustration can be on the card, with all monies loaded onto it. Salespeople can call an 800 number or go online for the balance on the card.

Consumer rebates and spiffs are marketing sales tools that contribute to a company's bottom line. These programs help to sell products, lower inventory totals, and better competition. They continue to be successful in a very competitive business environment, especially when a company needs to jump-start sales or even launch new product categories. All in all, the future should see an increase in all types of incentives.

Q: How Should You Handle Rejection?

James Callander
The Customer Perspective

If you're in sales, rejection is something you'll face on a regular basis. How you handle rejection is key—not just in your work, but in all areas of your life. Some people want to point fingers in every direction but at themselves. Others use rejection as a tool to pinpoint areas for improvement. Still others take the rejection personally, blaming themselves.

But let's be realistic: Rejection—at least in sales—seldom relates to you as a person. Most likely, something else caused the negative response. Maybe the last person who held your position made a bad impression on your client. Maybe your company didn't resolve an earlier issue to the client's satisfaction, meaning you're dealing with the fallout. The point is, rejection can result from any number of things.

When I request pricing proposals from vendors, only one of those vendors is going to win the business—meaning there will be at least as many (and usually more) rejected vendors as vendors whose proposals are accepted. The very nature of bidding out requisitions means someone is going home without an order to show for his or her efforts. When I decide against placing an order with a specific vendor, that decision is almost always based solely on the merits of the offering; the proposal simply didn't measure up to the competition. I seldom reject a bid because of the salesperson—although it has happened in cases where I deemed the salesperson incompetent. In such cases, however, I'd avoid giving that vendor or salesperson the opportunity to provide a quote unless there were some compelling reason to do so.

Some of our vendors might receive inquiries from us weekly or even daily; their hit rate will depend on the merits of their proposals. Many vendors I deal with, however, are starting from scratch with me and my company. They have no clue who we are or what we do, and so we are constantly working to bring these vendors up to speed on how to deal with us—meaning they are frequently rejected.

I've had vendors supply quotes on 10 or 20 requests before receiving an order. They could have given up, but they didn't. Instead of taking those rejections personally, they saw them as opportunities to sharpen their pencils and prepare more competitive offers.

Unfortunately, most people take rejection personally. They feel they did something wrong. Don't do that! Enter the land of self pity and disbelief will make you less effective in dealing with others. Instead, use the rejection to evaluate how you can improve the next time you are given an opportunity. You might even ask your client for feedback. If you suspect that it was you, not the proposal, they were rejecting, then ask them point blank. I doubt the answer will be that they awarded the business to another vendor because of you.

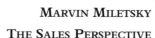

MARVIN MILETSKY

THE SALES PERSPECTIVE

You've just lost an order that you were counting on and thought you had in the bag. You worked on it for quite some time, dedicating every ounce of your being into its successful award. Naturally, you're disappointed, not to mention angry. Actually you're *beyond* angry; you're downright pissed. You're trying to make some sense of this when you remember some advice you read in *Selling for Dummies* (published by John Wiley & Sons): "You can get angry and be unproductive [when you lose an order] or you can investigate the reasons for failure. I recommend the second of these two options, because when you discover what went wrong, you can prevent those pitfalls from happening again."

They're kidding, right? I mean, maybe we should discuss how to write a proper thank-you note to the person who just screwed you! Granted, the advice is right on in telling you to learn from the experience, but you've got every right in the world to get upset and angry. If you can swallow defeat in such a matter-of-fact manner, then you're probably more suited to another profession. Staying hungry keeps us sharp. Never accepting defeat must be part of your makeup.

Obviously, the larger the requirement and the more you've put into it, the greater the fall. Just remember: It's not an order until it's an order. Don't get ahead of yourself; there are no sure things.

Of course, the way you react to rejection in front of a client is not the same as when you're by yourself. I needn't remind you that you're in this for the long term, and maintaining an open door must be your priority. The customer has already shown he or she can obtain your product elsewhere; that's why you lost the order in the first place. There's no reason you can't share with your customer your disappointment at the loss of this order (as long as you do so in a professional, non-threatening manner), but needless to say, blowing up in front of a client—no matter how angry you may be—is not your best move. I typically walk away from these types of situations to vent—not to be introspective, but to calm down a little.

Once you've vented, your anger has subsided, and your pity party has come to an end, it's time to make some positive use of the experience. Go to school on the loss:

- Ask your customer where you went wrong. You're looking for an answer that might shed some light on your letdown. Maybe you didn't understand the original criteria of the request.

- Think back to when you started the project. Were you realistic in your expectations, or was this order a reach for you?

- Do a little soul-searching. Did you do or say anything that contributed to the loss? (You've already read the answer to Question 14, "Is It Okay to Stretch the Truth to Win an Account?" which notes that you sometimes do have to stretch the truth to get a positive result, haven't you?)

- Review whether your fundamentals were in proper working condition. Was your product acceptable? Were you presenting to the right people and to the ultimate decision-maker?

Be realistic. You've got more than one customer, and odds are slim that you'll be 100-percent successful with each one. In fact, being too successful *could* be a sign that you're doing something wrong—for example, pricing your materials far below what a market will bear, and perhaps even losing money as you fill your orders.

My philosophy: If you *really* want to get even with people, sell to them! There's no better way to stem your anger than to make a profit off this individual in the future—and the future is usually right at your doorstep. Let's sum it up: Get angry, control it, get over it—and turn it into a profit!

PART THREE

Pitching, Negotiating, and Landing the Account

Q: Is There Really Such a Thing as a Free Lunch? Does the Salesperson Really Ever Give Anything Away?

MARVIN MILETSKY
THE SALES PERSPECTIVE

I sell for a living. That probably makes me a hard sell when I'm buying—especially when someone is giving me a free something-or-other. I'm a born skeptic, and I'm also a realist. I know that everything has a cost. There must be payback for everything we get and give—including a free lunch. That said, I've always seen a free lunch as a component of my selling effort, not as a means to an end. Translation: Don't expect to spend $10 for a lunch and get a commitment for an order. It ain't gonna happen. Your profit will be in getting alone time with your prospect, and your goal should be to learn as much as you can about that person's company—but in a social way.

You're probably going to find that the best place to do business is at the client's office, where you've got their attention, and a great way to put the cap on the meeting is by continuing on to a social event like lunch. Keep this advice in mind as you entertain your clients:

- Be natural and friendly. Let the conversation flow in any direction—but look for opportunities to dig a little deeper into their likes and dislikes and perhaps even for some more information about their company.

- Try to find out how others have failed, and what you can do to avoid making some of those same mistakes. Just keep in mind that these and other important questions cannot come out as if you are interrogating a suspect. These people are out on their time, and they can well afford to buy their own lunch. They don't need some sales jerk trying to put some pressure on.

- Never lose sight of the fact that the meal you are sharing is called a "business lunch" for a reason. These are not your friends. Your purpose is to sell, so don't get too comfortable. By the same token, do understand that the lunch hour is not their working time; it's their personal time. I once saw a salesman sitting at a table near me in a restaurant take out a sample of a product to show his prospect. His timing couldn't have been worse, as the client had just put a forkful of food into his mouth when the sample was pulled out.

The look on the poor guy's face as he chewed his food told the whole story of how annoyed he was at this blatant attempt to push a product at a most inopportune time. Your prospect knows the underlying reason you're there, so don't abuse it. Try to follow his or her lead. If you're asked a business-related question, hit the answer as briefly as you can and continue with your lunch, always keeping respect for his or her time in the forefront of your mind. Use your meal as an opportunity to build your relationship, subtly infusing some of your business objectives into the conversation if you can.

- If more than one of your prospects accepts your lunch offer, great. The old adage "the more the merrier" could not be more accurate here; the opportunity to meet several contacts at one time is priceless. You won't be able to talk much to each person individually, but you'll be able to identify the people in power and who among them could eventually be an ally to you.

- Letting your client suggest a restaurant relieves you of any responsibility for the service being too slow or the food not being up to par.

- Eat responsibly. Ordering ribs and having your fingers knuckle deep in barbecue sauce probably is not a look you're going for.

- Some clients may take your offer as permission to indulge, perhaps at a restaurant with far-above-reasonable prices. Protect yourself. Don't simply accede, and don't be afraid to speak up; you—not the client—must be the one in control. Use a rational excuse, like you don't have the time to devote to a lunch at such a formal place. You'll have learned a valuable lesson about your prospect; chances are if he or she will attempt to take advantage of a simple thing like a lunch offer, he or she will be even worse to deal with to obtain an order.

I've always tried to have some fun with customers, including during any meals I've shared with them. Once, one of my best clients and I were both rushing to get to a meeting, so we drove through a fast-food place to get sandwiches—which I paid for—so we could eat on the way. Several weeks later, when I was looking to get a particular order from him, I reminded him that I had bought him lunch, and I needed the order to cover expenses. "That damn lunch was three dollars!" he said as he declined to place the order as requested at that time. After issuing several more similar reminders over the next few months, I arrived at my office one day to find an envelope from him on my desk. In it were three one-dollar bills and a note that read, "Here's your damn three dollars back. Now leave me alone!" I called him immediately, as he knew I would, and asked him what he was doing for lunch; he laughed, called me a name not fit for print, and told me never again. He'd pay his own way, thank you! We laughed for years about that three-dollar lunch. But before you go pulling a stunt like that, you'll want to make sure you know who you're playing with!

JAMES CALLANDER

THE CUSTOMER PERSPECTIVE

Promotional materials such as pens, pads, hats, etc. are meant to be given away, just to get your name in front of the client. Your company may provide you with ample supplies of these or may require you to request them for your clients. Either way, dole out these supplies effectively; you don't usually have an endless supply to work with. And when you give these items out, don't expect anything more from your client than a simple thank you.

Another tactic your company likely supports is entertainment—taking clients out to lunch or dinner, depending on the occasion. When clients get away from the office, they are more relaxed, and usually more talkative. Golf outings, which are very popular during the months when prices and weather are reasonable, also fall into this category. Golf outings in particular offer real benefits—most notably that you'll have four hours with the client alone and away from distractions. I don't know of many other circumstances in which a client is going to agree to a four-hour meeting with you!

Should a salesperson expect anything from clients if he or she takes them out to lunch, dinner, or a golf outing? I believe the answer is yes—but let me explain. When clients agree to enjoy themselves at your expense (or rather, your company's expense), your expectation should be to bond with those clients. This bonding is critical to your success. The more comfortable your client is with you, the better your chances of maintaining his or her account. Spending time with your clients in this manner builds a level of trust that enables you to serve like no other vendor. The client will turn to you first when he or she needs quick action.

Unfortunately, if your clients are government or public entities like schools, utilities, etc., you may find that treating them to lunches, dinners, rounds of golf, or what have you involves many hurdles or is outright forbidden. This is true of some private companies as well. Make it a point to uncover what is acceptable in this regard during your visits so as not to accidentally embarrass yourself or your client by making an inappropriate offer. If clients are open to being entertained by vendors, improve your relationship with those clients by spending time with their personnel outside of the office.

Q: ARE SALES DECISIONS BASED MORE ON THE PRICE, BRAND, QUALITY, OR SALESPERSON?

MARVIN MILETSKY

THE SALES PERSPECTIVE

 Yes!

Oh, you wanted more than that? Well, okay, if you insist.

I wish I could tell you that there was one thing that would seal every deal, but I can't. I've lost orders where I had everything accounted for—all the angles covered, the right price at the right time, and the delivery. And then there've been times when I've had nothing positive to offer and was awarded an order— and I can guarantee it was not based upon my good looks.

Part of the fun of selling comes from the surprises you experience. You'll walk out of a presentation thinking your prospect didn't understand a thing, and then you'll get a call thanking you and asking for more. You'll be sure you've priced yourself out of the market, but unexpectedly the order will arrive. As they say, "It ain't over 'til the fat lady sings."

That's not to say you shouldn't do all you can to prepare. Stay sharp and alert as you present your products and make your offers. Make sure you touch all bases, but know that just when you think you've covered everything, in comes another consideration from left field. And remember: Whether they're new or long-time clients, whether it's a new or a repeat opportunity, treat each as if it's your first and most important. Don't assume that past performance is a guarantee of the future. Earn your way in each time.

When I started my sales career, I used a checklist to make sure I addressed every requirement. Here's a partial version of it; perhaps it'll help you. Add to it, alter it, use what's valuable to you—just develop some sort of list that will keep you on track. Forms like these keep me focused, especially given that I have more than one customer at a time.

Item	Comments
Date	Date of inquiry
Proposal Number	I always give proposals a number and reference that number as I go along.
Client	Name, phone number
Contact Name	Person's name
Due Date	When the quote is due
Decision Date	When the order will be placed
Formal or Informal	Is a written quote required? Or can it be delivered by telephone?
Competition	Who I'm up against
Previous Results	Have we bid this? Did we lose the bid or receive it? If we received it, at what price?
Submittals Required	What literature is required with the bid?
Delivery Required	When do they need to take possession?
Follow-Up Phone	Comments on your phone follow-ups
Follow Up in Person	Make an appointment to follow up

Discussion with your prospect should reveal what's important to him or her. Make sure you understand from the beginning what these things are. Don't make the assumption that because you satisfy one criterion, you satisfy them all. Part of you is a detective; investigate your client and pull from them their most important requirements. Of course, it's going to take some prodding to elicit this information; do it as subtly as you can.

A good way of judging your negotiation might be based upon the delivery requirements, as this is often of prime importance. Make sure you know what your lead time for delivery is, as many of your customers will wait until the last moment to place an order. Read their body language as you inquire about their schedule and press them a little to find out how firm that schedule is. Often, you'll find that the availability of your product can be a major influence on the total negotiation. This should be considered as your first and most important question when you start.

A little word of advice: We discussed earlier whether it's okay to stretch the truth a little, and my ability to deliver is an area where I've had to do that on occasion. (Note to my current customers: I don't do this anymore. Really, not ever. I swear.) Don't lose an order due to delivery issues. Agree that you can meet the requirements and then find a way to make it happen. Don't close a door before you've even had a chance to make your proposal.

JAMES CALLANDER

THE CUSTOMER PERSPECTIVE

Buyers consider many factors when evaluating vendor proposals, and salespeople must identify those factors that are most important to each request if they want to land an order. Each of these factors—price, brand, quality, and salesperson—can play a pivotal role in a buyer's decision-making evaluation of vendor proposals, but in different ways:

- **Price:** Price is always in play when a buyer looks at your proposal. Many times, price is the only consideration, especially if all other aspects are minor or if all vendors are submitting the same item. This is especially true for items that are purchased repeatedly, where the buyer has data on previous purchases that enables them to evaluate what price is acceptable and thereby manage their costs. When price is the major factor in the buying equation, the buyer is in the driver's seat. The buyer places the cost he or she has determined to be acceptable in front of vendors to accept or reject; this forces vendors to lower their margins to generate an order.

> If you are dealing with a client who is basing his or her purchase decision solely on price, remember that you probably aren't the only vendor that person is shopping the inquiry to. Your competition may in fact have seen the same request and politely declined.

- **Brand:** When brand preference is part of the evaluation, you may find yourself on either side of the selection depending on your offering; obviously, it puts added pressure on you if yours is not the preferred brand. In that case, you might offer a deeper-than-usual discount to sway the buyer, assuming the buyer has the leeway to use an off brand. Some specs don't allow for any other brand than what was called for, however—in which case vendors can expect to pay a slightly higher price due to the lack of competition.

- **Quality:** The quality of the product, which is related to brand preference, is usually already established prior to the bid process—meaning that unless there is an apparent difference between competing vendor proposals whose pricing is similar, the quality of the product normally won't be the determining factor in the final decision.

- **Salesperson:** All other things being equal, the vendor whose salesperson has fostered a strong relationship with the client based on trust, respect, and reliability will be given a slight edge. This edge diminishes, however, with inquiries that are less critical or less time-sensitive. In those cases, buyers might consider accepting an offer that's equal in cost, brand, and quality from a salesperson who is looking to establish a working relationship and needs an opportunity to begin the process. Buyers would never give an untested salesperson a critical or time-sensitive order unless they had no other options.

Q: IS THE PROMISE OF FUTURE WORK ENOUGH TO MAKE UP FOR LOWERING PRICES AT THE OUTSET OF THE RELATIONSHIP?

What's your perspective on this question?
Let us know at PerspectivesOnSales.com.

MARVIN MILETSKY

THE SALES PERSPECTIVE

Each and every step you take to engage your prospect should be with an eye toward developing a relationship in the future, and not just in the moment. All too often, however, the future is not as clear as it might seem, and promises made by a client may not be fulfilled. Promises are only words. They cannot be taken to the bank. The decision-maker could change, a new product by another vendor could replace yours, or the prospect's business could change, thereby eliminating the need for your product. There are a million reasons your client may fail to live up to the promise.

You've got to protect each order at the time you're negotiating it. You're promoting a complete package that includes service, availability, and reliability—all at a price that's fair both to yourself and to your customer. Sure, you'll have some customers who'll use you for your pricing only and don't want the extras that your sales efforts bring, but basing your business solely on its pricing structure does not allow for a relationship or loyalty to develop.

Tell your client that your pricing, which is based on the requirements stated in the bid package you were sent, is firm. If a price reduction for this order is sought in exchange for some promise of future business, make that future happen now. Ask for a firm commitment for the next order as part of this one and base your total price on the larger amount. Alternatively, tell your customer that a credit to his next order will be given if it is placed in a timely fashion. Just remember: It's not an order until it's an order.

JAMES CALLANDER

THE CUSTOMER PERSPECTIVE

↳ This is a huge gamble—a crap shoot even when clients have the best intentions. Obviously, most clients don't look to take advantage of their vendors. In fact, the opposite is true. They are looking to the vendor to provide a win-win, a proposition that satisfies both parties. But the fact is, things change in business —sometimes dramatically and swiftly. What was once offered by the client as a future opportunity may vanish before it can come to pass, leaving you with nothing but an empty promise.

I believe if your clients want you to lower your price, they should ask you directly—not with the carrot of future work. Nonetheless, some clients do employ this strategy. If you are dealing with such a client, you'll have to consider many factors when deciding how to respond to his or her offer. Make sure to cover all the angles, both the pros and the cons. If you are new to sales—heck, even if you aren't—you should seek guidance from your superiors before making your decision. This prevents you from going out on a limb to satisfy your client and finding out later that your manager doesn't approve.

> Be aware that while an offer may seem lucrative, it may also include misleading statements and hidden agendas.

Here are some things to consider:

- What prior experience do you have dealing with the client? How strong is your relationship?

- How much do you know about your client? If you've studied your client and have a strong understanding of their business, you'll make a better decision.

- Does the client actually have work you value that could be obtained in the future by agreeing to the current request?

- What exactly will be required of you to secure this future work?

- How much of the future work would you need to obtain to consider such an offer?

Another piece of the decision-making puzzle is that putting all your eggs in one basket, so to speak, by accepting an offer like this one will foster your client's confidence in you—which is always a good thing.

One approach might be to discuss partnering with your client to tackle a business opportunity you know they will attempt to secure together. Partnering requires both parties to share information and resources differently than a simple inquiry followed by a priced quote. It also becomes central to the success of each party to plan for the opportunity.

Q: WHAT CAN YOU OFFER YOUR CUSTOMER THAT WILL BE SEEN AS A BENEFIT IN THEIR EYES?

MARVIN MILETSKY

THE SALES PERSPECTIVE

All things being equal, the difference between what you offer and what anyone else offers might well be the customer service you provide. We've discussed in other areas of this book ways you can stand out from the crowd, such as building trust and quickly responding to their problems; these two strategies, along with your availability and the fact that you care about their business, will add to the benefits of dealing with you in their eyes. Along these lines, here are a few points to consider:

- Your response to emergency situations will set you apart. If a buyer divulges that he or she forgot to enter an order, and as a result will not be able to get your material in a timely manner without a penalty, arrange to forego as many if not all added charges normally associated with expediting an order in order to help him or her out personally.

- You can be creative with your invoicing. For example, arranging for an invoice to be mailed somewhat after the order has shipped will enable your customer to make use of the product and realize extra profit in their cash flow.

- If you're in a position to do so, offer "special" payment terms to a prospect in order to gain their attention and see an added benefit in dealing with you. For example, while most companies are pretty set in their ways of making payments, with the overwhelming majority being within 30 days of receipt of invoice, I sometimes offer terms such as a 2 percent discount if paid in 10. Even though I know full well that the client probably won't take this option, it still attracts the buyer's attention, and he or she will likely see it as a benefit. (Of course, you should make sure you have your company's blessing before messing with their terms of doing business; otherwise you'll likely find yourself in hot water!)

In the beginning of any relationship with a customer, during those formative first meetings and presentations, in the follow-up calls, and with all that you do to court the account, there'll be little you can do to build the confidence you're looking to garner. That confidence will only result over time. But once you've received that first order, do everything in your power to make sure your spoken word becomes a deed that can be used as the basis for building the relationship in the future. This then does become the benefit they seek: consistency and reliability in you. Success breeds success; failure often takes you in a wrong direction.

JAMES CALLANDER
THE SALES PERSPECTIVE

 Price and availability are the obvious answers to this question, but they are far from the only ones. Beyond these, clients expect a certain level of support from all their vendors. Providing what the client considers good service requires you to ask questions and apply the information you obtain as a result across all sections of your company. Indeed, the stronger the support from all levels of a vendor's organization, the more I will rely on that vendor to handle my business. I want vendors that understand and respond appropriately, and are thoroughly engaged with me. Are you capable of providing this level of service and support? If so, you should communicate this quality to your clients.

Technical expertise is another benefit in your client's eyes. The ability to discuss the technical merits of your products and services helps remove doubt and confusion among client staff, both of which must be overcome to ensure that new inquiries are presented. Technical selling can also be seen as a benefit to your clients. Can you notify me about a product that has become obsolete and tell me what product will replace it? Can you offer alternative solutions that are innovative design-wise and reduce the cost of labor or materials or both? This will be a huge benefit for your clients. I find this type of salesperson to be the most successful in my industry. Having the product and service expertise gives them the edge in most of their visits with my company.

If you don't have technical knowledge about the product or service you offer, do you have access to someone who does? If so, take advantage of that person!

In addition to being able to provide excellent support and technical expertise, you'll find that having certain attributes will be a benefit to your clients:

- **Reliability:** The price and delivery date you quote are meaningless if I cannot rely on you to make good on both. If a salesperson makes promises he or she cannot keep or fails to communicate challenges, he or she is not likely to have another chance at my business.

- **Timeliness:** Did your quote arrive on time with all of the information I needed, or did I have to chase you down?

Baseball great Pete Rose earned the nickname Charlie Hustle because he gave his best effort in every game. He made sure no one in the ballpark played harder than he did. As a purchasing agent, I am looking for salespeople who want to be Charlie Hustle. Are you asking the right questions, communicating challenges, formulating solutions, and following through after the sale?

Q: • What Are the Most Important Things • a Salesperson Can Do to Gain Trust?

Marvin Miletsky

The Sales Perspective

Merriam-Webster Dictionary defines the word *trust* as "assured reliance on the character, ability, strength, or truth of someone or something." My own definition would be "consistency of actions." It's what allows any relationship to flourish and grow; indeed, I can't see how any relationship can take root without this key ingredient as its base. However you define it, you can't expect to build trust overnight. Trust becomes deeper with each experience.

I once knew a salesman whose business card could have included the following motto: *Never a repeat customer.* He would tell any target anything they wanted to hear to close an order. His vocabulary consisted of one word: Yes. As a result, his career was defined by a series of one-time users, none of whom would ever repeat. It took years for the word to get out on him and for the burned bridges to fall, but he did finally run out of people to target and companies willing to be represented by him. If he's reading this book, chances are he'll skip this section, as "trust" was never a part of his vocabulary or selling philosophy.

Be consistent in everything you do. As you pursue your career, remember the expression "The road to hell is paved with good intentions." If you tell someone you're going to something, *do it*. If things change and you can't accomplish what you promised, pick up a phone to explain your delay. Notice we're discussing *your* delay, and not that of your staff or co-workers. You're the one who made the commitment; it's your responsibility to see that the mission gets accomplished.

In this day and age of electronic gizmos, you've got more than enough tools at your disposal to remind you of dates and times. You've also got co-workers and support staff. Make use of them! You're not a one-man band; you should rely on those around you to carry out the minutiae of the actions required to satisfy your customers' needs, whether for delivery, information, or pricing. That said, it is *your* responsibility to be in touch with the client to make sure things have been taken care of. You cannot assume anything. You want to be remembered by your clients for the things you do, not the things you forgot or avoided. Be the one that your client never has to call back for information owed, and who he or she calls for progressive business opportunities.

One last point: You're the contact with your customer. Sure, you like giving good news, but it's your responsibility to give bad news as well. This should be done personally, not by e-mail or by voicemail, and not by one of your associates. You face the music and let your client know that you are doing all in your power to rectify any negative occurrence.

JAMES CALLANDER
THE CUSTOMER PERSPECTIVE

Where does trust come from? Trust is earned. Knowing how to earn it requires that you understand your customer, identify the best way to meet their needs, and proving that you are the person best able to get the job done. Ask yourself: What traits instill trust in the customer's mind? To determine which actions will best gain your customer's trust, review these trust-building equations:

ANTICIPATE + COMMUNICATE = TRUST

Does the buyer have specific reporting requirements? Does the buyer need to update management as to progress in the purchasing process? What information does he or she need and when? Are you dealing with a small company, ordering materials and services on a "just in time" basis? Where is the flexibility in their schedule? Asking questions that allow you to anticipate the customer's needs and communicating the needed answers on their schedule build trust. And although the customer may not be happy to hear news of a problem with their order, your willingness to anticipate the impact on their business, propose a solution, and communicate both builds trust.

MEETING THE REQUIREMENTS + GOING THE EXTRA MILE = TRUST

In my answers to earlier questions, I discussed the importance of developing your understanding of your customer's requirements. This understanding plays a key role in building trust. A basic understanding of your customer's business and clarifying every element of a proposal request are things you can do to ensure your ability to meet the customer's requirements before an order is placed. Following up on an order to ensure that delivery of the goods and services is on schedule and updating the customer as needed will help you to meet the customer's requirements after the order is placed. Doing these things—without the customer asking—goes a long way toward building trust.

RELIABILITY + EXPERTISE = TRUST

Your customer's trust increases when he or she can rely on your availability, your quick response, and your ability to answer questions. How easy is it for your customer to reach you? There is a vast array of technologies designed to make it easier for customers to reach you, but the ability of those technologies to promote sales depends on your response. Quick response to initial contact is essential—even if all you can tell them is when you can call them back. Once the customer makes contact, they are relying on your expertise to assist them in solving problems and making purchases. Your customer needs to see you as the person he or she can rely on to supply the answers to questions—maybe even to answer questions he or she has not thought of yet.

If you are just starting a career in sales, your expertise may be limited, but you must be committed to learning. Even if you have been in sales for years, you need to be looking for new ways to build your expertise and keep up with new developments. Continuing education is essential.

DOING A GOOD JOB + HAVING PEOPLE KNOW YOU'VE DONE A GOOD JOB = TRUST

Doing a good job of meeting the customer's needs is an obvious trust builder, but that is not enough. Your customer needs to *recognize* that you have done a good job. You can do this by providing performance information to the customer in the form of periodic reports. You might also want to consider using performance surveys. Not only are surveys a means for gathering information as to how you can improve your performance, but they encourage the customer to take stock of your performance and recognize the value of good service. Customers are busy people with a lot on their minds; there is nothing wrong with prompting their memory of a job well done.

Q: • How Important Is a Factory • Visit by the Client?

Marvin Miletsky

The Sales Perspective

↳ I've invited far more people to visit our location than have actually come. In fact, it's extremely rare for people to actually show up on our doorstep. But my story has always been about our products and the people behind them— which is why I always extend an invitation early on in my meetings with prospects.

They say a picture is worth a thousand words; a factory or home office visit is probably worth more than a million. How often has a potential client shown up in my office for a tour and spotted something totally unrelated to the thing he came to check out in the first place? It's like a gigantic show and tell, only this time instead of being in front of your the first-grade class, you're impressing at a much higher level. We've gone so far as to leave documents regarding other work we've done for other clients in a place that the prospect is sure to see; I can't tell you how often they've taken the bait and asked if we'd be interested in looking at a similar project for them.

No matter what business you're in, what could be better than to show your prospect where it all comes from? If your company is in the service area, a stroll down the aisles of your home office filled with the smiling faces of people at work is a wonderful sales tool. If your company manufactures a product, taking a walk in your factory among the machinists to show how things are made can be quite impressive. There might be things in your office or factory that people had no idea you were involved with; this can open their imaginations to using you for other areas that you might not have considered.

When customers come to visit, make sure that you use their time responsibly. Ask up front how much time they have, and make sure you hit any areas they're interested in—as well as the areas you want to impress them with—early in the visit. Also, remember that this is *your* prospect. There probably isn't anyone else in your company who cares more about the success of the visit or knows the direction it should take than you. So make it your business to be there to host the event.

Clients who come to your home office might well be ones who are interested in developing relationships not just for current requirements but for future opportunities as well. Make sure you have the proper personnel on hand to greet and work with them. In particular, make sure you have technical people around to answer any questions that go beyond your expertise. When your client is touring, make sure you greet the people you see along the way by their first names; there's no reason you can't introduce your client to these people as well. It's important that everyone you work with understands they are *all* members of the sales department. How they act during a client visit goes a long way toward showing one uniform, positive view of your company; that can leave a lasting impression.

If you are in a particular area of your office or factory where you're not expert on what is going on, get someone who is. Always remember the old adage—the one that goes something like, "It's wiser to keep your mouth shut and have people think you're an idiot than open it up and prove it." Don't go beyond your abilities. People won't blame you for not knowing an answer, but they'll never forget that ridiculous one you gave.

Before you invite anyone to your plant, make sure you've got a story to tell or something positive to show. You run the risk of damage if your office is not typically in good shape or your factory in a state of disarray. You're probably kidding yourself if you think you can do a quick clean-up and fool the client; after all, you can't change the personnel who've been willing to work under those substandard conditions.

JAMES CALLANDER

THE CUSTOMER PERSPECTIVE

For many companies, this question doesn't apply. It's really only relevant if your company is or represents a manufacturer. In that case, a scheduled factory visit by clients who are either the end users of the product or clients who install the product could be helpful. Clients generally appreciate the opportunity to see first-hand where and how an item is made. And in some cases, these visits may be required. For instance, in the transit industry, end users require first article of inspection for equipment they plan to install, the goal being to ensure that the manufacturing process meets the quality requirements. Without the end user's approval of the process, the vendor cannot proceed with making the equipment. This inspection consists of a visit to the manufacturer's facility when the equipment is being made. The goal of the inspection by the end user is to ensure the manufacturing process meets with the quality requirements. Without the end user's approval of the process, the vendor cannot proceed with making the equipment. The factory visit is now not just a benefit, it is a necessity part of an order. End users may also visit your facility during the testing phase to verify the testing specifications—established and communicated prior to the vendor being awarded the order—after the equipment is made but prior to it being delivered.

The interest in the visit by the client visiting your facility will likely vary depending on that person's role in his or her company:

- Buyers typically are interested in the process; this gives them a greater understanding of the delivery timeframe. They are also interested in quality-control measures used to maintain a constant, repetitive result. If I were to visit a vendor's production facility, I'd also review the process they use to maintain control of their information. I rely on their staff to provide information and assurance that we are staying on course with no issues; during a factory visit, I want to find out whether the information they provide is reliable.

- Installers tend to focus on production, engineering, and design areas. They are looking to these departments for information to support their installation requirements. Factory visits give installers access to product group management and staff who control the means and methods that bring the products to market; access to these individuals gives installers the opportunity to ask questions about issues they will face during the install. The open nature of the visit enables installers to receive specific answers from these departments that a salesperson more than likely wouldn't be able to supply.

If you are in an industry where factory visits are mandated or encouraged, you should use them as a selling tool. Factory visits can offer a tremendous advantage in the selling cycle (assuming the client can see the benefit of such a visit). But you should carefully plan any visit by a client. You'll want to determine the likelihood of the client accepting, the accessibility of key personnel at the factory, and which areas of the factory should be covered during the visit. A little bit of planning will make for a very successful visit indeed!

Q: • SHOULD YOU BRING YOUR
• MANAGER/VP IN ON A SALES CALL?

MARVIN MILETSKY
THE SALES PERSPECTIVE

You want to present an air of independence when dealing with prospects and customers. You want to be the go-to guy in your company from their point of view. Before you've even presented your company's credentials and far before you discuss specific products, you must sell *yourself*. Your personality and the confidence you exhibit will convince them that you are someone worthy of their business. The first impression you make will lay the groundwork for all future relationships, so make sure it's positive. Let them know that you can handle—either by yourself or by reaching out to others—any challenges you and your prospect or customer may face together.

> You have these qualities, don't you? If you don't, you're not quite ready for this step. Build that confidence and let that personality flourish.

That said, just as there may be times when you may need to bring technical help with you on a sales call, you might encounter situations where bringing a top executive will help win an order. Once, my company was extremely close to landing our first order with a new target. The project was massive, which made the bottom-line profit exciting—and the challenges daunting. I was the only person the prospect had ever met; I represented all my claims alone and without support. When I sensed that the customer was reluctant to start a project of this magnitude with a company that was, to him, an unknown, I brought out the big guns—the president of my company—to personally give his assurance that we could and would handle this project. That did the trick; we received and completed the order.

So yes, there can be times when dropping your ego and bringing a higher-up on a sales call can serve you well. But as you're probably guessing, there's a "but" in there. Most likely, your superior has fought the fights you're currently trying to win—meaning that he or she has more experience and may have developed a more effective personal style than you. Indeed, your superior's presentation and charisma may be so comforting to your target that he or she wants to deal only with him or her in the future. Worse, your superior might be equally taken with the prospect and want to infuse himself or herself on a more regular basis. Your superior's ego might need feeding, prompting him or her to take over, try to outshine you, and even encourage your target to reach out to him or her directly. So guess what: You've just become your superior's assistant! All past efforts have been undermined, and you've lost your customer not to some competitor, but to your superior.

So what's the bottom line? Unless bringing your superior along is absolutely necessary, you should go it on your own. You must carefully weigh the benefits of bringing a superior with you on a sales call, always keeping in mind your reason for making the call in the first place: to make the sale and build a relationship. Your reason for bringing a superior along should be goal-oriented, not just for the sake of working together or showing off to your superior how good a job you're doing. The positive results of your work will be clear in the amount and quality of the orders you write, not in your ability to get along with your potential or existing customers.

JAMES CALLANDER
THE CUSTOMER PERSPECTIVE

In my position, I typically see salespeople bring their manager or vice president into our meeting more for their reasons than mine. Yes, the manager or VP usually wants to ask how our business is and how he or she can be of help, but rarely does he or she show more than a casual interest. Most visiting managers are disconnected from the actual selling process; they are little more than cheerleaders. Sure, I'm open to meeting with them, but I'd prefer if the salesperson have more for the manager or VP to do than look good. That is, clients generally do not mind when you bring your manager or vice president to a sales call—when there is a point to the visit.

So when should you bring your manager or vice president on a sales call? Obviously, if you are a new salesperson, you'll want to bring your manager along when calling on established clients for the first time so he or she can introduce you. Beyond that, you'll want to bring your manager or VP to sales calls when that person can make a difference in the sales process. For example, say a negotiation is at an impasse. Both you and the client want to make a deal, but you do not have the authority to make certain decisions for the company. This is a perfect time to bring in your manager. He or she serves a purpose, becoming a key element in the sales process from which both you and the client benefit. As an added bonus, the client will make himself or herself available as needed for both the salesperson and the manager in the future.

If you do bring a manager or vice president on a client visit, do some planning well in advance to make the sales call a success for everyone. On your end, use the visit to establish new contacts within the client's organization by maximizing your manager's or VP's exposure during the visit. Orchestrate meetings—however brief—with as many contacts within the client as possible, and make sure you have an agenda with each person you contact. (Give your client plenty of advance notice so he or she can schedule the necessary appointments.) Also find time before the visit to discuss with your manager or VP who you are seeing and why. On the client's end, make sure they know what the visit is about and how it can benefit them. Your managers and especially your VPs have access to company personnel and processes that you do not have, and they can use their influence to help the client. And a VP in particular may be able to provide the client with support on more complex selling issues. VPs can also offer help with estimating and engineering challenges; try to secure time with either of these departments during your VP's visit.

Q: • IS A DIRECT APPROACH OF • ASKING FOR THE ORDER OKAY?

MARVIN MILETSKY

THE SALES PERSPECTIVE

↳ Okay, you've come this far. You've read the parts about building trust, being honest, setting up relationships, and servicing the prospect or customer. You've held meetings, given presentations, distributed samples and literature, and provided your quotation. After all this, do you really think your customer thinks your objective was just to engage in some sort of exercise? Of course not. From the beginning, your purpose should have been perfectly clear: to win the sale. So you asking for it should not be seen as a surprise to anyone. If asked properly, the worst that can happen is you'll receive a polite negative response that you can follow up on in the near future.

There are different ways of asking for an order. One is to state that an order is needed now to guarantee timely delivery. Use your sense of humor to assist in your customer's decision. I once told a customer that we were having a limited-time special spring clearance on industrial merchandise (of course, it was the middle of the winter). Other times, I've told clients that there was going to be a price increase in around 10 minutes, and I wanted to protect their interests by writing an order immediately, before the increase took effect.

Create your own light methods of asking for an order. Try telling them you're having a special sale, buy one for full price, and the second unit will be the same price. If they tell you that they are required to get three prices for your product, volunteer to give them three prices yourself. Alternatively, tell them that as a service, you will forward their request for purchase to three of your competitors—but that if the three do not respond, they will have no choice but to place the business with you. Even if the order is not placed immediately by the client, that person will get the idea that his or her business is important to you.

There have been times in my career when I've been more aggressive with a customer in seeking an order. I've put pressure on customers right from the beginning, telling them that their order is important to me and my company and that I expect to win it. I've also taken a position of control with customers as I follow the flow of the negotiation and keep the pressure on. I can't say that this is a style that should be used often, but with the right timing and a receptive customer, pushing a little has had positive results. The meek may inherit the earth, but they'll only get whatever has been left by the aggressive. Go for it! Ask and ye shall receive—well, sometimes maybe. You'll never know unless you try.

JAMES CALLANDER

THE CUSTOMER PERSPECTIVE

Asking for the order is part of your responsibilities as a salesperson. You do not want to become a quote service for any of your clients. Of course, many of your proposals—especially for repetitive off-the-shelf–type products and services of minimum value—will become orders based on their merits. With day-to-day buying, clients don't always need hand-holding. But when the dollars associated with an inquiry start adding up, your client will ratchet up their scrutiny of all vendor proposals. Sitting back and waiting on the results only raises the chances that your proposal will fall out of favor.

On repetitive-type requests, the best time to gauge the client's acceptance of your offering is right after submitting. If you are handing in your proposal during a visit, this is a good time to ask questions. How do we look? If you are not dropping off your proposal, you can ask this question over the phone. The client may comment in the affirmative or ask questions that could lead to you modifying your proposal—which could tip the balance in your favor and lock in the order. Your goal is to close an order by verifying you have submitted the correct information. There's nothing worse than having a vendor submit a request lacking specific information I asked for and need to make my award decisions; doing this will certainly hurt your chances. Finishing a close second is the vendor who fails to prepare his or her offering to meet my requirements.

Asking for an order with client requests involving substantial dollars requires a mixed approach. You should clarify whether you have provided what your client asked and, if you have cultivated additional contacts within the client, you should gather additional details. Are there alternative solutions you could offer that would benefit your client? Asking all of your contacts questions during this phase should yield any significant missing information. These types of requests typically involve an extensive number of details, so your understanding of these details can affect the client's award decision.

You must keep in contact with your client throughout the proposal process, beginning with clarifying the information the client provided. Know, too, that issues sometimes arise after the client has sent the inquiry to vendors; you should follow up throughout the process to confirm that nothing has changed. You do not want to be the person who missed important changes that could affect your proposal! And once you submit your proposal, you should commence the process of following up as often as the client allows.

The type of inquiry can be useful in determining when to ask for the business. Gauge the average order size from your client. When a request comes in above the norm, you have a good guideline as to when to start asking for the order.

Experience selling to your client or experience gained from selling to other clients can also play a part in how and when you ask for an order. People new to sales might find it helpful to follow up on most of their proposals—even ones for day-to-day–type items. Those starting out may not have the necessary insight to gauge the necessary cost structure for the client to award you an order. Remember, too, that your competitors are also calling on your client, and depending on their experience, they are asking for the order, too. Their relationship with the client may sway the buying decision in their favor if you are not attempting to do the same.

Q: WHAT IS THE IMPORTANCE OF HAVING THE POWER AND AUTHORITY TO MAKE A FINAL DEAL?

MARVIN MILETSKY

THE SALES PERSPECTIVE

↳ Can you imagine bringing your discussion with a client to the point of final negotiation only to find out that you are not dealing with the actual decision-maker? Well, just as you need to target the right person at your client, the buyer needs to deal with the proper authority in *your* company—or at least someone empowered to bring things to a close.

If you've ever purchased a car, you've no doubt reached that point in the negotiation where you've made your offer, only to be told by the salesman that he'll have to consult with his manager before he can accept it. Inevitably, he leaves you sitting at his desk as he purportedly fights on your behalf to make the deal happen—only to come back and inform you that the manager needs another few dollars to seal the deal. Not coincidentally, it is at this point that I get up and leave, never to return—not even after the salesman says they've reconsidered and will accept my offer. (You might have guessed from this story that I hate buying cars!) These days, when I go to purchase an automobile, I deal directly with the manager of sales so that I can in fact negotiate with someone authorized to make a deal.

Make sure you know your limitations when sitting down to present and discuss your offer. Your attitude will speak volumes to customers, enabling them to become comfortable with the knowledge that they are dealing with the right person in your company. Calling a time-out in the middle of a final negotiation to make a call to your office in order to confirm that you can meet your customer's needs can be enough to change the whole complexion of the meeting and even jeopardize the end result, so try not to do it. In earlier days, I actually took some liberties with my power to enter into orders on behalf of my company, but was never met with resistance when returning with an order in hand. Be judicious, but take some chances; they will pay off in the future. You might actually become empowered to make some of the decisions you've already laid down.

James Callander
The Customer Perspective

⌐ Government agencies on the federal, state, and county level use formal bidding for the majority of their needs. The rigid nature of the bid process means that they derive no benefit from working with a vendor salesperson who has the authority to cut a deal; they simply need vendors who can complete and submit the bid form on behalf of their company.

Not all clients, however, employ such strict bid processes. In some cases, such as the following, clients seek negotiated solutions:

- **Emergency requests:** In these cases, the client must obtain a product or service by any means necessary. Time is of the essence; any delay will cost the client money. Often, I am asked to handle rush orders for materials needed by my co-workers. When this happens, I contact vendors who I know can act quickly to support my pending order. These vendors are capable of tracking down all the pertinent information needed for me to release an order to them the same day the request comes in. I may even need salespeople to make important decisions on the spot—for example, to modify their quote. So the salesperson's ability to make decisions is one of the reasons I select that vendor in the first place. Dealing with a salesperson who constantly checks with management on what can and cannot be done would not support my needs when urgent requests are in play.

- **Engineered solutions:** If you have technical knowledge of your product or service, you can benefit from a negotiated award when the information you possess helps with the solution. Clients do not always understand everything associated with your product or service. Providing support to the client through a technical review gives you the opportunity to show the merits of the product or service and to guide the client to a better solution— with you receiving the order. The client requirements may in fact cause you to make changes to your proposal or agree to terms not previously known. Understanding the client's need and the capabilities of your offering, and conveying changes you are willing to make to satisfy the client, help put orders in the win column.

Clients will benefit from salespeople with the authority to make decisions. Salespeople who are capable of handling requests quickly and efficiently stand to gain the most from clients looking for fast, accurate responses from their vendors. Your relationship with a client will also benefit, affording you more opportunities to serve.

Q: REGARDLESS OF LEGALITY, DO KICKBACKS OR EXPENSIVE GIFTS PLAY AN IMPORTANT ROLE IN LANDING A NEW CONTACT?

MARVIN MILETSKY
THE SALES PERSPECTIVE

I'll eliminate one part of this question immediately by stating that the word "kickback" should be offensive to you and has no place in helping to shape your career. I'm not denying they take place, but you're way off if you think that they can be a component to any sales strategy. Yes, there are legal rebate programs that reward companies for their loyalty, and these work quite well—but the term "kickback" flies in the wrong direction.

An expensive gift—any gift, for that matter—that is given in trade for a positive result is not a gift at all. It's a bribe. I have never participated in this type of selling, and I never will—although it has come up in conversations with clients, either overtly or as a hint. My answer has always been the same: My company does not participate in this sort of marketing. The reason gifts should be given, if they are to be given at all, is to celebrate a relationship and to express your intention to keep building and enhancing it—and that's the *only* reason.

JAMES CALLANDER
THE CUSTOMER PERSPECTIVE

↳ Do kickbacks or expensive gifts play a role in landing a new contract? Not in my book! If that is what it takes to do business with a client, then you shouldn't call on them. Your integrity must be without question. The deep and unforgiving ditches along the heavily traveled road of sales are littered with the bodies of those salespeople who couldn't conduct business without providing a bounty of extras to supplement their proposals. Just as dodgy are those clients who reward this inappropriate behavior with their business. You only need to look at the news to realize this practice still occurs (although not to the extent it was when I first started working).

Salespeople don't need to offer gifts or kickbacks to foster favoritism. There are many more important things they need to do to be successful—most notably burying themselves in learning. Besides, your workload—prospecting for new clients, maintaining existing clients, and growing your business yearly—is already a full plate without the added burden of dealing with greedy clients. If you find yourself in a situation where you think a client is suggesting you engage in some sort of underhanded activity, make sure you understand exactly what is being asked, and then take this information directly to your manager. Better yet, find a new customer.

Q: THE CLIENT IS WILLING TO PAY FOR PRODUCTS OR SERVICES THE SALESPERSON KNOWS THEY DON'T REALLY NEED. SHOULD THE SALESPERSON ALERT THEM?

MARVIN MILETSKY
THE SALES PERSPECTIVE

↳ I don't want to sound too calculating, but your first responsibility should be to yourself, and your decisions should be based on doing the right thing for you. I'm also not a fan of taking advantage of anyone, and I take pride in being a partner to those I deal with—but only to a point.

That said, sometimes your focus should be the long-range goal of fostering a long-term relationship with a customer versus the rewards of one sale. A customer who attempts to order a commodity from you that you know won't sell in his area will only try to return it after it sits in his inventory. Your company probably allows returns of this type merchandise in exchange for other more popular items, but wouldn't you be better off warning that these items don't sell in his area and suggesting an alternative? And if your company *doesn't* allow returns for any reason, wouldn't it be better to warn your client of this beforehand rather than risk making an enemy of the client down the line who could lose faith in you and that partership you have been purporting to be building?

I once befriended the manager of a distribution company that sold both commodities and project-oriented products on a wholesale level. He told me to work up a suggested quantity of inventory to be put on his shelves for distribution. I was to be given a blank order to do with as I pleased; who could ask for more? It came as a shock to him when I thanked him but refused—although I was probably doing myself as much a favor as I was him. By way of explanation, I told him that his sales people didn't have sufficient knowledge of my product line to sell it from stock, and there wasn't enough familiarity among consumers for them to ask for it by name. The bottom line was, in six months he'd be asking to return the unsold material. We both won, as I didn't have to take back material that he couldn't use, and he was spared the expense of the investment.

Of course, in this case, we were discussing commodity items. In other areas of selling, the product or service is used for a specific application. Your job description includes your use of whatever tools you have to put your company's products into the hands of the buyer. You might be aware that if your client's designers took a different approach, they could use less of your product than they have requested. Your experience might tell you there's another product out there that, if specified, could eliminate the need for yours altogether. Purchasers might ask for snow-melting equipment to be used on projects in the deep south or other apparent mismatches of material and need. In these cases, you must remember: You are not the designer or consultant. You are the salesperson. Handle the requirement as you would any other and let the buyer do with your product as he sees fit.

JAMES CALLANDER

THE CUSTOMER PERSPECTIVE

Many customers purchase the same or similar products and services repeatedly. Often, the history of these purchases is available and utilized during the evaluation process. When this is the case, the customer is, or should be, more informed about their needs than the vendors who serve them. This question comes into play when the customer has no purchasing history or experience with the product or service.

Some examples of why customers might request a product or service that is more than they actually need include the following:

- The client is attempting to purchase a product or service with a variety of optional features and may be requesting quotes on a product with unneeded features. In this case, the client may be able to lower costs by selecting a product with only the features required.

- A product or service has special technical issues of which the customer is unaware that could affect its effectiveness.

- If the customer's intended use of the product or service is infrequent, the customer may not need to pay for a higher-grade product designed for constant use.

- The purchasing agent does not have the authority to purchase anything other than the specified product or service. This is an example of where your relationship with multiple contacts within the customer's organization can be beneficial.

- The customer is inexperienced.

In all of these cases, you can best serve customers by informing them of your observations (although the customer may or may not change his or her purchasing decision). Even if the customer spends less money on this purchase as a result, you will have established yourself as reliable and as having valuable expertise. This perception of you on the part of your client will pay off in future sales.

The same scenario is true when you can inform the client of possible improvements to his or her current selection. An example might include upgrading to a newer version of software or hardware. If the costs associated with the upgrade are insignificant, your client benefits from the newer technology. Another example is if the client has requested a hard-to-find or limited-supply item involving extensive lead time and cost. If you can suggest an alternative that is readily available and lowers his or her costs, the client more than likely will look at the information.

Finding an opening to engage your client on either side of the selection request provides you with the chance to build trust and acceptance. The client may not agree to what you are offering, but that doesn't mean he or she doesn't appreciate the support. If your competition provides the information you considered providing but didn't, they gain the recognition you need and want. Don't let a few dollars stand between you and doing the right thing when dealing with your clients.

Q: THE CLIENT IS IN A BIND AND NEEDS A PRODUCT OR SERVICE IN AN EMERGENCY. SHOULD THE PRICE GO UP?

What's your perspective on this question?
Let us know at PerspectivesOnSales.com.

MARVIN MILETSKY
THE SALES PERSPECTIVE

Take a good hard look at the cost structure for the products or services you produce using controlled methods. Now take a look at the extra money your company has to spend to produce the same product under emergency circumstances, and you'll realize that not only *should* the price go up, it *must*. It doesn't make a whole lot of sense to satisfy a rush requirement that costs you money, does it?

Even when you think you've accounted for all the additional costs, there are subtle ones that may not even register. One is the cost of breaking the normal flow of your business to satisfy a rush requirement. For example, you might interrupt another requirement that you're working on in order to handle the emergency. Inevitably, you'll return to the original job and find that the time you took to handle the emergency has put you behind schedule. You can't let this customer down, meaning you'll have to take extraordinary measures to catch up, which can mean added personnel or overtime—for which, of course, you can't charge your current customer. All this is to say that emergency production is costly and unproductive and should be avoided if at all possible.

I was once in a manufacturing business that catered mainly to contractors and industrial users. They were not the best planners, and frequently relied on last-minute orders to save their hides. Eventually, we came up with a way to combat the steady stream of "emergencies" that seemed to permeate our business: we instituted a flat "emergency services" charge on all rush orders, above and beyond the charges for the material or service we were going to provide. By the negative responses we got, you'd have thought the world was coming to an end.

We were told that these charges were unfair—and lots of other things, many of which don't belong in print. The amazing thing was, many asked what the normal delivery would be without those charges and were quite satisfied with the standard delivery we offered. Even if we asked whether they wanted air freight as part of the service, they informed us that standard delivery arrangements would be satisfactory. The moral of the story is, make sure you're dealing with a true emergency before you commit to the service.

There's a tenet that selling price is often based upon what the market will bear—and during emergency situations, the market can bear a little more. But I'm not encouraging you to be usurious. You're not in business to handle a single order; your relationship with your customer is built through your total service to them under standard and non-standard conditions. The emergency service you provide for customers should pay dividends in developing and keeping their loyalty in the future. Follow-up calls to see how things went and whether their experience with your company was positive should be made. Keep the service you provided fresh in their minds; it could play a role in breaking a tie in the future. Just remember that a relationship is two-sided. The same response and pricing should not be given to someone using you for this emergency only. You've done your due diligence in trying to court this target, but now, during their hour of need, you become convenient. Make a very handsome profit, serve them well, and try to use this as a stepping-stone for future business—but don't count on it, as they've demonstrated in the past that they already have their standard suppliers lined up.

JAMES CALLANDER
THE CUSTOMER PERSPECTIVE

As a client, I have to manage and satisfy the needs of both management and co-workers. When an emergency arises, my first priority is making the deadline for availability as needed. The second priority is the price. If I can receive product or service within the time allotted from only one vendor, I am willing to pay more to make that happen. If two or more vendors can handle the timing, then price can be a major factor in who gets the order.

If you are faced with a client emergency, you must find the answers to these questions in your attempts to determine your price strategy:

- **Why is the client in this situation and what is expected of you in your attempts to serve the client?** Knowing this enables you to respond in a way most likely to meet the need. At the same time, understanding exactly what is expected provides direction necessary to escalate the proper response within your busy schedule and that of others needed to support the inquiry. If you require others in your organization to assist in managing the solution, then the price should reflect the time and effort you and others put forth in submitting the final offer. What is required internally to satisfy the client's request often helps determine your markup. Things like special handling, expedited delivery, and technical support all play a role in determining the final price. Extensive effort on your part and that of others you need to manage a solution should not be free.

Clients that ask for support to a time-sensitive request that do not accept enhanced costs become a nuisance to the rest of your client base. Let's face it: The last thing you need is to drop everything to support a client that doesn't value your time. Keep this in mind if you find that one of your clients repeatedly cries wolf.

■ **Is the product or service readily available?** Regardless of the urgency of an inquiry I send to vendors, if the product or service is readily available, your chance to raise the price is limited. If your competitors can provide the same or equal item immediately, then you have no advantage to offer. If, however, you have an exclusive selection or if sole-source capability permits you to raise your price to support my need, then I might not be thrilled to pay more, but I will be forced to balance cost versus time issues in my decision.

When I'm dealing with a situation that requires immediate support from my vendors, I'm usually attempting to fix a problem that has popped up unexpectedly. This forces me to lean on my vendors to work under pressure as I am doing. Those vendors who understand this and rise to the challenge do so with a sense of expectation—specifically, that an order will be the result of the vendor's ability to provide the necessary solution in the established timeframe.

Gathering the right information and evaluating your ability to handle the client emergency is the starting point. Once you have determined what you can do to address the problem, your attention should shift to developing your price. The amount of effort, the exclusivity of your offering, and the handling and or expediting required to deliver must all be weighed when determining whether you should expect to increase your margin. Do not forget, however, that in most cases, you are not the only vendor contacted by the client to help with the inquiry.

Client emergency requests are a constant part of doing business. You never know when an emergency is coming, but I am confident you will deal with them regularly. (Any type of next-day or second-day-air requirements applied to your client's request should raise the red flag.) How you handle the challenge can affect your business both positively and negatively.

Q: HOW EFFECTIVE ARE SCARE TACTICS IN SALES? ("YOU'LL LOSE MONEY IF YOU DON'T..." "YOUR BUSINESS COULD BE IN DANGER UNLESS YOU...")

MARVIN MILETSKY

THE SALES PERSPECTIVE

Once, a salesperson came to my house to do an inspection for evidence of termite infestation. He began the inspection by asking us a series of questions. As he did, every once in awhile he would swat at something that was disturbing him, look around in search of a fly or some other airborne pest, and then swat again. We looked closely but could not see what he was swatting at; the same thing that was assaulting him was not anywhere near us. After several swats, he finally put his pen down and said that in all his years of working, he had never seen such obvious infestation, and that we must take immediate action against the offenders. If we would just sign on the dotted line, he told us, he would handle the rest. He couldn't have been more shocked when I asked him if he enjoyed making a living preying on the fears of others as I escorted him off the premises.

If your sales career will be based upon such tactics, you really don't require this book or any other. The main purpose of a guide like this is to further your skills in relationship building, with the net result being to sell a product on an ongoing basis. Although scare tactics could enable you to successfully make one sale to one buyer, it's not a style that would make anyone's top 1,000 list of sales tools. That said, legitimate cautions do have their place in your sales technique—for example, if you know of a price increase that's coming or if the product your customer needs has a long lead time, which could jeopardize the schedule of the project he's working on if not ordered right away.

Another piece of information you might want to pass on to your client might be your knowledge of a failure on the part of one of your competitors to perform. Of course, you don't work for your competitor and can't make absolute statements about anything you've heard, but you can encourage customers to check them out for themselves.

In such situations, you might suggest that your prospect issue either a letter of intent or a hold for release order, thereby reserving the product or service you're proposing at the current price and guaranteeing delivery. You'll be doing your customer a service by giving him a little more time to take positive action on his requirement without actually making a final commitment. (Make sure there's a clear understanding as to how long the items the client is seeking to protect can be held; it cannot be open-ended, as your costs will rise, and you cannot safely predict availability in the future.) Once such a document is issued, you might find that the client will go no further in his search for other vendors—in other words, the requirement is "off the street." The key now is to get that all-important release for delivery of the material; follow-up is a must.

JAMES CALLANDER
THE CUSTOMER PERSPECTIVE

"Pricing is going up tomorrow if you do not release the order today." Over the years, I have heard this more times than I can count. Was it my luck that I requested pricing the exact day before a major price increase was to take affect? Doubtful. At this point, depending on the vendor and their track record working with me, I usually ignore this statement altogether.

Using these tactics puts salespeople in danger of alienating client buyers and driving a wedge between those buyers and other client personnel who support you. In the case of the former, if you alienate the one person who releases orders to you and your company, you have a real mess on your hands. In most cases, the buyer is your champion within the client. That person helps you gain access to others and runs interference when others in the office object to proposed solutions you offer. Managing this relationship is critical to your path to success with any client. As for the latter, realize that scare tactics can affect the other personnel at the client you call on. A client's decision to move quickly forward with a purchase solely based on the pressure you bring to bear can backfire on you—especially when the information is investigated and found to be lacking. Either way, the end result may well be that the client opts to use other vendors.

That said, if the information is genuine, I want to know. You should communicate what the increase is and the date it will take place. I do appreciate advanced notice of increases; this information will be important in our procurement decisions. And the earlier the notice, the better I can manage our costs; indeed, such information may well force me into buying sooner than I had anticipated so that I can maintain our projected budget.

Unless you are a sole source for the request, the client will probably have heard about a price increase or other major change from other vendors. When talking to your client, keep this in mind. Instead of presenting the information as a statement of fact, pose it as a question your client can answer, as in "Did you realize there is a price increase going into effect tomorrow?" If the client does not know, then you can educate him or her without sowing any resentment.

Managing your client involves providing good, useful market intelligence. Any information you can provide on, say, future price increases or availability—preferably weeks or months in advance—will help your clients plan and schedule more effectively and will help support your efforts to improve your relationship and grow your business with clients. Putting pressure on your client during the quoting phase, however, only places them in a defensive mode.

Q: YOU AREN'T GETTING ANYWHERE WITH THE PERSON YOU'RE TRYING TO SELL TO. SHOULD YOU SEEK A HIGHER AUTHORITY?

MARVIN MILETSKY
THE SALES PERSPECTIVE

⤷ The president of our company once received a letter from a vendor who was attempting to do business with us, complaining about how difficult the purchasing agent was. The vendor explained that each time he tried to do business with us, he was greeted with a barrage of questions and qualifications he had to meet that were burdensome and time-consuming. The attitude of the P.A. was equally displeasing to the vendor, who went on to suggest that the president consider his immediate replacement. He argued that without the purchasing agent's blockade, the doors to doing business would be open to lots of new vendors, which would ultimately be more profitable for our company. In his communication back to the vendor, my company's president thanked him for his letter. He then advised the vendor that he was putting the purchasing agent in for an immediate raise and future promotion because the P.A. was doing exactly what he was being paid to do: Seek out qualified providers for the best product at the most competitive price. The purchasing agent, who was copied on the letter, never heard from the vendor again.

In an effort to conduct some very unscientific research, I questioned quite a number of people in various businesses—from manufacturing to service to business-to-business and even some consumer-oriented—for their opinion on this issue. There wasn't a single case where going above the decision-maker had made a positive impact.

That said, while some companies give their purchasing department the power to make decisions on their own, others are set up such that buyers gather information required to purchase an item but rely on others to guide them. I mentioned earlier in the book that you should get to know people within the company— for example, people in this planning or budgeting department—who might have the ear of the purchaser. While it's never a good idea to go above the buyer, it doesn't hurt to enlist the assistance of these people in putting in a good word on your behalf. In the end, though, these situations should be rare; if you've positioned yourself correctly from the beginning, you should be able to determine whether your efforts have some chance of success.

For more information, refer to the answers to questions about dealing with more than one target at a client and identifying and targeting the actual decision-maker in the organization (Question #31, "How Should You Identify the Actual Decision-Maker and All Players Within the Company?" and Question #34, "How Do You Approach Multiple Contacts in the Same Company?").

One more thing: No matter how a company is set up, the person who served as your initial contact should be included in all correspondence and conversations ongoing. His or her inclusion might appear to be clerical in nature, but you can never be sure of his or her power. Treating everyone on an even basis will prevent you from inadvertently stepping on someone's toes.

JAMES CALLANDER

THE CUSTOMER PERSPECTIVE

Throughout your sales career, you will deal with obstinate clients. While you may believe you have plenty to offer them, they will not give you the time of day to speak with them, let alone visit with them. These individuals may be rigid in their unwillingness to visit with vendors for any number of reasons, chief among them that they have already made their assessment of you or your company—most likely based less on personal experience than on the opinions of others, be they others on their own staff or representatives from your competition. It could be, however, that there is some other issue that needs to be uncovered and dealt with for you to move forward. In that case, you should attempt to identify and resolve the issue. Look for opportunities to make recommendations, suggest alternative solutions, and be proactive.

If, after identifying the issue, you determine that there is at present no way to resolve it, you have two options. One is to refrain from continued efforts to move this item forward; you might be able to bring it up again at a future date if you find an answer. Another is to seek a higher authority to circumvent your contact. I should warn you, however, that I have yet to see a vendor who has failed to convince me of his or her ability to succeed in establishing himself or herself with my superiors. The vendor who finds the road difficult working through me will not find a better avenue going around me; instead, trying this maneuver is almost certain to result in an even larger wall between us. Before attempting such a strategy, ask yourself: How much harm will gaining an audience with the manager cause? How much do you value your current relationship with the client?

While jumping to the next level of authority is an option, I strongly advise you to avoid doing so at the first sign of resistance. And if you do decide to pursue this avenue, I suggest you ask for permission from the non-receptive individual to speak with his or her manager on the subject. The worst thing that will happen is he or she will say no. Asking gives the individual authority, which is important to maintaining a healthy relationship with that person or client. You may, in the course of asking, find out why the individual has a negative attitude to your offerings. A clue could lead you in a different direction and possibly resolve the original objection. Either way, always ask for permission first. If he or she does not respond, you have a decision to make: whether to proceed with contacting the manager or dropping the subject all together.

So whom should you contact if given permission? If your original contact reports to a department manager, then that's who you should contact. Be aware, however, that if the person reports to a vice president or the company president, you will have a difficult time involving that higher authority in the sales process if his or her subordinates are not already on board with your efforts. Indeed, I have yet to see a vendor start their relationship with our company president or vice presidents. Typically, sales efforts focus on the lower- or mid-level members of my company. This "low hanging" fruit, which is easier to access, provides many vendors the contacts needed to develop their relationship.

Q: Is There a Time When You Let an Order Go to a Competitor or Even Suggest That It Does?

Marvin Miletsky

The Sales Perspective

After you've taken on the challenge of answering the customer's requirements for product or service, your every effort should be directed toward one main goal: the sale. Letting an order go to a competitor or even suggesting that it should shows a weakness in your company. Just as you've waited for your opportunity to get in, your competitor could be lying in wait for his; don't help him. If an order has to go elsewhere, the customer agent should be the one who makes that decision based on all the facts that are presented to him. He doesn't need your help!

Ask yourself if some responsibility for this negotiation getting to the point of even considering this question can be attributed to anything you did or did not do. Were you as prepared for this request as you should have been? Did you understand the requirements of it, including the delivery needs and the time for quoting? Did you do your homework to understand the exact product that was needed? How about your competitor—did you underestimate him, the product he is offering, or his ability to perform? Did you take into consideration the pricing structure that was needed in order to win the award?

Like the Boy Scout motto: "Be prepared." Enter every negotiation with a checklist of what will be required to land this order and make sure that you are capable of satisfying each and every one of the items. Take a look at the list in my answer to Question # 47, "Are Sales Decisions Based More on the Price, Brand, Quality, or Salesperson?" and use it to keep track of your efforts and to determine from the beginning whether your efforts have a chance at being successful. Once you've decided that you've got a chance, do everything in your power to bring it to that happy ending: the sale.

Things can happen during the course of your proposal estimate that could jeopardize your ability to successfully handle the project if awarded to you. Your stock situation might change, you could received other business that would interfere—any number of things can happen. In such cases, I would be careful not to share this information. Instead, find some other method to avoid getting the order, such as pricing yourself out of it.

There might be times when you're doing some work for a client and they ask if you can take on another project that is not within your company's ability to handle. Or some new company may send an inquiry that is out of your scope of supply. While you're outer self won't want to walk away from any opportunity and might consider finding some way to entertain this new request, trust the inner you who knows this is not your bailiwick. See this as the wonderful opportunity it is to help a customer and further build that trust thing we've discussed by sharing information and suggesting an alternative means to solving their new requirement. You'll have done the right thing, saving yourself from failing at something you should not have gotten involved with in the first place and winning the respect of the client.

JAMES CALLANDER
THE CUSTOMER PERSPECTIVE

Sometimes you cannot miss. Everything you touch turns into an order. The phone rings off the hook every day. You hardly have time to breathe; before you know it, it's time to go home. Other times, the order you were sure you had won is awarded to your competition, or you go a week without so much as a peep from your clients. Naturally, that little voice inside you starts asking questions of what you did wrong. The life of any salesperson is full of these high points and low points. The expression "feast or famine" will play out daily in your sales career.

I bring all this up so you can prepare for the day when you are working with a client who has rejected your original proposal, which was thoughtfully prepared, and is aggressively attempting to negotiate a better price, better terms, better delivery, or what have you. While the purchase would be a feather in your cap and a nice increase in your wallet, and the client has offered to award you the order if you meet their new requirements, you realize the new requirements are not acceptable; agreeing to them to satisfy the client would put your company at risk. But at the same time, saying no puts your relationship with the client at risk.

You are at a crossroads with your client that potentially could cause future opportunities to dry up—but I believe your only recourse is to turn the client's offer down. The client obviously will not be happy about the turn of events—indeed, your relationship with that client may become icy for a time—but you can rest easy knowing you did nothing wrong. Odds are you'll be able to turn the corner with the client at some point, but even if your client decides to cut ties with you and your company, you can console yourself with the knowledge that your company did not have to suffer through a bad order. And while you may not receive much in the way of praise by your management, your leadership in this situation will have made the difference. Besides, you can replace a customer that stops working with you—after the kicked-in-the-gut feeling goes away.

The time to let an order go to a competitor is when you have little or nothing to gain by accepting the order—for example, when you know the delivery-of-goods requirement is outside a timeframe you can support. You might also let an order go because of payment terms. If the client starts adjusting payment terms beyond 45 to 60 days, there may be something wrong with the client's finances—and if there's not, then the client is simply hoarding capital at the expense of others, which is equally problematic.

Q: CAN A PITCH OR PRESENTATION BE COOKIE-CUTTER? OR DOES IT NEED TO BE COMPLETELY CUSTOMIZED FOR EACH PROSPECT?

MARVIN MILETSKY

THE SALES PERSPECTIVE

There's no such thing as a "one size fits all" sales presentations or sales call. There are as many variations as there are people in the business. Just as the circumstances and surroundings constantly change, so too should your delivery.

Imagine you're a mechanic who is about to embark on a repair project. The challenge has been laid out and you understand the target end result, which is to put whatever it was that was broken back together. When you pack your bag and go on your way, you should take every tool you own. You really will not be able to tell ahead of time which tools you'll need—and once there, you can't return home to pick up one that you've forgotten. Approach every sales presentation with this level of preparedness. You can't predict what you'll encounter and which tools will serve your needs. Having too many tools is a good thing; having too few can be a nightmare.

As your presentation progresses, you'll have questions and reactions from the current group that might be similar to another presentation, but these can take a different direction in the blink of an eye, and still others will have no similarity at all. Be prepared for any occurrence and stay loose.

Don't ever let your delivery become routine. You'll wind up being bored with it, and your approach will suffer. Your main message might be the same for the product line you're pushing, but you should spice it up a little and adjust it to different audiences. I like to include a cover sheet on handouts and a screen at the beginning of my presentation with the client's name on it, thereby personalizing it.

Your presentation should be an extension of your regular personality—the one you use when you're one-on-one with someone. Only this time, instead of just trying to impress one person, you've got a group to deal with. Be yourself and have fun.

JAMES CALLANDER

THE CUSTOMER PERSPECTIVE

↳ Yes, a canned message can be effective—provided you believe in the message and know your material. Standard statements are nothing new; they are part of your selling vocabulary. The message about your company and who you are is a form of canned message that is used particularly when meeting new clients for the first time. This message usually provides details your client can use to understand what they can gain from working with you. Another canned message used when meeting new people is your background. This information enables the client to assess whether you are qualified to help him or her. Particularly if you are new in sales, you will use these types of messages. They are easy to remember and provide you with a point of reference in the event nervousness kicks in.

That said, many companies provide for their salespeople the base outline for PowerPoint presentations, which they can then modify as needed either by changing or omitting the individual slides in the presentation or by inserting new ones. This provides the salesperson the ability to take a canned message and tweak the information to focus specifically on a client, market, or industry. Modifying a canned presentation in this manner improves your chances of a productive outcome. You've done your homework on your client and their business; now you can use this information to tailor your presentation to cover those areas that will most benefit the client. This supports your goal of gaining preference with your offering.

For the most part, your level of experience will determine which type of presentation or message you are going to give. New salespeople will typically rely heavily on canned messages to get their point across. They still need to do their homework on the prospect or established client. They also need to spend time preparing for the visit. The seasoned salesperson, however, will rely on his or her experiences in preparing for and managing the actual appointment. These experienced salespeople often adapt canned messages to a specific audience and customize presentations that suit the client's needs, reflecting a relaxed and confident salesperson. They still do their homework; the difference is that they apply this information better, painlessly adapting the canned message and presenting it at the appropriate time. Whichever type of salesperson you are, you have to place importance on preparation. Otherwise, you invite problems that can be avoided.

Q: • CAN A SALESPERSON RECOVER
  • FROM A BAD PRESENTATION?

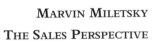

MARVIN MILETSKY

THE SALES PERSPECTIVE

I had my share of clunkers in the beginning—enough of them that I sometimes still wonder how I got past them. I remember thinking that I was glad *I* didn't have to sit through the torture of my own presentations. I wish I could tell you that the customers were salvaged after these poor efforts, but I'd be lying; there were no storybook endings. You know how first impressions are the most important? So too is the first presentation you give for a client or prospect. Get it right the first time!

I don't mean to sound so fatalistic. Although that first presentation is dead and buried, there'll be other opportunities for presentations in front of the same company or new ones that you'll ace. Look forward, not behind!

The fact is that I was ill-prepared for my presentations. I thought I'd be able to wing it as I went along. In hindsight, I probably went before an audience without proper guidance and too early in my sales career—although I did have an excuse in that the company I worked for had no formal training, and I was forced to learn while in the field of battle. (You'd have thought I could have picked up a book and read a little something, wouldn't you?)

To give yourself the best chance for success, prepare the presentation well in advance and blend some simple and tested ingredients into your own version of a soufflé extraordinaire:

- Get in front of a mirror, some friends, or family to get used to being in front of an audience. Know how you're going to start, and practice your opening remarks.

- Start your meeting with a broad smile and a welcome greeting in a strong voice that can be heard by all. Most importantly, the tone in your voice should be your normal, friendly one; don't try to be someone you're not. If you relax and enjoy yourself, the participants will be able to do so as well.

- State the purpose of the sales meeting to the assembled: "We're here today to discuss your requirement for the design proposal for your new office building" or "Today I'm going to show you how you can satisfy your need for a speedier, more reliable copier service" or whatever it is. Stating the customer's requirement provides you with a target and should serve to keep you on course during the meeting.

- Make sure you know the key point to your presentation before starting. It's that point, if you make no other, that absolutely must to get across.

- The decision-maker is your most important target. Be aware of this person's time constraints—often, the decision-maker is the busiest, with the least time to spare—and make sure your timing allows him or her to witness your main selling point. (For more on this, refer to my answer to Question #29, "How Do You Make the Most Out of a Product Demonstration Meeting?")

- If you're going up against other presenters for the same piece of business, try to go last; the last presenter is typically the one who stays in everyone's memory. If you wind up early in the lineup, see if you can create an excuse to return to provide some additional information or literature or a sample.

- Dress for the occasion. You're from the home office, not a member of your customer's staff. Gentlemen, wear that tie; ladies, a conservative pants suit will do just fine.

- Bring visual aids with you to support the points you're trying to make, but don't rely on them. They are for accent only. You're the star; be it.

- Bring the proper amount of literature with you, but don't pass it out until the end. You don't want people scanning literature while you're talking.

- Identify your competitors and make sure you know the products they offer that compete with yours—but don't put them down during your presentation. I've never been a believer in negative selling; I prefer to stress the positives of my company and product. I confidently throw out a challenge to anyone who can find a better product by some other company, and I speak with an air of confidence when I'm tooting my own product's horn. Besides, you run the risk of getting into a debate if you make a negative statement about your competitor's product, which can detract from your presentation.

- Try to keep your prospects involved with the presentation by asking questions and letting them have the floor. I like to ask customers questions about their understanding of my product, its use, and how it could satisfy their needs.

- Avoid getting into a discussion about pricing—not even guesstimates. I usually state that our company has a strict policy that all quotations must be written.

You're the chef, and you've got the recipe in hand. Take a little pinch of this advice, add a tablespoon of your experience, toss in some imagination, and stir it all together. There you have it—the recipe for great presentations: confidence!

JAMES CALLANDER

THE CUSTOMER PERSPECTIVE

 Bad presentations can happen to good salespeople, but taking swift and appropriate action to gain the client's trust and goodwill can make a huge difference in your ability to recover. Areas that can negatively affect your presentation include the following:

- **Showing up late:** Never schedule a presentation and then show up late. You'll start off on the wrong foot. If you are running late, you absolutely must communicate with the client to let them know.

- **Lacking key materials:** Be sure to bring plenty of catalogs, flyers, samples, etc.

These are only a couple of examples; clearly, you should prepare well in advance and attempt to be early for any presentation regardless of whether it's for one person or several.

The type of presentation can determine how much damage you might have done. If you were doing a one-on-one presentation, you only disappointed one person if things went badly. That person might not be satisfied with how the presentation went, but you should be able to manage a recovery.

I believe you can recover from a bad presentation—but only if you know one has occurred. Often, you will recognize when you gave a bad presentation; other times, your client will inform you. But if neither of these occurs, you must be aware of certain signs and monitor how your client responds in future dealings.

Measure your effectiveness daily when selling to this client. If, after a presentation, you see a drop-off in business, inquiries, or the availability of the staff, you most likely have an issue. The effects may appear minor, but repercussions may follow.

After a bad presentation, regardless of how it is revealed to you that one has occurred, you must determine what went wrong and decide how to go about patching up your relationship with the client. One place to start might be to visit the person you worked with to schedule the presentation to ask for his or her assessment of the situation. Use that person's response to determine the best method to get back on track; I suggest you double your efforts to support his or her every request. If your contact within the organization tells you about someone else who was disappointed by your performance, find out who the individual is and what the issue is. Then attempt to contact this person directly and demonstrate your sincere concern. The individual may or may not accept your request, but you must try.

> Access to other staff members can be limited or eliminated altogether because of a poor presentation. Your efforts to gain preference as a salesperson and to gain preference for your product and service offerings could suffer. If you are not capable of effectively building relationships with multiple departments within the client's organization, your potential is limited. I believe your ability to recover in this situation is critical to your success.

Of course, while you can recover from a bad presentation, your best tactic is to avoid making a bad presentation in the first place. Here are some pitfalls to avoid:

- Starting late is annoying to the client and may cause you to edit your presentation on the fly, leaving you open to making mistakes. You may not be able to control delays caused by the client, but you must ensure that you are not the cause of a late start.

- An unorganized presentation is confusing and often does more harm than good. Information should flow from one point to another in a logical progression. If you find yourself jumping between presentation slides to illustrate a point, you need to reexamine the flow of the presentation.

- Technical problems involving computer programs, overhead projectors, sound, and lighting call kill a perfectly prepared presentation. Never wait until the last minute to set up. Give yourself time to recover from unanticipated mishaps. Always have extra batteries, bulbs, and backups. If technical problems arise before or during the presentation, you must determine the best way to proceed. Is it better to limp through an inadequate presentation or ask to reschedule? How difficult was it to bring the group together? Does the client need the information you are presenting to meet a deadline?

Given the amount of time required to deliver a presentation, if you are not prepared to present and answer questions, you will most certainly have a difficult time recovering. Your goal when requesting to deliver a presentation was to inform the client of your product or service. If you were not able to be effective, chances are you will not be doing another presentation for the client in the near future. It goes without saying that basic planning goes a long way toward increasing your effectiveness. Include the following in your planning:

- Make literature and samples available to keep your attendees focused on the information you are presenting.

- Your appearance and attitude have a direct bearing on how people accept you and what you are saying. Make sure your appearance is appropriate to the setting.

Q: • How Important Is Determining When • the Buyer Requires the Quotation?

Marvin Miletsky
The Sales Perspective

A proposal that arrives after the client needs it is of no value. You could spend a month preparing it, but if you miss the time to submit it by just a moment, it could be the difference between success and failure. And if you're in a business that caters to government agencies, the bid instructions come complete with an absolute date and time by which your bid must be in. If you don't submit on time, your bid will not even be considered.

Recently, a planner called me to provide a budget price for a grouping of my material, which he needed for an upcoming meeting. My first question to him was how soon he needed it. Tongue in cheek, he answered that if he had wanted the information tomorrow, he would have waited until then to call me. He needed my information in a matter of hours or it would be of no use to him. So I became a purchasing agent myself for a few minutes, calling one of our vendors for a price on a very important component of my product. Although they said they'd need a few days to work up a price, even for budget purposes, I told them they had 20 minutes, adding that if they couldn't come through I'd take my best guess—and I'd make sure they *weren't* considered if the project did in fact come to fruition. Within 15 minutes, they had provided a price, and I was able to respond to my customer in plenty of time. (Note to my purchasing department: I know I'm not supposed to do that. I realize it causes confusion and embarrassment when the vendor calls you to follow up and you know nothing about the project. I won't do it again!)

Knowing when your customer needs your proposal is important to your ability to quote intelligently. In the example I gave, the requirement was for budget pricing and allowed for some educated guessing. But guessing cannot be a component of a proposal that commits your company to provide material or service for a fixed price. Knowing the customer's deadline for your proposal will enable you to judge whether you have enough time to prepare based on the complexity of the requirement. Determine immediately whether you're being given enough time to prepare; any mistake made during the preparation of the proposal could haunt you through the term of the order. Don't be afraid to request more time for preparation. I've actually told clients that if I'm forced to prepare an estimate or proposal without sufficient time, I will always protect my company by adding lots of dollars to cover the costs of unknowns. For their benefit and mine, I advise them that they'll achieve better results by allowing enough time. They are usually reasonable and acquiesce.

JAMES CALLANDER
THE CUSTOMER PERSPECTIVE

This should be part of the inquiry submitted to vendors. If you aren't sure when the quotation is required, you could wind up submitting your quote late —and not many buyers are going to accept a late quote late unless there was communication preceding the submission and an agreement allowing the vendor to do so. If this information is missing, you should contact the client immediately to determine the timing for producing a proposal. It's generally simple enough for the client to provide, but sometimes information is overlooked.

Having this information is critical to your ability to manage your time. Rarely do we finish tasks weeks or months ahead of schedule. We tend to apply ourselves toward the end of the allotted time to complete tasks. If a sales request is due in three days, people are inclined to wait until the final day to begin and finish what is required, whereas if the request requires immediate action, you will focus on how best to go about providing the needed information right away, which may involve reshuffling your schedule. The chances that you will require support from others can also play a part in managing the request properly; if you need others to review the information, provide comments, or supply you with pricing, then you must juggle the client request and keep track of your requests to others.

If the request for a quote lists ASAP (as soon as possible) as the due date, beware; ASAP can mean right now or it can mean as quickly as you can provide the information, which can create confusion for vendors. To avoid disappointing your client, you should contact them and ask them to clarify exactly what they mean. This will ensure that you understand the client's needs and will help you determine the best course of action for completing the request on time. If you are given weeks to provide your proposal, the client's inquiry most likely has significant requirements. This may involve a blanket order, a large volume, or even a highly specialized product. Spend some time up front reviewing the information provided and make notes to help you prepare your proposal. These notes should also include any questions you have for the client.

If the date supplied by the client is too aggressive—that is, if there is no way you can produce your offering in the time allotted—you must let your client know; it's possible they will grant an extension. If you client allows you more time, then great! But if you are forced to comply to the original deadline, then you have the added burden of pushing the request through your system, your vendors, and your schedule. Managing your time and that of your vendors becomes critical to keeping your other commitments in all areas of your day. You will need to devote extra time to assembling important information to complete urgent tasks.

Learning to juggle multiple tasks and deadlines is part of selling. Make sure you know the required date for all clients inquiries so you can incorporate them into your daily and weekly planning.

Q: • How Important Is Determining When • the Buyer Requires the Material?

Marvin Miletsky
The Sales Perspective

↳ You've got to ascertain the delivery requirements of the merchandise or service you're proposing in order to provide the most intelligent quotation possible. Material for immediate delivery can be priced based upon current costs as opposed to those required at some future date, where the cost basis is not as clear or predictable. In the latter case, your proposal must include escalations to protect you against cost increases at the time of shipment, as customers are often unwilling to renegotiate cost in the future, expecting you to take all the risk.

In times of volatile price fluctuations, it might be impossible to hold pricing for more than a very conservative period of time. One way of guaranteeing the price is to propose to take an order, manufacture the item, invoice, and store the item until the actual delivery is needed. Your customer will benefit by controlling his costs and ensuring material delivery precisely on his schedule. His downside is the payment of your invoice before taking possession. You've also got to ensure there is sufficient room to store the material at your location.

Another major reason to determine the delivery requirements is to enable your company to plan its workload to ensure the order's on-time completion. Your pricing could be affected by the need for overtime to fill a requirement. Conversely, if your customer has lots of time for receipt of the product, this could enable the production to be done at a more leisurely pace and as "fill-in" work when production time is available, not under the usual stresses of tight deadlines.

JAMES CALLANDER

THE CUSTOMER PERSPECTIVE

There are several quick evaluations you can use to determine if you understand the client's delivery requirements:

- **Short term and short lead time:** Requests of this type are typically daily inquiries, usually associated with off-the-shelf products or services that are readily available. Short term refers to how quickly your quote is due back to the client; this might be an immediate response over the phone or via e-mail, a response delivered within an hour, or a response delivered within a full day.

- **Short term and long lead time:** Requests of this type require the same turnaround period for the quote as the short-term and short-lead-time requests, but the client must wait a few days or weeks for delivery. This type of request typically occurs when a client accidentally failed to order an item that is required to complete a piece of work.

- **Long term and short lead time:** Requests of this type are generally for items that are not recurring purchases and usually require vendors to source with a company or division they represent, which stocks the item in question and can ship quickly. The short lead time indicates that the client is ready to use the item right now and may be willing to pay a premium to receive it quickly.

- **Long term and long lead time:** Requests of this type are generally for items or services that require manufacturing, engineering, or designing. These types of inquiries are usually associated with a large-value vital need with multiple requirements from the client and their customer. These requirements are one of the main reasons for the extended period the client allows for to the vendor to develop the proposal. Another reason may be the sheer volume of the inquiry.

While your client will normally list the requirements of their request, at times you will find that there is missing information. Your experience managing your clients will help you find the areas that require your attention. One of the obvious ones is when the item is needed; another is when the quote is due. A quick glance at your client's inquiry will determine whether this information has been provided; if not, you will want to contact the buyer to find out. If you aren't sure what the client is asking for, pick up the phone and talk to them. They need you on board and fully engaged with their requests.

Q: • SHOULD YOU EVER LOSE AN ORDER • BECAUSE OF DELIVERY?

MARVIN MILETSKY

THE SALES PERSPECTIVE

When it comes to inquiries about your ability to furnish a product or service to meet an immediate need, there's not much room for fudging. You either have the item or you don't. There's no middle ground. If you can fill the order, you reap the benefits; otherwise, you'll have to wait for the next opportunity.

When following up on such an order, use the fact that your customer required immediate delivery as an opening for a larger discussion. If you were able to satisfy the customer's requirements, try to capitalize on this by asking your client for his feedback on your response. It's a good way to keep you and your company fresh in the client's mind and could lead to additional orders as reward for the one you just handled. You might even want to inquire whether your customer sees a need for this item again in the future and, if so, whether they want to place an order targeting a distant delivery date. If the item is required on a regular basis, you might propose that the client place a blanket order—that is, an agreement that sets both price and delivery over a long period of time, thereby eliminating the last-minute hysteria that inevitably arises when the customer realizes they didn't place their order on time.

While orders requiring immediate delivery don't allow much in the way of wiggle room, you can be a bit more creative with requirements involving a longer lead time. While I'm not advocating straight-out lying to close an order, a little stretching of the truth with respect to delivery might be the difference to swing an order in your direction. Chances are, most order requests will have delivery requirements stated in weeks if not months in the future. These dates are typically not cast in stone; they should be used as guides, not absolutes. You might know your company's ability to ship is outside the requested schedule, but you'll have to worry about that upon receipt of the order. (If this makes you uncomfortable, take comfort in knowing that your competition won't be above doing this, too.) You may be required to do a bit of tap-dancing as your late delivery starts to become apparent; call your customer in advance of the due date to let them in on the bad news and assure that you are doing everything in your power to expedite things. And don't just *say* that; *do* that by using all your resources to push your company to fulfill the order.

JAMES CALLANDER

THE CUSTOMER PERSPECTIVE

Should vendors lose orders due to delivery? Yes, of course they should, and they will—every day. For clients, delivery requirements, when known, can and will be a part of the decision-making process. When a client provides specific delivery requirements in a request, this becomes one of the benchmarks vendors must meet. Indeed, I believe delivery is a major consideration for awards —as much as price, all other things being equal. Generally speaking, neither price nor delivery on its own is strong enough to evaluate on its own merits, but combining the two provides the buyer a level of information necessary to make a decision. The vendor that cannot hit the date risks losing an order because of it.

Suppose a client issues an inquiry for a product or service with a long lead time—say, 14 weeks or longer. (Generally, a long lead time will apply for items requiring extensive production by manufacturing, is made to order, or requires a very complex production process.) Using a grading system, which may have been purchased or developed by the client's own staff and assesses various aspects of a vendor's proposal, the client will evaluate each proposal received in several areas for compliance to their inquiry. Pricing is always a factor, as are other specific requirements, including delivery, which can and sometimes will be the major factor on award. If a vendor cannot accommodate the required date, the client will focus on proposals that can.

When I request pricing, the delivery requirement, if known, becomes part of my inquiry. The ball is then in my vendor's court to provide me pricing that meets or exceeds my expectation. During my review, I evaluate the delivery information along with all other aspects of the vendor quote. Obviously, if I need the item or service next week and you quote four weeks, I am going to have a hard time justifying an award to you—unless my other vendors quote similar lead times.

Once the client sends their vendors the inquiry, the vendor must adhere to information provided by the client. They should list any exception when submitting their proposal. Even though the proposal needs reviewed, the client is optimistic that the vendor submitted a proposal that at minimum meets all of their requirements.

I believe delivery is a major consideration for awards as much as price when all things are the same. If pricing can and does determine the award, so can delivery. Usually neither is strong enough to evaluate on their own merits, but combining the two provides the buyer a level of information necessary to make a decision. The vendor should always consider their capability to deliver on any order.

Q: • Should "Fine Print" in Your • Quotation Be Divulged?

Marvin Miletsky

The Sales Perspective

↳ Recently, while on vacation, I witnessed first-hand two very different styles of divulging fine print. I had asked a salesperson about a tour; in response, the salesperson said there was plenty of availability, but cautioned that I would be required to sign a release absolving his company of any responsibility should I get injured while participating. (The tour included a little hiking on steep and uneven trails.) I thanked him and told him I would think about whether I wanted to participate. Later that day, I returned to find another salesperson. I told him I wanted to sign up for the tour; he pulled out the credit-card form for me to fill out and made the necessary arrangements. It wasn't until after the process was complete that he said, "Oh, by the way, I need you to sign this waiver for my records." I asked him what it was, and he replied that it was just standard operating procedure—nothing I needed to concern myself with. Two different salespeople, and two totally divergent techniques.

I was on vacation, so the likelihood of these people ever seeing me again was remote—meaning their efforts were targeted for the immediate sale, not a long-term relationship. Still, I appreciated that the first person gave me the warning up front, enabling me to make my decision based on all the facts, not just on the positive ones that the second person had presented. As it turned out, I did go on the tour, but I did have reservations about the document they wanted me to sign. It made me wonder whether the hike was more aggressive than I was interested in. (In hindsight, I wish they had warned me that my calves were going to ache the day after; that really would have gotten my attention.)

Your customer has every right to expect you to look out for their interests as you serve your own. That's what relationship-building is all about. You're not in this for just one order with this customer, are you? That fine print that you might be inclined to hide will show its face sooner or later—and when it does, your credibility will be compromised, as will any chance for a relationship to blossom. Every industry has its own sets of standard caveats—the terms and conditions comprising the fine print—that should be brought to the attention of the buyer.

You should be familiar with these and point them out as a part of the quotation if not discussing them individually. Be up front with all the finer points, and you won't have to deal with any headaches later.

Be aware, too, that there might also be some specific quotation modifiers geared toward a specific customer or order. It's as critical to discuss these as it is the actual product you're offering. I once had a quotation that required the customer to front 50 percent of the cost within 30 days of the order placement and the balance upon notification that it was ready to ship. You can guess the customer's reaction when he was asked for the money after that 30-day period; he had not been made aware of this provision and could not come up with the money on such short notice. As a result, we changed our policy, requiring our salespeople to include any such terms as a part of the written purchase order.

JAMES CALLANDER
THE CUSTOMER PERSPECTIVE

It's a "buyer beware" world, and most purchasing agents know it is their responsibility to read the fine print in any quote or purchase agreement. That said, there may be times when you are dealing with an inexperienced purchasing agent or someone unfamiliar with your product or service. To answer this question, ask yourself what the potential negative consequences of failing to divulge the information are. Is there something in the fine print that will make the customer angry, eliminating the potential for future business? Will there be an impact on cost or delivery? Is there something out of the ordinary in the fine print—something a reasonable person would not expect to see? Knowing the answers to these questions will help you decide whether you need to bring the matter up to your customer. And if you know there is something in your fine print that may cause a customer to balk, telling them in advance may even help promote the sale.

> Often, contracts include verbiage to protect against legal action, but what's discussed is not part of a company's normal operating procedure. Your ability to explain this and reassure the customer that there will not be a problem can go a long way toward building a good sales relationship.

Of course, before you can inform your customer of any issues covered in the fine print, you must be aware of them yourself. I frequently encounter salespeople who are unfamiliar with the contents of the terms and conditions section of their own sales contracts, where most of the fine print appears. This lack of knowledge may never be a factor, but could make the difference between making a sale and losing it. It can even cost you money if the customer discovers an error or omission you did not know about. By familiarizing yourself with your own contracts' fine print, you can protect yourself and your customer.

As a purchasing manager, I respect and value salespeople with widespread knowledge of their business and at least a basic understanding of mine. That respect increases when the salesperson can put that knowledge to use in preventing and resolving conflict through communication. If you send out a quote that includes information in the fine print of which you are not aware, you appear unprofessional. If you *are* aware of something in the fine print of a quote and do not communicate it to your customer, you appear dishonest—which is also unprofessional.

Payment schedule is frequently covered in the fine print. If your customer purchases goods and services from you in order to create a final product for sale to their customer, delivery and payment schedules may be in conflict. Reviewing these issues with your customer in advance will help ensure neither party is disappointed in the transaction.

Q: • HOW IMPORTANT IS IT THAT YOU • UNDERSTAND THE BUYER'S REQUISITION?

MARVIN MILETSKY
THE SALES PERSPECTIVE

Receiving a requisition is no different from receiving an invitation to a formal party. The invitation tells you place and time, the reason for the celebration, when you should respond, and the expected manner of dress. And just as you have to pay attention to all these details when responding to an invitation, so, too, do you have to keep them at the forefront when handling a buyer's requisition. So to answer in just a few words: You'd better take the time to understand the requisition.

When you first receive the requisition, you'll want to do the following:

- Call the buyer to confirm receipt of the requisition and thank him or her for considering you. While you're at it, ask some questions, like when he or she expects to make a decision on your proposal. This can open the door to other areas, such as who you might be competing with and whether there are any important areas that you should stress in your proposal.

- Look at the commercial terms right away, noting specifically the date on which the customer requires your proposal. A quick scan and your experience should give you an indication whether the time to quote is sufficient. (If you're not that experienced yet, ask for help from someone in your company. There's no shame being seen as inexperienced by your co-workers, but there will be raised eyebrows by your customer if you miss their deadline.)

- If you determine that you require more time to prepare the bid, call to ask for an extension—and make that call immediately. There's nothing more frustrating to a buyer than having someone ask for an extension at the 11th hour. Any verbal correspondence on this matter between you and your client should be followed up in writing by memo, mail, or e-mail; keep a hard copy in your file for future reference.

Fortunately, you'll more than likely have support staff to analyze the details of the requisition and help provide a cost estimate upon which to base the bid price. Nonetheless, it's important that you understand at least the basics of what's being called for so that you'll be in a position to answer questions during negotiations. Have enough knowledge to potentially question some of the conclusions your preparers have made, always keeping in mind that it will be you in the customer's line of fire during the bid presentation and follow-up. Also, be sure to guide them in a direction that satisfies the minimum terms of the requisition without going beyond. If the requisition calls for "an automobile with four wheels and engine," your bid should not be a Cadillac; a Ford will do. Your competition will submit the lowest-value product possible that will satisfy the terms of the requisition—meaning you might actually be priced out before you even start.

Once you've handled the basics of the bid requisition, try to add proposals for items that could benefit the buyer but that were not called for in the original requirement. For example, the requisition might have described components individually that you know your company can offer as a package, thereby saving your client money. Keep this information until the end of the proposal and add it is an alternative, thereby showing your knowledge and interest in being of service to your client.

JAMES CALLANDER
THE SALES PERSPECTIVE

Ever heard the phrase, "The only stupid question is the one you don't ask"? It holds especially true when it comes to requisitions. If you don't make absolutely certain you understand every aspect of my requisition, you risk the following:

- Failing to provide the necessary information

- Failing to identify the correct pricing

- Failing to provide the correct product or service

- Failing to meet my deadlines

- Failing to utilize the correct shipping

- Wasting your time

- More importantly, wasting my time

Even if you have previously handled requisitions from a customer, verifying the terms of a new requisition is still a good idea. If they are using the same material or service in a new application, some variables may have changed. Far from being bothersome, your attention to detail will be appreciated by your customer.

Not all vendors find the time or consideration to review the buyer requisition. These same vendors normally do not see an order from the client due to their failure to provide all the information required by the client. If this were to continue as the normal operating mode of the vendor, the client more than likely would just stop sending requests. Obviously, continuing would be a waste of time for the vendor, and it certainly is for the client! The saying "the devil is in the details" holds true during the quotation phase. If you are missing important details, you are causing grief for your client—especially if the client placed the order with you, as mistakes are inevitable. In that scenario, you're also causing grief for yourself and your company due to added costs involved in double-handling an order that contains mistakes.

When clients submit requisitions with major contractual requirements, you must bury yourself in these requirements to understand them completely. As an example, extended or firm pricing over a period of months or years read wrong could spell disaster for your company. As another example, blanket pricing based on quantities "not guaranteed" by the client could expose you to higher costs when the client orders a much lower volume of material and your own suppliers set higher costs based on the lower volume. And not reading the "not guaranteed" statement will put you on an island if you price aggressively and the volume is not in line with expectations.

When I send out a requisition, I spell out the information I need my vendors to reference. Even so, I call vendors every day to confirm information that is missing. The request that's omitted most often is lead-time, followed closely by freight terms—both of which I use to evaluate vendor offerings. A vendor might have a great price compared to others, but knowing there is a two-week lead-time is important when I need to have the item in two days.

Not following instructions can and will cost you orders—and possibly clients— if you make a habit of not working within the guidelines. You must invest the appropriate amount of effort and manage all areas that support your client's interests. Guard each step in the sales process to ensure everything is going as planned and stated.

Q: WHEN IS A VERBAL AGREEMENT OKAY?

MARVIN MILETSKY
THE SALES PERSPECTIVE

↳ Simply stated, an order's not an order until it's an order! Lots of things can happen between the "saying" and the "doing." The best way to protect everyone's interests is to get it in writing.

Once, a customer told me that an order was on its way but that he needed me to start on it immediately due to a very aggressive delivery requirement. I can spare you his long story of why he couldn't get formal paperwork in my hands, but the bottom line was that we made the investment, we started the process—and we were left holding that proverbial bag when my client called to say that an order would not, in fact, be coming in our direction. He didn't even apologize (although even if he had, it wouldn't have made up for the time and money we lost).

A purchase order is a legal document that represents a commitment between buyer and seller. It removes any questions and confusion between the two entities and serves as the blueprint for the project. To get a sense of what one looks like, look for any number of standard purchase orders available from online providers. Some computer word-processing programs also feature standard purchase orders. In my early days, I got copies of the orders we sent from my company's purchasing department and reviewed old orders that my company had filled in an effort to understand what to be on the lookout for.

Always review your customer's P.O. to identify whether there are any special conditions set forth that could hold you liable for something you did not expect.

But, okay, there might be some times when taking an order verbally can be part of an aggressive selling strategy. Here's an example: The accounting department at one of my customers deemed a purchase requirement as unnecessary and therefore refused authorization, noting that they would only authorize "emergency" spending for the balance of the fiscal year. Still, the operations department needed the equipment. So we accepted a verbal order from the operations department and manufactured what they required. We then contacted them upon completion of our manufacturing process, at which point they went ahead and "created" an emergency—which allowed them to formally enter the order. We shipped the item—which should have taken two months—in one week. The operators were happy, the accountants stuck to their guns, as we looked like heroes to all involved.

Similar opportunities to be creative with your customers will present themselves, offering a wonderful way to satisfy your customer's needs while securing an order for yourself. But you must be very careful when deciding whether to take the risk, as you'll have no recourse if circumstances change and the material is no longer required. Here are a few points to keep in mind:

- Make sure that more than one person at the customer is aware of what is going on and that one of people on board with the scheme is in a decision-making position.

- Avoid accepting a verbal order that involves manufacturing an item that cannot be used by anyone but this customer.

- Only stick your neck out for your most credible customers—ones who have demonstrated loyalty in the past. Entering into such an agreement with a new or unreliable client can result in a dramatic loss for your company and your own credibility within.

James Callander
The Customer Perspective

For vendors, accepting a verbal agreement has its pros and its cons. On the pro side:

- **The order is received:** Even though it's verbal, the client has awarded you an order.

- **You have the opportunity to build trust:** The client is giving you an opportunity to prove yourself.

On the con side:

- **The client may have a hidden agenda:** The client may give you a bad order that other vendors have turned down based on the requirements.

- **There could be payment issues:** Possible issues with payment terms not spelled out during the conversation could emerge that require the vendor to hold invoicing or allow additional time for the client to pay.

- **There's no hard copy:** Without a hard copy of the agreement, you may not *really* know what you've signed up for.

- **There may be problems with other terms:** For example, any freight charges may become the responsibility of the vendor to absorb.

If you are new to sales, I strongly suggest that, if you accept any verbal order from a client, you do so with some concern. I'm not suggesting that every client is out to take advantage of you, but that "ounce of prevention is worth a pound of cure" quote comes to mind. I'd rather you prepare for the challenge than be blind-sided by it; attempt to secure the hard copy of the purchase details as quickly as possible.

If you are working with a new client and they ask you to accept a verbal agreement, you may feel as though you are in a difficult position. You have yet to develop a history with that client, so you don't know whether there is reason for concern; at the same time, failing to accept could slow your progress with the client or, worse, put your efforts at risk. If you're not sure how to proceed, seek counsel from your manager; that way, if an issue were to come up from the verbal agreement, you'll be covered.

Allowing verbal agreements with established client business is another matter altogether. A client's relationship with key vendors affords them the opportunity to place multiple verbal commitments prior to processing the hard-copy purchase order. This is important to the client, especially on time-sensitive orders. For example, suppose it's late in the day and I need to overnight something to one of our job sites to have the item there next day. I know the carrier's cutoff time doesn't afford me the luxury of calling for prices, writing up the order, and confirming the receipt of the order; I need to get the pricing and availability information and immediately place the order. Any delay could cause the vendor to miss the pickup, meaning my job site has to wait another day for the item. Both the vendor and I must trust in each other to complete the transaction. Note, though, that I would not put a new salesperson through this exercise. In this situation, clients choose their vendors based on the vendors' capabilities and experience. As a client, I rely on these vendors to make the commitment; in turn, I am obligated to take care of my end and process the hard copy of the purchase order so they can invoice us properly.

Q: • Must You Know Your Competitor's • Weaknesses and Strengths?

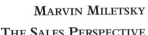

Marvin Miletsky

The Sales Perspective

Knowing the strengths and, more importantly, the weaknesses of your competition may well make a difference to your success. Why? Because with this knowledge in hand, you can concentrate your efforts in the area of those failures. The trick is, however, to avoid belittling your competition, as this may be received poorly by your client. A better approach is to concentrate on presenting your company in the best possible light rather than trying to speak from a position of speculation or conjecture about your competitors.

So how do you gather intel on your competitors? Most of what I've learned about the competition has come from my clients. Elicit information during your conversations with prospective buyers. Listen to them. If prompted correctly, they'll reveal all sorts of answers that will help you in your quest—many of which will help you determine where your competitors' weaknesses lie. I usually like to take a casual approach; I try to ask in a matter-of-fact way as part of something else we're discussing. For example, while discussing the date they require delivery, I might throw in a question about whether the customer has had experiences with any other vendors who have failed to deliver. This may well open a door that allows further discussion of contract failures or other sources of disappointment to the client. Don't be afraid to admit that you're trying to learn as much as you can to ensure that your company doesn't make the same mistakes.

Store any information you obtain in a safe place in your memory or, even better, in some hard-copy notes that you can refer to at some later date—for example, during your next negotiation with this or some other prospect.

Don't allow information you gather go to waste. It'll prove invaluable on future sales calls with this or other prospects. Share the information with others in your company and elicit from them their experiences. But use the information cautiously when presenting your case. Rather than overtly referencing your competitor's failures, just plant a seed of doubt. For example, you might question things you've heard about the company or its products that might open your prospect's eyes to problems they could experience with other brands that they won't experience with yours.

Recently, I dealt with a situation where I quoted a price that was higher than my chief rival's (I'll call them Company X). I had learned from an associate of the buyer, however, that they had recently had a terrible experience with Company X. Apparently, they had tried to get Company X to address a problem that had occurred after delivery of a recent similar order, to no avail. Rather than point out Company X's weakness, however, I proudly tooted my company's service department's horn. It turned out to be the deciding factor in the buyer's choice to go with us. A positive for my company was used as a reminder of a negative of our competitor's. Ah, the positive effects of subtle negative reinforcement!

There might be some times when knowing and citing a competitor's weakness is a requirement. I recently discussed this very matter with an area manager for UPS. He revealed that just because they were the market leader in ground shipping, that didn't mean they didn't have to fight each day to maintain their position. He talked about threats from upstart companies that always targeted UPS, claiming that they were cheaper than UPS and could deliver on a similar basis. The way he saw it, it was absolutely his responsibility to know his competitors' strengths and weaknesses, to be able to challenge the claims of those seeking to take away his business—and to inform his customers of what he knew. In one case, a competitor that claimed to be able to deliver a package to a remote area in a Midwestern state in three days in fact had to pass the package along first to one cooperating and independent local carrier and then to a second, each carrying it the short distance they covered—a journey that in fact lasted closer to *six* days. On top of that, the competitor's system for tracking packages was abysmal, and the weight limit for packages they were able to handle was far less than that offered by UPS. He had done his research on the competitor and was able to defend against them by using his knowledge of this challenger. In doing so, he not only performed a service for his customer, he prevented any interruption to his own business.

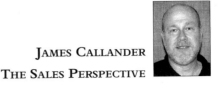

JAMES CALLANDER
THE SALES PERSPECTIVE

If you are new to sales, you should make it a point to understand who your competition is and how they go to market. This applies to every client you have in your account package. Once you undertake the task of documenting these competitors, you will see that each client presents a different challenge based on who your competitors are. Why is this important? Your clients are relying on these vendors for many different requests throughout the year. Any opportunities you receive are more than likely heading to at least two or more other vendors. I seldom request pricing from one source—and when I do, it is for a specific item that others do not handle or do not handle well.

So what do you stand to gain by knowing who the others vendors are?

- You might be aware that a particular vendor is notoriously slow to respond to client inquiries. I constantly see vendors—understaffed and overburdened with account responsibilities—struggle to respond to simple requests. This would be helpful to know because many clients must act quickly to put out their own fires. If you can respond in kind, you can get a leg up on your slower competition.

- What if your competition delivers their own goods, without charging the client freight? That would be good to know, because you normally would ask the client to pay freight. The chances the client would accept your proposal plus freight would then weigh heavy on your costing.

- The salesperson at your competitor may hold the key to whether you can grow quickly or slowly with a client. If a new salesperson calls on me, looking for an opportunity to serve, that person may see a few inquiries from my office. But if this same person is with a vendor that competes with one of my key vendors—i.e., a well-seasoned salesperson who has handled our account for years—he or she will have a more difficult time getting a foothold. Why? Because my key vendors understand our processes and can easily comply with changes required from time to time. These vendors have also developed multiple contacts throughout my entire office. They can visit almost any day, and most times unannounced. They have a good ear and know about future opportunities before I send them out for bid. If you don't run into this type of salesperson at any of your clients, count your blessings; this is the type of salesperson you should want to become.

Evaluating what your competitors can—and cannot—do better than you is part of managing your clients. If you know what your competitors do well, you can stand toe to toe on those key points. If you know what your competition lacks, you can use this against them both in your proposals and in direct contact with the client. Having insight on your competitors gives you an advantage. Knowledge of their strengths and weaknesses is available to you if you look for it.

How do you find out about other vendors? Your clients are great resources for gathering this information. Many times, I have been asked for support from a vendor. While I may have some interest in using their services, I also have a valued set of vendors with whom this new vendor competes. If the new vendor wants my business, they'll need to step up. Inevitably, the conversation turns to what support I receive from these other vendors that I find particularly helpful. If the new vendor is taking notes, they can apply this information to improve their position with me. Multiply this conversation by the total number of clients you currently deal with, and you have a wealth of information at your fingertips.

Q: • AT WHAT POINT DO
• YOU JUST WALK AWAY?

MARVIN MILETSKY

THE SALES PERSPECTIVE

I can almost hear the echoes of Sir Winston Churchill bellowing, in his speech that inspired a nation to battle on for an Allied victory in the face of overwhelming odds, "We shall fight on the beaches, we shall fight on the landing grounds, we shall fight in the fields and in the streets, we shall fight in the hills; we shall never surrender!"

Churchill was a realist, however. He knew that winning a war did not necessarily require you to win every battle. Just like Churchill, you've got to remember to keep the big picture in your sights. When negotiating a specific requirement, there may come a point when your efforts become fruitless, and continuing will add no value. Indeed, your persistence may actually have a detrimental effect on your ability to work with this client in the future. How do you know if you've reached this point? One of the signs might be the expression on the face of your prospect—a normally affable guy who now wears a scowl that screams displeasure. So too might his attitude and brevity in conversation tell a story. It might be that when you call to make an appointment, this usually very accessible client is too busy to see you. Or if he starts looking at his watch, it might be time for you to take the hint and leave.

When faced with signs like these, it's time to cut your losses. Learn to be a good loser—or, more specifically, learn to portray yourself as a good loser. Never let on how annoyed you are. Send a note or, even better, make a telephone call to thank your prospect for allowing you to be part of the negotiation and to tell him that you look forward to the next opportunity. Your goal is to cast yourself in a positive light while keeping doors open for the future. This may also the perfect time to learn why you lost the order (or, if not now, then in some future exchange—but not too far in the future, as you'll want everything to still be fresh in your contact's mind):

- Was your price too high?

- Were you able to meet their delivery needs?

- Were your solutions to their requirement satisfactory?

- Was your proposal clear to them and easily understood?

- Did your proposal address every requirement in the request?

- Was your company deemed competent to handle the project?

- Were there outside influences, such as their ultimate customer's preference on the product as a component?

- Did any past experience play a part?

- Did any individual within their company push in the direction that the negotiation finally took?

Remember: You're not interrogating your contact. Be careful not to sound that way in your follow-up.

I'm not one who stubbornly proceeds in the face of overwhelming odds just to satisfy my ego that I can conquer whatever it is that I've come up against. My advice is for you to make an assessment of your overall situation and come up with a real-life understanding that you cannot be all things to all people. You do not have to have everyone you pitch to as a client. They've got competitors who should still be targeted. In other words, your time must be managed in such a fashion as to fight the fights that you have a shot at winning and leave those others for another day.

There's another consideration to your thinking that might have to be made: we've been discussing walking away from a prospect when it's obvious that your efforts for a specific negotiation or building of a relationship are fruitless. However, there's another side to this coin, and that's when *you* determine that you do not want these people as a customer or client. I've had people who've given me an order and for some reason become the enemy as soon as they sign. Their demands become overwhelming, and the amount of time required to satisfy their most inane comments is both draining and costly to your company. We were doing business with just such a sort on a project that should have been profitable to both our companies. No matter what proposal we made or prototype we submitted, it was refused out of hand. We finally told them that their confrontational attitude and lack or cooperation were leading toward an eventual failure, as there was nothing that could be done to satisfy their baseless demands. We had to take a stand in order to get the project moving forward. Some time later, we did actually finish the project, but when approached again by this same company, we politely refused to quote, citing our busy work schedule as the excuse. It does actually work both ways; there'll be people with whom your not going to do business, and there might be some people you are not going to let into your business life.

JAMES CALLANDER
THE CUSTOMER PERSPECTIVE

Through the course of your career in sales, there will come a day when you have to decide whether to walk away from a client. There are various factors in making this decision, but the client's ability to work with you is at the top of the list. Working with clients is not as easy as some might imagine; it takes hard work and dedication to satisfy your clients. Clients must strike a balance on costs, brands, features, and benefits; they don't have to make it easy for their vendors, nor should they.

Here are some instances when you may need to consider walking away:

- **The client already juggles large numbers of vendors:** Clients' goals are sometimes the opposite of those of their vendors. For example, while you may want to establish yourself as a vendor with a client, the client may be looking to reduce the number of vendors used for products and services. Indeed, many clients' vendor list is reason enough for them to make it hard for you to break in and establish yourself. Just because a client has the ability to source a product or service from 10 vendors does not mean it is productive for the client to solicit 10 different bids. Instead, they select a shorter list of vendors to request quotes. If you are on the outside looking in, you may find it necessary to evaluate how much time and effort you have versus what is required to get your footing with the client.

- **The client is using vendor proposals to support its own bid:** In certain industries where there is a request to provide pricing to clients who are bidding their own work, vendors are submitting proposals to support the client's bid offering. In these situations, clients commonly use the low price submitted by a vendor along with their other cost estimates to formulate their own bid; if the client is awarded business from their customer, the award usually supports the vendor who was low. If you determine this is the situation with one of your clients, you should confront them; if it happens frequently, you should consider dropping the client. Obviously, the client does not value you or your company enough to award you the business outright or even negotiate with you to bring about a satisfactory conclusion for both.

- **The client's business doesn't measure up to your expectations:** Many vendors use a simple formula to determine the potential value of a client's business. For example, the electrical industry uses the contractor's or end user's total sales to gauge the value of their business. Another gauge might be the client's number of service trucks or employees. But a client's potential does not necessarily match the reality when you begin serving the client. The threshold you set in your goal to obtain business from your clients should guide you yearly. Throughout the year, you should evaluate your efforts—both those that are successful and those that are not. If you notice that lost opportunities are outpacing awards, you probably are missing sales goals. Here again, you have a choice to make: Keep serving your client and attempt to gain acceptance or remove them from your list of accounts.

One more thing: Many clients make new salespeople pay their dues before giving them larger opportunities. New salespeople will typically be asked by the client to handle orders other vendors do not want. If you are new to sales, keep this in mind. The first year dealing with clients is usually the toughest and most demanding. Avoid making the decision to walk away from a client without management's consent in the first year.

Q: THE CLIENT HAS CALLED THE SALESPERSON'S BLUFF. CAN THE SALESPERSON STILL BACKTRACK AND SAVE FACE?

MARVIN MILETSKY

THE SALES PERSPECTIVE

↳ A wife returns home to find her husband in bed with another woman and demands to know who she is. He responds by asking her "what woman? There's no woman in this bed, you're imagining it!" Deny, deny, deny! That's the joke; unfortunately that's not real life.

As we go forward in our pursuit of business, there might be times that we have to embellish our stories or even make some sort of bluff in order to close. And as with anything we do that stretches the truth or at least rearranges it, we stand the possibility of being caught. I can't say that bluffing is a sales technique, but I'm sure that I've done it more than once. In the end, I really have had to be creative in certain circumstances in order to close an order, and the art of misdirection has been included. It's never anything I plan ahead to do, but when push comes to shove, I would rather bluff in an effort to get the order than walk away without giving it that good ole college try. Before you even consider such a tack, make sure you know the prospect well enough to be able to survive if you are caught. Try never to consider the person you're trying to deal with as an imbecile. He probably didn't get to his position of authority by being a fool, so don't treat him as one.

I can remember bluffing my way into an order by telling the prospect that we'd require six weeks to satisfy his needs and that the only way we could succeed was by starting immediately on it. My bluff landed me the order, and all was well with my world. That was until my company shipped the merchandise within a week, as we had the material available at the time of our offer and I had neglected to coordinate with the shipping department that we hold these items for several weeks. There was another time that I urged a prospect to act swiftly on his decision because a competitor of his had also been inquiring about the same product, and we had only enough to fill one requirement. My ploy worked, and I got the order away from a competitor of mine and at a higher price due to my bluff. My strategy was exposed the very next week when an employee from the competing company hired on to my customer's company and exposed the fact that his original company was never interested in my material in the first place. Who could have known?

In the rare occasions that my bluff has been caught, I found myself having to face the music with my clients. We've discussed the importance of building a relationship that usually has as its foundation the component of trust. Based on the circumstances, I was unable to actually come clean and admit that I was bluffing or embellishing. I apologized for leading my customer astray and attributed it to poor information I had received when we had originally discussed their project. I took total blame rather than try to blame others in my organization because, I told them, no matter what, it was my responsibility to get everything right, no matter who gave me the information. In our discussion of the situation, I have always tried to get the upper hand by speaking in a confident yet apologetic voice. I also have brought the discussion to a quick end by getting into some other business topic, perhaps a new product or service we have just introduced.

There have been times when the end of this discussion has occurred with the customer still a little leery and suspicious and not quite accepting my story. There's little you can do at this point other than to be contrite and let the conversation come to its natural end. I've actually never had a circumstance where the bluff was so outlandish that we couldn't recover from it. Hold your bluffs to a minimum; the more often you try, the harder it gets to recover if you do actually get caught.

JAMES CALLANDER
THE CUSTOMER PERSPECTIVE

You can backtrack from any statement, and you will from time to time. For example, when information based on current circumstances changes, then you should inform your client. But you should never try to play games with your clients. What do you hope to gain by inviting trouble? Your client is looking to you for guidance through any lengthy process associated with an order. They use the information you provide for planning and scheduling. You must keep this information clean and to the point, and not overstate your capabilities.

Bluffs typically are one of three types:

- **Bluffs about availability:** Your proposal indicates delivery is four weeks; you know it is closer to six. When week four rolls around and your client has scheduled installation based on your proposal date, guess who is going to have a bad day? That's right: you! And what do you think will happen if your client knows that the information you've provided in your proposal is bogus? They are not going to let it slide; they will ask you directly about how you can make a six-week item ship in four.

- **Bluffs about terms:** On most vendor proposals, the payment terms are typically net 30 days. When the dollars become excessive or there are terms on which the client must insist, however, both parties must negotiate. That is, the client needs better terms on large-dollar orders. If you as the vendor insist on standard payment terms, the client will certainly wonder whether you are bluffing with regard to holding firm on the terms, whether you simply don't know what you can provide, or whether you have even asked your management for guidance. Regardless of the reason, the client will look to other vendors to negotiate better terms. And once that happens, you will have lost your competitive edge—at which point there is no backtracking or saving face. Worse, it will likely become a source of resentment for the client and may color their opinion of you in future dealings. I doubt the client will be anything but cordial, but they will not easily forget, either. If you are ever presented with this situation by one of your clients, I suggest communicating with your management for direction.

- **Bluffs about price:** Clients have various tools, some precise and others more like barometers, for determining the current market value of their inquiry—meaning that the vendor who inflates prices is usually easy to spot. Clients who see a vendor trying to make a fast buck tend to challenge the proposal to uncover why costs exceed their estimate; the explanation given by the vendor weighs heavy on the client's acceptance. If the client is not satisfied with the answer, the vendor may get the order at the requested price, but future consideration could suffer. To save face, the vendor could decide to adjust pricing to satisfy the client, which will go a long way toward maintaining trust built up with the client.

PART FOUR

Managing the Relationship

Q: • SHOULD WORK EVER GET STARTED
• BEFORE THE CONTRACT IS SIGNED?

JAMES CALLANDER
THE CUSTOMER PERSPECTIVE

↳ Earlier, we discussed those rare occasions when you might accept a verbal order from your client and proceed with supplying materials or services—for example, in an emergency, when the dollars and risk involved are minimal. Asking vendors to proceed without a written order is not the norm, however. The preferred approach is for the client to write a purchase order beforehand and submit it to the vendor for completion. This protects both parties from unforeseen issues down the road.

For items that require manufacturing—as well as software systems and high-dollar goods—a signed contract should always come first. In all these areas, your clients are going to process the required paperwork for the sake of both their company and yours. In the case of items requiring manufacturing, the costs associated with producing the wrong material make this a necessity. In addition to a signed contract, the production process generally warrants signing off on drawings submitted during the bidding process. The vendor must then ensure nothing changes during what is typically a lengthy production process. Any miscommunication could result in part or all of the production being scrapped.

In my industry, the electrical industry, clients do sometimes ask vendors to lock in copper pricing prior to actually writing the order. The amount of copper used in this industry is simply massive; every single home, office, manufacturing facility, and power plant is loaded with copper wiring. Given the volatility of the metal markets over the last few years, the purchase of copper wire for construction work has required a level of scrutiny never before seen. The difference in cost on certain buys from day to day can be measured in tens of thousands of dollars, and can swing over the $100,000 mark when measured over the course of a month. So by asking vendors to lock in a price per pound as it is listed on the commodity section of the stock market, clients are in effect requiring a commitment from the vendor prior to the actual release of the purchase order; this enables them to move forward with an accurate cost estimate instead of missing a window of opportunity pricing-wise. Many of the vendors that supply copper to this market, however, prefer to mandate a hard-copy order prior to locking in the copper due to the fact that copper prices can only be locked in between 9 a.m. and noon. This moves the risk onto the client, even though the vendor selected for the award still must lock in the copper price. Clients must search for vendors who can manage this type of transaction in the preferred manner, thereby reducing or eliminating upside cost risk.

If you do proceed without an actual written order, I recommend you send your client an e-mail that recounts exactly what was discussed and requested and confirms your intent to act upon those requests. You should also maintain contact with the client in the unlikely event they do not process their order in a prompt manner.

MARVIN MILETSKY

THE SALES PERSPECTIVE

Would the contractor you've hired to work on your house ever start work before he had a signed agreement clearly outlining the details of the project and how his invoices would be handled? Hell no. In fact, the times I've had dealings with contractors, nothing was started without the contract being signed and, usually, a deposit being paid.

I've tried to apply this contractor/homeowner way of doing business to my everyday sales proposals to see if this method might work for me. Not surprisingly, it doesn't. I think the main difference between my business and a contractor's is the number of one-time clients a contractor must deal with. As a result, the contractor requires more in the form of guarantees to protect himself or herself. That is, most contractors won't have built a relationship with their customers that ensures future business, so they've got to protect themselves early on as they don't really know me nor do they expect repeat business.

Salespeople are often caught between that proverbial rock and a hard place. Often, customers require your product on an absolute, dead-nuts date. There's no room whatsoever for failure to deliver by the deadline; your product will be useless after it passes. Delivering Easter eggs in May or Valentine's Day candy weeks after that holiday has passed or sending direct-mail pieces you produced after the event being announced has occurred will not ingratiate you with your client—and you can forget about getting paid for your efforts, not to mention any future business!

By now, you probably know enough about your business to know what it takes to get the final product into your client's hands. Often, however, the amount of time available to you is reduced by the client's inability to get a contract or purchase order into your hands. For the customer, the clock starts ticking as soon as he or she gives you the go-ahead. Your clock, however, technically shouldn't start until receipt of the signed papers. That's in a perfect world, however. In our world, there are times when we have to take a little risk to satisfy the customer's requirements on time.

I recently had just such a problem with a customer. He required my product in eight weeks, which already stretched my lead time, but couldn't get the paperwork to me for two weeks. Because I had a relationship with this customer, his problem was to become mine. If I would not ensure delivery without the proper paperwork in hand, one of my competitors right down the street would almost certainly be willing to stick his or her neck out. So I took the order from him verbally, and everything worked out fine.

If you find yourself in a position where you need to start an order before receiving the signed paperwork, there are some steps you can take to mitigate your risk:

- Try to reserve this course of action for only those people with whom you have a track record of past business and who have displayed loyalty to you.

- If you must proceed with an order for a new customer or one that you have been courting, your requirements for the contract should be stricter than those for a regular customer.

- You should only go so far into production that your company won't be hurt in the event of a cancellation or if the contract is not received. Progressive work should be done, but only to the extent that another customer could make use of this same material at some future date. Starting your work with no firm guarantee in your hand will prove to be costly to you—but adding to that being stuck with merchandise that can't be used by any other entity is just not acceptable. Your company is not in business to take a loss; there should be limits to the chances you are willing to take.

- Make sure you e-mail the person who authorized you to go ahead with the project to confirm that you are proceeding and will expect his formal paperwork shortly. Follow this up with a letter sent through the regular mail.

- Confirm with your superiors that this course of action is agreeable to all and that they understand the risks you are taking as a company.

- If you don't receive the signed contract in the agreed-upon timeframe, follow up with your customer. You've really got to put some pressure on to ensure that your company doesn't take all the risk but receive none of the rewards.

- Get as much mileage as you can from the satisfactory completion of the order and all the agreed-to conditions with your customer. Let them know that the job wasn't easy and thank them for giving you the business. Let their upper management know the heroic steps your company took to bring this project home in accordance with their needs. You're going to need some payback; that should come in the form of their loyalty to you and the awarding of future orders.

Q: THE CONTRACT IS SIGNED. HOW OFTEN SHOULD THE SALESPERSON STAY IN TOUCH?

JAMES CALLANDER

THE CUSTOMER PERSPECTIVE

Responding to an inquiry from a client is an involved process, with the obvious conclusion being an order awarded to you or one of your competitors. Throughout the process, you attempt to understand all the requirements and uncover items not clearly noted so your proposal meets the client's expectations. You work at breakneck speed to achieve this, navigating options and alternatives that might result in an acceptable solution. But once you have been awarded an order, there are not necessarily any specific rules on how much to follow up. Each client and each order will be different. It's up to you to determine how much effort will be required.

To make this determination, begin by considering the size and complexity of the order. An off-the-shelf–type purchase does not require a lengthy or in-depth follow-up—although, depending on the circumstances, a short, intense focus may be required to produce the desired results (that being the client awarding you the business and your company providing a smooth transaction for the client). In contrast, a client buying a major piece of equipment or service will require more attention up to and even after delivery.

There are too many types of purchased items to list where maintaining contact with the client after the contract is signed becomes part of the sale. Your experience will provide you with some level of guidance with respect to how much contact is required. If you don't have much experience to fall back on, I suggest you speak directly with your client. Your client should offer his or her recommendations based on similar past purchases. Another person who can provide some direction is your immediate manager. He or she will most likely have participated in sales prior to accepting his or her current position; he or she also likely deals with every client your company is actively pursuing. Your manager's extensive knowledge ought to help steer you toward the right approach with client contact after the sale.

Why is following up so important? After the award, there are many ways sales-people can bring value to the purchase. One is by communicating the delivery schedule. Here, the goal is to maintain a constant vigil for items with long lead times. Another is by keeping abreast of changes to the order in the days or weeks after the award is made—for example, changes in quantities, special notations associated with the items or purchase order itself, or technical questions that arise after the release. By being proactive and following up after being awarded an order, salespeople can resolve any issues for the client more quickly. Buyers reward vendors who meet or exceed their expectations and drop vendors who do not perform—and one of the biggest mistakes vendors make is failing to follow up.

> Don't just follow up on orders you're awarded; also follow up on ones you lose. This can help you determine what changes are necessary to improve your hit rate. Both you and your prospect will benefit— the prospect by improvement in sourcing, thereby lowering costs, and you by gaining additional sales.

A consistent follow-up routine for client purchases that are complex or that require manufacturing over a long period of time should be developed by the salesperson and adopted as part of the normal ordering process. Vendor sales personnel who support clients from a central point (i.e., inside sales) must know the requirements in this area to be effective. The inside sales staff can and will affect the outcome on many orders they handle. As a salesperson, you must manage this area by educating the support staff daily to any changes or new procedures required to meet the client needs.

MARVIN MILETSKY
THE SALES PERSPECTIVE

There's really no formula for the number of times you should be in touch after the contract has been signed and the order is being processed, but keeping in touch after the receipt of an order is as important as doing so during the "courtship." Keeping in touch after the order shows the interest you have in developing a relationship for the future. It shows that you care, and that will go a long way in any future negotiations. Remember to always target that *relationship* as your main goal! In fact, I've actually gone so far as to tell customers that when I receive an order from them, I no longer work for my own company, but become an employee of theirs. That is, I now represent them to my company.

Besides, there are lots of things that can happen between order entry and shipping. Unless you're up on the progress, you could wind up unpleasantly surprised by obstacles that get in the way to prevent the successful conclusion of the project. For one thing, it is you on the firing line, providing that buffer, should anything go awry during the course of the order. You're the one your customer will hold responsible. And your staff may not understand the urgency your customer feels with regard to this project, meaning that if anything were to slip, it will not have the same impact on them that it does on you and your client. You were there for the fun of landing this order, and you did what it took to get it. You can't walk away until it's been successfully completed.

When things do go off course, make it your responsibility to be in touch with the customer to inform them of the progress (or lack thereof) and the steps that are being taken to rectify any situation that has arisen. Don't let them find out there's a problem from someone else in your company or by your failure to deliver on time. Relationships aren't based solely on successes; to maintain a good relationship, you must handle the full gamut and address each item within.

I've discussed how success breeds success; the truth is, the contract you're currently working on could be a stepping stone for expanding your current business with this client. Visit the client and take advantage of this success to meet new people within the company or to simply reinforce the ties you've already made by sharing good news about the current project. Of course, don't show up *too* often or overstay your welcome; use care to avoid being intrusive, as that can have the opposite effect to the one you're trying to achieve.

Q: • SHOULD THE SALESPERSON BE
• PRESENT AT PROJECT MEETINGS?

JAMES CALLANDER
THE CUSTOMER PERSPECTIVE

Not all salespeople will be able to relate to the question, insofar as not all salespeople deal with clients who conduct these types of meetings. If your clients do conduct project meetings, however, attending them can provide some benefit for both the vendor and the client in certain circumstances.

Project meetings form to review progress on a multitude of tasks required to complete a project or to discuss other significant developments. For example, project meetings would be held on a regular basis throughout the implementation of new operational software or the construction of a building. In my industry, the electrical industry, we regularly hold project meetings. These are generally attended by the project manager or the assistant project manager along with engineering, craft supervision, safety, and quality-control personnel. During these meetings, we review the progress of work scheduled to determine whether things are going according to plan. Any issues are identified and a course of action to address these challenges is developed; progress on this course of action is then reviewed in the next meeting. We then review safety and quality of work following this same approach. If no issues are identified, the meeting then moves on to discuss other topics. If, however, problems are noted, the meeting shifts to resolve them. Work stoppage due to safety or quality concerns is a major red flag.

If you, as the salesperson, are simply supplying off-the-shelf–type items, then it's probably not necessary for you to attend a project meeting. If, however, you are supplying your client with more specialized goods or services, then your participation in one or two project meetings during the life of a project will pay dividends for the client. Your role while in the meeting will be, for the most part, information based only. For example, your client might need details from you about the engineering, manufacturing, or delivery of your product or services, or information that may affect the client's project schedule. Technical issues are another thing your client might call you in to discuss. For example, the client may have identified a problem and ask the vendor to discuss what action is necessary to resolve it. (Of course, any resolution must enable the client to maintain the current schedule.)

When attending a project meeting, I recommend you keep your comments to a minimum. Injecting information not requested into the conversation may cause more damage than good, as you may find yourself in the position of being asked questions to which you do not know the answer. Remember, too, that project meetings are to advance the client's schedule of work. They are not a selling opportunity—although attending them can be very informative when it comes to future visits with the staff and potential selling opportunities.

If a client asks you to attend a project meeting, I highly recommend you make yourself available. Be aware that project meetings tend to be lengthy events. Your schedule should allow for extra time, as chances are good the meeting will run long. The information in which the client is most interested typically relates to delivery; look to follow up weekly on any long–lead-time items to check the progress.

MARVIN MILETSKY
THE SALES PERSPECTIVE

Know who's out seeing your customers while you're attending those very interesting and satisfying project meetings? Yup, that's right: me. You know, that competitor of yours who's just been waiting his opportunity? Hey, your competitor's salesperson might have been attending a project meeting when *you* called on *his* customer. Your main function is to bring opportunities to your company, *not* to attend project meetings. Let the cooks do the cooking. It's your job to fill the restaurant.

That said, there is one meeting I recommend you *do* attend: the first one, or kick-off meeting. This is the meeting that will define your company's understanding of the project and set the tone for its completion. Who better to set the gears in motion than the person who has the most intimate knowledge of things—you?

After you attend the kickoff meeting, however, it's time to get on the road again where you belong: in front of your customer to communicate that his order has been entered and is being worked on and, by the way, do they need anything else at this time? After you've brought that customer up to speed, get out of his or her office and do what you do best: Pound the streets, develop new prospects, and visit existing ones.

One more thing about project meetings: Although I would no sooner advise that you attend these than work a drill press in a factory, you must keep up with the results of these meetings. Make sure you're on a distribution list for meeting minutes or ask any inside contacts who attend these meetings to report the results to you. Make sure you are aware of anything that can adversely affect your order so it is not sprung on you at the last minute. Even if there is something that will negatively affect your order, there still is no reason to attend the meeting yourself; go to a responsible attendee or executive who can make things happen to put it back on track.

Q: • Are Web Meetings Acceptable?
• Or Is Face-to-Face the Best Way?

James Callander
The Customer Perspective

Gone is the day when the only methods of talking to another person were by telephone or in person. Even mail-type correspondence has given way to the fax machine, which has in turn been replaced by e-mail. The changes that have occurred over the last 20 years are impressive—and daunting.

Vendors are the victims of these changes. The time allotted by client inquiries to respond to requests and complete tasks has compressed into a smaller and smaller window. We now see response demands measured in hours that 20 years ago we would have measured in days or weeks. Both vendors and clients must utilize all tools at our disposal to complete our daily workload if we are to be successful—including Web meetings.

A year or so ago, I was looking into a tool-management system. I was impressed with its features, and the training available was in-depth and flexible. At the point that buy-in from my senior management was required before we could proceed with awarding an order, the vendor was more than willing to fly in and give a presentation for all concerned parties, but getting everyone in place on the same day proved easier said than done. We decided to do a Web-based presentation and were able to quickly secure a date and time that worked for everyone. Not only did this mean we were able to meet at a central point in cyberspace sooner than later rather than waiting for a date far in the future when all key personnel could be in one place at one time, but it allowed for a noticeable cost savings. For one, the vendor didn't have to fly or rent a car to meet with all of us. The vendor was also able to bring into the presentation one of the designers to provide technical support—something they probably wouldn't have been able to do otherwise. The presentation was efficient and effective and minimized the amount of time and effort required by both parties to participate.

Web-based presentations and meetings will never replace their face-to-face counterparts, but Web-based technology does have a place in the selling process, offering advantages to both parties. But while my industry commonly makes use of this technology to conduct weekly, monthly, and yearly meetings, other industries are farther behind. If your company supports the use of this technology, I suggest using it. (If you don't know how to use it, then apply yourself and learn.) I suspect you will find your clients very agreeable to employing it. Indeed, I predict that in the next few years, you will see a substantial increase in the use of Web-based presentations both in your company and with your clients.

While I'm on the topic of technology, let me add that I attempt to keep up to date on newer forms of communication that allow me to compress the time needed for various work activities. Inevitably, I find myself educating my vendors on the potential of using some of these methods. I am selfish in this area; I want my vendors to make my life easier—and in turn, by following my lead, they become more efficient. But not all vendors have the resources available to them to support their efforts to manage their business. Personally, I find this unacceptable, especially when you compare the cost of providing these resources to the upside of using them. For example, I still see fax quotes and memos from some of my vendors. But when a fax is sent, document management becomes more labor intensive. Many of your clients are serious about document management; if you have the means to e-mail information rather than faxing it, I recommend you do so.

MARVIN MILETSKY
THE SALES PERSPECTIVE

I can't imagine anything replacing face-to-face interaction between salespeople and customers. Looking a customer in the eye and and being able to judge by his body language when to change my course has proven invaluable to me. And the way a face-to-face conversation can flow from business into a discussion of some sporting event or news of the day often has the effect of easing tensions, providing a relaxed atmosphere in which to continue my quest for an order. Often, face-to-face conversations lead right into lunch—always helpful when it comes to building relationships. I've gained so much through face-to-face communication with my customers; it's always proven to be a stepping stone toward getting an order.

I believe that face-to-face encounters will always be the most valuable weapon in your selling arsenal. That being said, I've used Web meetings to follow up on face-to-face meetings. For example, there have been times when I've needed to draw upon my company's technical team to answer a question for a client and wanted to strike while that iron was still hot. In these scenarios, Web meetings are ideal; they enable my technical representative to answer the client's question —without having to take a trip. Web meetings are also great if you deal with clients with offices all over the country. For example, my main contact at one company set up a Web meeting to enable us to introduce a new product to a great many people across a huge area, all at one time—although after the meeting, I did follow up with personal calls, individual thank-you notes, and face-to-face visits.

Now to the question of whether Web meetings are acceptable. Depending on your industry, these meetings might enable you to approach a vast and varied audience in a short period of time—and at a dramatically reduced cost compared to traveling to each and every one of your targets. These meetings could allow you to address people in remote areas that you otherwise would have little chance of visiting in person.

There are lots of opportunities to use Web meetings in a sales effort. I recently saw a newspaper ad that invited interested parties to e-mail or call for a password that would grant entry into a Web meeting that focused on financial planning. Similarly, certain travel planners use Web meetings to expose large numbers of potential clients to some of their properties, some even offering premiums and discounts to attendees just for logging in to the meeting.

If you conduct a Web meeting, make sure you do so in such a way that will keep everyone's interest. It's far easier to absent yourself from one of these meetings when you're are not physically in the presence of others. The Web meeting is the newest of tools available to you; research them well and see where they can fit into your sales effort.

Q: CAN THE CLIENT AND SALESPERSON EVER REALLY BE FRIENDS? OR WILL THE SALESPERSON ALWAYS LOOK FOR THE UP-SELL OPPORTUNITY AND THE CLIENT ALWAYS BE SKEPTICAL?

JAMES CALLANDER
THE CUSTOMER PERSPECTIVE

The natural tendency of many salespeople is to make friends with clients first and then move on to business. Our culture plays a large part in how we develop this mindset, which may be further promoted by training by your company (although depending on your company, your training may be designed to offset this tendency). While I'm not saying your business will suffer if you become friends with a member of your client's staff, I am suggesting that many salespeople erroneously assume that clients want to be buddy-buddy.

More than friendship, the one thing I require from all vendors who call on me is professionalism. Before I accept any vendor, that person must demonstrate the ability to conduct himself or herself in a professional manner, regardless of the type of communication. My focus, and the focus of most people in my position, is on the salesperson's ability to articulate information and serve my account, as well as the type of products and services the vendor offers.

While I'm not looking for a friend per se, I don't mind if the salesperson and I get along. In fact, I prefer my dealings with a salesperson to be pleasurable. Even a vanilla type of client-vendor relationship is preferable over one that is ugly. Unpleasant vendor-client relationships cause indifference, which inevitably leads to a heightened level of hostility that neither of us enjoys. A friendly relationship is also helpful in the event a problem arises. If my relationship with a vendor is friendly, then chances are that, even if the situation becomes tense, we will work through the issues. This becomes less likely in cases when I have a combative relationship with a vendor. Working through problems becomes tedious, even for the simplest of issues. Naturally, when I find myself in a situation such as this one, I start looking to replace the vendor.

One more thing: Depending on your target industry or market, you may find clients more relaxed with their vendors, allowing friendships to develop without restraint by management. Certain industries, however, have rules or guidelines that prevent interaction between clients and vendors outside work. Government agencies on the federal, state, and local level, for example, insulate their staff from even the perception of favoritism when dealing with vendors. Other industries and businesses have similar policies regarding conduct to which their employees and vendors must adhere. You should familiarize yourself with any policies your clients have that might affect you.

If a friendship does develop between a client and a salesperson, both parties must separate work from their personal lives. If you believe the friendship is more important than the business you conduct with the client, then you should consider giving the account to another salesperson. If, however, the current and potential business is the driving force behind your relationship, then you should be able to manage the account successfully.

MARVIN MILETSKY

THE SALES PERSPECTIVE

You know that old saying, "Familiarity breeds contempt?" There's no situation in which this is more true than when two people are trying to do business together. Perhaps in an ideal world, such a scenario could take place, but in the world of salesman-buyer relationships, I've never had or seen such a friendship develop. I've developed a multitude of "business friends" as my career has unfolded, but I can't think of one where I could actually say that while we were doing business, it was on a level equal to any relationships I had developed outside of work.

Once, I did witness a friendship develop between an owner of the company I was working for and a major supplier. Their friendship, which had developed as a result of their interaction while doing business with each other, appeared strong and committed. Eventually, the owner could no longer devote the time needed for purchasing, so he turned over that responsibility to me; I found myself in the position of needing to buy a commodity from the owner's "friend." The problem was, another vendor was offering the same product at a better price with speedier delivery. It didn't matter, though; the boss's friend got the order. As it turned out, this guy had been hosing us for years—and he continued to do so, as the owner of my company would tolerate no questioning of his friend's company or its product line. My thoughts then (as they are now) were that a business friendship is only as good as the next order. I do have some good news to report, however. Although I've never developed friendships with people with whom I was actively doing business, I've become true friends with several people after they've changed careers or retired.

Q: HOW MUCH OF THE SALESPERSON'S PERSONAL LIFE CAN BE SHARED WITHOUT TURNING OFF THE BUYER?

JAMES CALLANDER

THE CUSTOMER PERSPECTIVE

Sharing personal information is how we get to know one another—and the more we know about someone, the easier it is to understand his or her motivations and expectations. When the conversation turns personal, you'll want to keep these points in mind:

■ People are busier than ever—meaning that it's often very difficult to meet the day's deadlines in the hours available, let alone spend time getting to know someone. As a result, the issue is not always how much you disclose about yourself but whether the customer actually has time to engage in casual conversation with you. Salespeople who cannot appreciate the value of my time are more likely to turn me off by their lack of thoughtfulness than by any personal information they reveal.

■ Until you have had a chance to get to know someone, you are at greater risk of inadvertently offending him or her. For that reason, it's a better idea to ask people questions about themselves than to give information about yourself. Someone once told me that since we have two ears and only one mouth, we should spend twice as much time listening as we do talking; I thought that was pretty smart advice. Of course, you don't want to appear nosy, but I suspect you'll find that people are amazingly responsive when you show genuine interest in what they have to say. Everyone has a story to tell. Allow customers to open up. Ask them about their family. Are they married? Do they have kids? Boy or girl? How old? Ask them what they do to relax. Do they play golf? Do they fish or hunt? Ask how they got into their business. Usually, people find their work in strange ways.

■ Think before you reveal. Before you launch into a story about how much you had to drink at a party last night, be sure the buyer you are talking to is not a recovering alcoholic or a member of a religious group for whom drinking is prohibited. Before you complain about a minor problem in your life, consider how it might sound to someone who is facing a major crisis in his or hers. Before you say something in jest, be sure the other person is going to think it is funny.

■ At the risk of sounding like an old codger, I should probably point out to younger salespeople that behavior considered perfectly acceptable to someone in your generation may not be at all acceptable to someone 20 or 30 years your senior. I might also point out that no one particularly enjoys being made to feel like an old codger by being subjected to tales of the exploits of a younger person.

■ It has long been considered taboo to discuss religion or politics in social situations, and for good reason. Even if the customer has revealed his or her thoughts and feelings on these matters, you cannot go wrong by withholding your opinions.

Abraham Lincoln said, "Better to remain silent and be thought a fool than to speak out and remove all doubt." Bear this in mind before you start revealing your personal thoughts and experiences.

MARVIN MILETSKY
THE SALES PERSPECTIVE

My original, knee-jerk response to this question was to advise you to keep personal, personal and public, public—and never the twain to meet. But then I thought back over the years and the miles, the airline flights, the traffic jams, the telephone calls and the e-mails, and I realized that I've always mixed both areas of my life. That's how relationships are built.

Can you imagine walking into a customer's office and saying, "Hello. I am here to sell you my product. Please sign on the dotted line. Thank you. I will see you on my next visit. Goodbye." Sounds kinda robotic, doesn't it? I don't think it's a formula for successful order writing! We're not robots, and neither are our prospects or customers, so getting personal is a great way to break the ice. It makes for a more relaxed visit on both your parts. It sets a tone that should enable you to enter into the business part of the meeting as a natural progression rather than in some forced or contrived manner.

Of the many people I've come in contact with over the years, I really can't say that any two have been cut from the exact same cloth. Although there are similarities, each one has been unique, with his or her own interests, sensitivities, and intelligence. So I've always individualized my approach to each, adjusting not only my presentation but the amount and content of any personal information I share with them. But that doesn't mean I've built personal relationships with each and every one of these people; that just doesn't happen. Even if it could, there wouldn't be enough time in the day to keep all of these balanced and still achieve your goal: the sale.

Personal information I've shared with my best customers has come as a natural extension of a relationship that's been built over a long period. It takes a long time to build your relationship to a point where you're comfortable in sharing details and they're interested in your outside life. But when you reach that point, it's great to show your human side. You must keep in mind, however, that your customers are not your friends. Although you want to be open with them, there are details of your personal life you should keep to yourself. For example, you might share that you're going on vacation in Florida, but not that you're flying first class or you're playing golf on an exclusive course or eating at a very fancy restaurant. Likewise, mentioning that your child has just been accepted to a prestigious school is not okay; mentioning that he has been accepted to a school is fine. Not everyone can afford your lifestyle; stressing the things that you have that your client may only dream of may well foster animosity and jealousy on the part of your client. No one likes a sore loser, and they dislike loud-mouth winners even more. Keep all your conversations about outside life informational and fun.

Avoid spending too much time on your own stories. Remember, you're not in your customers' office to satisfy *your* needs; you're there to satisfy theirs. This is not about you, it's about them. You should be taking an interest in their personal lives, not the other way around. Allow them to do the talking; you do the listening. Take an interest. Draw out of them as much as you can about their outside life. Spend the time they need on these subjects as you ease into your main purpose for being in their office in the first place: to conduct some business. Next time you visit, continue your last conversation by inquiring about any of the information they shared during your last call.

Never lose sight of the fact that you're not visiting a customer for social reasons. You must keep it foremost in your mind that your purpose for visiting is business. If you can conduct business while being social, that's a great combination. Doing business without being social is acceptable; being social without doing business is not.

Q: How Important Is Loyalty?

James Callander
The Customer Perspective

As a purchasing manager, my loyalty is to my career and to the company that pays me. While I may feel loyalty for a particular salesperson and appreciate his or her past performance, I am obligated to make decisions based on what is best for my company and internal customers. I prefer to do business with salespeople I know, like, and trust, but if another vendor can best meet my employer's needs, I must go with them.

That said, I am more than willing to give vendors who have won my loyalty first crack at a quote. I am also willing to take the intangible benefits of using a particular vendor into consideration when awarding an order. That is, if the vendor and his or her product or services are known by me to be reliable, this may in certain circumstances outweigh a minimal price difference. If a vendor has demonstrated excellent follow-through skills and I will not have to do my own expediting, I may add that to the mix of information I use in making my decision. Price and/or availability are not my only priorities when I make my purchasing decisions. Not all buyers are able to say that, however. Particularly in large organizations, buyers must follow strict guidelines when making purchases, and loyalty may not be a part of the picture.

Loyalty plays a smaller role in today's business environment than it used to. When I first began my career in January of 1983, I often worked with people who had been in their position or with their company for decades. That is no longer the case. People change employers and positions much more frequently now. Add that to a changing economy in which companies once thought to be "blue chip" are going out of business, and it's easy to see why there has been an overall decline in loyalty between customers and salespeople. Despite these changes in the marketplace, however, it's still wise for salespeople to attempt to build their customer's loyalty.

To build loyalty with me, salespeople need to do the following:

- Respond promptly to my requests.

- Communicate new information to me without having to be prompted.

- Make my life easier, whether by tracking and reporting an order's status or working directly with my internal customer to resolve issues.

- Have expertise in your field, allowing me to rely on your knowledge.

Different clients have different ideas on the extent to which loyalty should influence their decision-making process. For example, clients that mandate strict vendor/client relationships may have different views on this issue than, say, a small, family-owned business. Make an effort to determine your own clients' views on this issue and how they put those views into practice. You don't want to find out a year after the fact, for example, that you have lost orders to a competitor who happens to be related to the client. And through it all, keep your eye on the prize. Meet or exceed your client's expectations, and you will find success in sales. You may even find this more rewarding than any perceived benefit of loyalty from your client.

MARVIN MILETSKY
THE SALES PERSPECTIVE

I've used the word "balance" more than once in discussing this line of work—and here I go again. I believe that relationships are one of the keys to success in selling, and typically that relationship involves a person, not a business entity. But in many industries—and here's where the issue of balance comes in—the relationship between purchaser and seller should also encompass the purchaser's organization.

Just to show you that I can still make mistakes at this stage of my career, I recently made a terrible mistake in judgment by not heeding some of my own advice. I had developed a wonderful relationship with a purchasing agent and was rewarded with lots of profitable orders and fun times during my visits to him. All was going well until he accepted a position at a new company that afforded him a move up the ladder toward an executive management position. I called to congratulate him and learn more about where he was going and what his new responsibilities were going to be. I was thrilled for him—and his promise to bring me along warmed my heart as I envisioned money pouring in from this old buddy and his brand-new employer. Talk about counting my chickens before they hatched! I was in for a rude awakening on two fronts:

- His departure from his original company left a void in my contacts there. I had spent so much of my time there with him, I had excluded just about everyone else. When he left, I had no ally in place to rely on or even talk to. I was in the unenviable position of having to build new relationships with people I hardly knew—people who saw me as opportunistic, as I hadn't really bothered to sell myself to them before my contact left. There I was with tons of product and no one to sell it to.

- On the day I walked into my old contact's new office to see what business we could do together, I discovered that his company was quite satisfied with their vendors, with whom they had a long history of success. Moreover, my contact's new position was more in the line of systems development and employee motivation. Of course, I was assured that when the opportunity presented itself, I would be among the first to be called—but that there was nothing in the immediate future.

There's a moral to this story: Make sure your relationships with individuals run deep, but that you become valuable to everyone you come into contact with (perhaps some more than others). Take your pal to lunch, but make sure to invite others along or even invite them separately for a one-on-one outing. You can't afford to be all things to just one person. Whoever the vendors at my contact's new place of business were, they had done a great job making themselves valuable to a broad spectrum of people, as the changing of the guard did not threaten their business.

All that being said, many service industries require just the opposite when it comes to relationship building. The business is done through one contact only, and it's important that you recognize the strength of that contact. In the advertising industry, for example, the decision-maker hires the ad agency of his or her liking—the one that he or she works best with and that can best interpret the message that person wants to convey. When that decision-maker leaves and a new one comes in, that new person will bring in his or her contacts that have served him or her well over the years—meaning the first agency is probably out. But there's a good possibility that the agency's original contact will bring the agency on board at his or her new company. It's the same with professional sports teams. When a team hires a new manager, that manager doesn't come in and try to reshape the existing coaching staff; the manager makes a clean sweep. And if you've worked with this manager before, chances are he or she will bring you along to the new venue.

Q: • CAN YOU WORK TOGETHER IN
• SPITE OF A PERSONALITY CONFLICT?

JAMES CALLANDER
THE CUSTOMER PERSPECTIVE

One of my first tasks before beginning a project in a new city is to establish accounts with vendors to support our office and materials needs. This requires me to do research in the local area to find the right logistical support ahead of time. During this process, I typically contact 20 or 30 vendors to discuss what we are looking for and evaluate their capabilities. Inevitably, some vendors struggle to grasp our needs and expectations. How they handle this gives me my first clue as to whether I will likely experience a personality conflict with this vendor. If the vendor manages the situation properly, I can overlook their initial difficulty grasping our needs for the moment and move on. But if the vendor becomes difficult—for example, if the individual assigned to our account is unwilling to accommodate our method of conducting business—this usually signals that there are more problems ahead. Would this be considered a personality conflict? It sure feels like one. Obviously, being new to us, the vendor might be apprehensive at first. I can understand that. But if I am asking for nothing more than for that vendor to help resolve an issue and all I get are arguments, I doubt very seriously I will need that vendor's phone number again.

Personality conflicts are based on perceptions that are rooted in emotion and tend to get in the way of conducting business. Personality conflicts can be difficult to overcome, but the fact is, clients can typically look to several different vendors for any product or service they require. Put another way, if a personality conflict arises between a client and a vendor, the vendor is usually the party that must make concessions. If there is a rift between the client buyer and the salesperson calling on that buyer, then the salesperson had better find a way to clear things up—for example, removing any emotional triggers from his or her communications. If he or she fails to do so, the chances of that salesperson continuing to sell to that client are marginal at best. If the issue is left up to the client to resolve, they will look to other vendors to fill the gap. The goal in sales is to book an order; salespeople should focus on achieving this goal every day. That means reacting to situations in a manner that is acceptable to the client.

MARVIN MILETSKY

THE SALES PERSPECTIVE

 Although you'll probably encounter lots of people with similar personalities during your career, no two will be exactly the same—and just because one person takes to you does not guarantee that another will. In fact, you might be welcomed like a long-lost family member by one person and as an enemy by another—and you're still the same person! One thing's for sure: There are no guarantees that your clients will like you. (Of course, there's also no guarantee that you're going to take to the person on the other side of the desk—but in that case, you'll almost always have to find some way of dealing with him or her. After all, that person can always find someone else to deal with, either within your company or at a competitor, with whom he or she can get along.) Just remember: In sales, it's never about you. It's about your clients and satisfying their needs. Adjusting your personality to meet their requirements is something you're going to have to decide to do or move on.

> One thing I've learned through experience is to be a good listener. I always try to allow the customer to set the tone for our conversation and fall into place with his or her direction.

Still, there are going to be people who just don't take to you no matter what you do. You'll see it in their reaction when you call, in the difficulty you have making an appointment, or in your inability to land any orders (or orders beyond the ones you know are the leftovers). You may ultimately need to decide whether you're wasting your precious time with someone who doesn't appear to want to enter into any short- or long-range business relationship with you—*ever*. Here's an expression you've heard before: Cut your losses and move on! Don't burn any bridges, but put these people on your lowest-priority list. Spend more time with clients with whom you have at least some chance for success. By the way, that guy with the attitude just might have done you a world of good. By signaling to you that you ought not waste any of your precious time on him, he enables you to spend more time with those prospects who are easier to get along with and will give you at least a fighting chance for success.

> Remember: You don't have to become friends with your client in order to do business. A cordial but professional relationship can do wonders.

Q: IS IT IMPORTANT TO WORK WITH YOUR CUSTOMER TO DEVELOP A NEW PRODUCT FOR HIM?

JAMES CALLANDER
THE CUSTOMER PERSPECTIVE

↳ "The customer is king" is an axiom of the sales industry, and putting it into practice is the test of any salesperson. One way you can make the customer "king" is to customize your product or service to meet that customer's specific needs.

When I am working with a vendor, I appreciate a salesperson with the creativity to tailor-fit a product or service to our business. I'm not suggesting you put on your engineering cap and design an entirely new product; often, by modifying an existing product, you can create something of greater value to the customer. Usually, this requires two things from the salesperson:

- A thorough understanding of the customer's product and services

- A competent understanding of the customer's needs, procedures, and working environment

> In an earlier question, I mentioned my niece, who successfully made the transition from engineering to sales. Because of her unique perspective, she is often brought in to help close the deal when a client needs a product that's slightly different from the "off the shelf" model. The customer needs assurance that the product can be manipulated to meet their specific needs; finding someone within your company who is capable of making and articulating such alterations can prove invaluable.

Tailoring a product or service to meet the customer's needs is often far more than a nicety; it's a requirement for doing business. Many customers operate in a business environment governed by federal, state, or licensing codes. Your customer's operations may be based on numerous contractual specifications, including tracking, packaging, and documentation. You may not need to make any physical changes to your product, but your flexibility in providing the product or service in accordance with your customer's procedural requirements gives you an advantage over other vendors being considered.

Being flexible enough to put together the perfect product for your customer can be challenging—especially if you are employed by a big company where most items are sold off the shelf. That doesn't mean it can't be done, however. You may have to get creative and put a little extra effort into making the sale, but this type of value-added offering is exactly what I am looking for as a customer. And remember: It may require a little more work on your part, but I am more likely to pay a higher price to purchase a product that is exactly what I need. And your flexibility in this area has the added benefit of ensuring that the customer will return to you for any repeat business.

Offering your customer a customized product may help you to make the sale, but being successful requires diligence after the sale is made. As a customer, I have many times experienced the unwelcome surprise of finding out the specified item or procedure promised by the salesperson is not what I received. If your offering is outside the normal scope of your company's offerings, you must ensure that everyone within your organization is clear as to what is expected. This may require you to invest time in educating others within your organization on the nature and requirements of your customer's business. I would rather have a salesperson tell me he or she can't provide the requested product than to promise it and fail to deliver.

MARVIN MILETSKY
THE SALES PERSPECTIVE

Working with your customer to develop new products or services for them can be important, and fits under the broad description of customer service and relationship building. Before you commit to such a project, however, you must study the situation and determine the possible return on your investment. We all like to extend ourselves for our customers, but you must make sure there will be a means for recovering your costs and, more importantly, turning investments into a profit.

My advice? Before even attempting to assist with the development of a new product or service for a client, make sure that you and your company have the time and wherewithal to actually invest in this sort of function. Confirm exactly who at your client is asking for this new item. Will that person be in the position to give you an order once you've completed your task? Make sure the item is not of the "one-time" variety, specific to their needs only. If it is, you might have to charge a fee for the development of the prototype and act more as a consultant than a producer of product.

There'll be times when developing a new idea or product might be advantageous to both you and your client. In such cases, you must make sure to take care of any legal ownership issues right from the beginning. Also, I have found that the best way to ensure the continued interest of a client and their sincere participation is to demand that they have a financial stake in the ongoing project. Recently, we were asked to develop a product for a transit agency. This is one of the worst situations to even *consider* such a task, as they, being a government agency, cannot buy from just one source; they must go out for public bid, meaning that you may well spend time and money designing and developing a product, only to lose the order to some Johnny-come-lately who has nothing to offer but a low price. To handle this, we arranged for them to pay for half the cost of the prototype; if it worked, they would be able to purchase the balance. A postscript to this is that the item *did* work, they paid for the other half, and we wound up with a new product to sell to others. On the next requirement, however, the agency came out for public bid, and we lost the job to someone with no experience manufacturing the item.

All this is to say there's lots of upside in helping your clients develop new products—but make sure you're covered for your efforts.

Q: THE SELLER HELPED THE BUYER DURING LEAN TIMES (OR VICE VERSA). WHAT, IF ANYTHING, IS OWED?

JAMES CALLANDER

THE CUSTOMER PERSPECTIVE

Every industry experiences ebbs and flows. While today, business in all sectors is slowing down, just a year ago most businesses were busting at the seams with trade. If you are fortunate enough to have a diversified client list in multiple sectors, you will be better able to weather the storm of a slowing business cycle. If your focus is on one specific sector or client type, any change in their business (up or down) will immediately affect your sales. Buyers often say to vendors, "You need to sharpen your pencil!" when the vendor's quote is high. During slowdowns, the sharpness of the pencil becomes your clients' friend. Their limited or lower-volume demand will require you to evaluate the effect of any lost sale. In down markets, competition heats up; because there are fewer dollars available, each one becomes more valuable to the vendor.

In the 25-plus years I have worked in the electrical industry, I have seen more than one slowdown. Each one forced consolidation on both the vendor and client sides. Vendors were sold or went under, effectively limiting clients' resources for securing pricing for inquiries. Likewise, many clients experienced a reduced call for their services, going out of business or accepting an offer by a larger competitor. This required vendors to scrounge for fewer dollars with a greater amount of competition. But belt-tightening measures employed during these times made both groups stronger when the slowdown period ended.

You should assess the likelihood of clients in your account package slowing down or even becoming insolvent on a yearly basis or at any indication of the economy hitting a snag. A client's payment practices during such times can be a good indication of trouble. If a client fails to keep up with their payments, you'll need to have some discussions with them and potentially make some tough decisions about whether to continue doing business with that client. You don't want to be left holding the bag if your client goes under!

During low points, you must supplement your standard account-management efforts. The shock of lost sales provides a sense of urgency to keep the sales coffers full. Client inquiries take on a new meaning for you and your company. In addition to all the normal correspondence and client visits, you'll want to make a special effort to follow up and carefully apply any information you gather to ensure you are in the know on all aspects. Making additional contacts within your clients is especially important here; each new contact can provide additional clarity with respect to the effect any downturn in business has on the client.

All that being said, I do not believe either party should benefit beyond the immediate need during lean times, except insofar as the relationship between the salesperson and the client may further develop. For example, vendors who manage to grow their business even during lean times may show themselves worthy in the eyes of their clients, thereby making them more reliant on the vendor both now and in the future.

MARVIN MILETSKY

THE SALES PERSPECTIVE

There may well come a time when your customer has hit a downturn in their business and you are in a position to ease their burden. For example, many companies in this situation experience cash-flow problems, and this is an area where you may be able to offer some creative solutions. Arranging to have your invoice due or paid over an extended period of time might be just what the client needs to bridge the receipt of their customer's payment with what is owed you.

That being said, while from the human standpoint you might want to do all in your power to support a client in this situation, you cannot be the hero to your client at the expense of your own company. Make sure that any help you provide doesn't create problems of your own. Also, limit your help to only those entities with which you have established a positive relationship over the long term. These companies will be more likely to understand the value of what you've done to help them and recognize their obligation to pay you back in the future in the form of their loyalty. A company that has never or only marginally supported you in the past is not likely to do an about-face in the future because of your help. While I hate this expression, it's true: A leopard never changes its spots. Any company that had the opportunity to support you in good times and chose not to should not be allowed to take advantage of you during their lean times.

One more thing: If you do want to help a client through the lean times, make sure your company is aware and approves of what you are doing. We once made special payment arrangements with a client but neglected to tell accounting what we were doing; accounting then proceeded to put the account out for collection to an agency. (Fortunately, once things were straightened out and the customer was back on their feet, they continued the pay us back for quite some time after.)

Q: WHEN THE PRODUCT DOESN'T WORK OR THE SERVICE IS POOR, DOES RESPONSIBILITY FALL ON THE SALESPERSON'S SHOULDERS? OR CAN HE OR SHE PASS THE BUCK?

JAMES CALLANDER
THE CUSTOMER PERSPECTIVE

Eventually, something will go wrong with your product or service. Typically, the client will discover that an item is defective or wrong at the time of install—which is unfortunately the worst time for them, as any resulting delays will cost them money, even if it is just for labor. The vendor replacing the item at no cost to the client is generally the preferred solution; hopefully, the product will be readily available, as the client most likely will want it by the following morning. If not, or if the client is located too far away for the vendor to deliver quickly by normal means, odds are the vendor will incur freight charges to rectify the issue.

An issue involving a mismatch with the application can be a bit more complex. In a best-case scenario, you can correct a mismatch by replacing the item you provided with another one. It may be, though, that you cannot provide a compatible replacement. In that case, the client will more than likely want to be compensated for your mistake. After all, the client will have to invest time sourcing the item from another vendor.

Most vendors have a staff of people in support roles working in a variety of departments, and these people do affect the salesperson's ability to serve clients in his or her account package. I may contact an individual in a particular department for help in the event an issue arises; if that person is able to handle the request effectively, then no additional communication with the vendor company is required. But if that person is inept, not only will I immediately contact the salesperson to provide me with a solution, but that person's failure to satisfy my needs will have an impact on my impression of the salesperson in charge of our business. Ultimately, in my view, any issue that arises as a result of a salesperson's efforts or the efforts of others working with that salesperson are the responsibility of that one person.

No one said managing clients was going to be easy. The fact you've decided to take on the responsibility of calling on clients for your company places the burden of handling issues when they arise squarely on your shoulders. While your clients may in fact deal with several people in your office, none of them has the relationship you possess with your clients. You are front and center on a weekly basis at the client's office, so when things go bad, it doesn't really matter whether or not it's your fault; your client is most likely going to turn to you to handle the situation.

The absolute worst thing you can do in such a situation is to hide from your client. This can destroy all the good you've built over months or years. I've never found a need to solicit business from a vendor after they made themselves scarce. I don't have the time for salespeople who promise the moon but deliver cow patties. If you are interested in my business, you have to handle the good *and* the bad. The salesperson who stands tall when issues arise and provides support, even if it is less than stellar, will command respect from his or her clients. If you make it difficult for the client to find you, don't be surprised when that client loses interest in doing business with you.

MARVIN MILETSKY
THE SALES PERSPECTIVE

The message on your desk indicates that your customer is trying to find you. They've called all over and must speak to you immediately. You feel a pit in your stomach as you realize they're not frantically trying to reach you in order to share happy news; something has gone wrong, and they need you to resolve the problem—*now!* At this point, how you handle the mop up will make all the difference.

Here are some great responses you can use if you are dealing with a customer after a problem has occurred (what, you thought you'd never have any problems?) and you expect to never deal with that customer again:

- My shipping department never pays any attention to what I say!
- The designers probably felt they had a better idea than you.
- Can you believe some clerk forgot to enter your order?
- They assured me this mistake not happen again. Oh well…I guess it did!

- Upper management cut some corners to reduce our costs and increase our profit.

- My secretary never gave me your message!

- A decision was made by someone to handle another customer's order before yours.

It's critical that you take responsibility for the failures of your company directly. In the eyes of your customer, you and only you are the responsible party. You can't be there only for the glory; you are a solo act with no one on stage to rescue you but yourself. You, not some support person, must respond. Distasteful as it might be (after all, you prefer accolades and sweetness), the customer is relying on you. You're their point of contact.

Once you are in touch with the customer, make sure you understand exactly what the problem is. If it's beyond your expertise, get your technical people involved immediately. Develop a plan that will fix the problem, and implement that plan quickly. The more time that passes between the problem and the fix, the more things will fester. And once the issues have been resolved, let the customer know that action is being taken within your company to prevent another occurrence in the future. If it was due to human error, convey that the personnel involved will be retrained or replaced.

In everything you say, be inclusive by using the word "we," not "I." "*We* make a great product." "*We* ship on time." "*We* care about your business." When the inevitable mistake occurs, "*We* fouled up"; when that mistake is rectified, "*We* were able to solve the problem." Not "I"; "we."

Q: • THERE WAS A MISTAKE IN PRICING. CAN • THE SALESPERSON ASK FOR AN INCREASE?

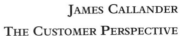

JAMES CALLANDER
THE CUSTOMER PERSPECTIVE

⤶ Speed kills. It's true with cars, and it applies to quoting, too. If you are moving too quickly, not reviewing your work before releasing the information to your client, you will likely make mistakes with some aspect of your proposal, such as pricing—for example, overlooking freight costs or other terms. My advice? Don't allow yourself to misquote. Of course, this is a simple enough statement—but one that's hard to comply with.

While the client is typically not obligated to relieve you of the effects of your mistake, meaning your company must absorb the difference, it's possible that they can work with you—but you must communicate the problem. Now and then, a vendor will approach me after determining that they have made a mistake in their calculations. Usually, this communication occurs during the quotation phase or shortly thereafter. If I am aware of the information prior to releasing an order, I can adjust for the increase. This may or may not affect the award of the order. If my primary criterion for awarding the order is price, the adjustment may put you out of the running—although I will give you high marks for having done the right thing.

Clients generally do not accept a change after releasing an order to a vendor, although if a situation develops in the order's early stages, you might find a receptive ear—provided the increase is relatively small. If you are looking for a major adjustment, I doubt your client will be receptive. Besides, the buyer may not even have the authority to make a large adjustment. In that case, the buyer would consult with his or her management, who is even less likely to be sympathetic to you than the buyer. Late in the order process or after the order is complete, the pricing mistake officially becomes your problem. No client will accept a change in cost at this late stage. The best you can possibly hope for is to never repeat the mistake.

Look, you will make mistakes from time to time. Limiting mistakes is important, but not making the same mistake twice is critical to your job. Even if a client does bail you out and accept an adjustment, you will quickly realize that their patience is short and their memory long if the mistake occurs again. Taking that extra minute to review all the information in your proposal is essential to preventing mistakes. The little bit of time you spend up front could save a whole bunch of time and money in the end.

MARVIN MILETSKY

THE SALES PERSPECTIVE

The order's been entered and the groundwork begun when you discover an error. No matter how many times you review your costing, you can't understand how it occurred. But there it is, right in front of you, and it's a *beaut*! Brace yourself; it's gonna happen. You've heard of Murphy, haven't you? We all make mistakes—usually at the worst possible times and with the most important clients.

In relationship selling, you would hope (and, really, somewhat expect) that your customer would give you some indication during the negotiation that something's amiss. That's not to say, however, that the indication they give will be overt. It's entirely possible you just missed it (one of the many reasons you should pay close attention to what they say). A simple question asking whether you have included a particular item in your bid should be enough to raise a red flag. The question in itself is strange and should prompt you to review your proposal.

You've got to judge the extent of the mistake that's been made and the cost impact upon your own company. The error might be so large as to threaten the very existence of your company. While I don't want to sound callous, the survival of your company is of the utmost importance. There's no sense filling an order and putting the health of your own company in jeopardy; in this case, not only should you inform your customer of the mistake, but you must seek their assistance in rectifying the situation. Remember: They need you as much as you need them. They make a profit off of you thanks to benefits of the product as well as the savings you offer. A true relationship can survive this sort of challenge.

If the mistake results only in a reduction or loss of your profit, or perhaps a small loss overall, it's probably better to eat the mistake. Let your profit from the order be in the form of lessons learned. Better that than admit to your mistake; doing so may diminish the client's belief that you understand your client's requirements and can satisfy their needs. After all, if this were strictly true, then you wouldn't be in this position in the first place, would you?

If you do reveal your mistake to your client and ask for a price increase, your customer might have some doubt about your honesty in your original proposal and ask for substantiation of your loss by asking to see your estimating backups. This is none of their business and cannot be given to them. By letting them in on your costing techniques, you might expose an area of your costing process that gives them better negotiating ammunition in the future. For example, you might have a standard figure that you use for your overhead and still another for profit. Or maybe you have a charge for "miscellaneous" items that is used to cover your mistakes. Whatever it is, it is *your* information, not theirs. Keep it proprietary and out of their sight.

Recently, I had reason to discuss with a customer a mistake on a quote that became an order. The mistake was not devastating, but it *was* going to cost my company money. Added to this was the fact that I had asked the customer during the negotiation whether they needed 20 of a particular item and was assured that they did—only to discover after the contract was awarded that they actually needed 20 *pairs* of the item. The order had been placed and the customer had no way of changing it as doing so would create problems with his superiors, so we resolved to make up the difference on some future negotiation. (In other words, he owed me one.)

One last thing: There will be times when you could win a battle and lose a war. You may very well get the increase you request, only to be eliminated from quoting on the next project. Choose your battles well and make sure the end result is what you want it to be.

Q:
• CAN THE DAMAGE DONE AFTER A FAILED
• ORDER EVER BE REPAIRED? HOW?

JAMES CALLANDER
THE CUSTOMER PERSPECTIVE

Most of the time, orders go without a hitch. The client takes delivery with no issues. But I doubt you will make it through your sales career without at least one order going wacko. There are just too many things that can pop up during the order and shipping process that can affect the outcome of an order. When faced with an order that seemingly has a mind of its own, the salesperson will usually find that putting a little extra time into following up clears up the issue—but every now and then, that extra effort won't fix the problem, and the client will be pushed to the breaking point.

As a client, I realize that my vendors probably aren't trying to trip up and cause me aggravation, but I also know that many vendors cause their own problems and are slow to correct them when they arise. Vendors who provide me with status reports on all my open orders with their company shine in my eyes. They are the exceptional ones who understand there is more to business than just taking an order. On the opposite end of the spectrum are those vendors who manage to win an order from me, only to quickly lose my confidence. They delay entering our order; they run out of the item that was in stock during the quote process; and they do not communicate any problems they encounter. Once I begin my follow-up—which I do, on orders large and small—they become hard to reach, hiding behind the growing list of voicemails and e-mails I am sending. And when they finally do answer, they act as if they are just now hearing from me. It only takes one or two of these experiences with a vendor to extinguish my belief in them and pass them over when future opportunities arise.

What I'm trying to say is, a single failed order won't necessarily damage your relationship and future opportunities with a client. All the things I have mentioned throughout this book will influence your client's decision to either continue to work with you or move on to other vendors. But if you have a "do not care" attitude going in, your client will see right through you.

It's important when issues do arise, such as a failed order, that you jump in with both feet to resolve things. The client needs to see that you care about them—especially when something goes wrong. Clients expect vendors to fix problems, regardless of how much it hurts, and they want the vendor involved immediately. Not tomorrow or next week; now! If you can't accommodate the client by taking action toward a remedy, they will find someone who can—namely, your boss.

MARVIN MILETSKY

THE SALES PERSPECTIVE

When I'm in presentation mode, trying to convince my prospect to favor me with an order, I stress all the positives about my company—its services, its products, and its reliability. My pitch includes the identification of the product or service that will best satisfy my target's needs. I demonstrate its worthiness and position myself so I have a shot at the order.

I've always taken the time to learn about the strengths of the company I'm working for as well as the strengths of the products or services being marketed, and have always been able to represent these with confidence to my clients. Over the years, I've learned that a great deal of successful salesmanship has to do with all those positives—in combination with one very important ingredient: a thing called trust. And that brings me to a very important part of developing that trust: the part wherein you share with your customer that your company is not perfect!

Yes, that's what I said. Admitting to some of your company's shortcomings is a very good way to gain a prospect's trust. If someone were presenting a product to you and claimed that it had a 100-percent satisfaction and reliability rating—that it never broke down or failed—you might listen with some suspicion. I, for one, would be more comfortable with someone who admitted that his company was not perfect but *did* have a service department in place to tackle any problems that might arise. This sort of honesty shows the human side of your company, as well as its ability and desire to address issues. It also prepares your client for the possibility that something could go wrong—but demonstrates that if it does, you'll know how to take care of it, and that you'll do so at once, in a professional manner, with the least disruption to your customer's business.

Things happen. And as Murphy's Law was written, they happen at the least convenient time in the worst of all circumstances. But you can repair the damage. You're the contact when things go right with an order, so it is you who will be contacted when a problem arises. Here's your chance to put your money where your mouth is with the customer as you coordinate your company's efforts to fix the problem in a timely fashion. And after all is said and done and the situation has been resolved, it's you who must put yourself right in front of your customer to take your licks. If the problem was a serious one, let your client vent. Even if you took care of it, they need to get their frustration off their chests. Remember, though, that your client isn't looking for a debate partner. Listen and give the assurances that any mistakes that were made have been addressed to ensure they won't happen again.

What if the mistake is of a catastrophic nature? Believe me, they happen. I know because I've made a few. Once, a customer became angry with us and demanded we finish his project immediately, noting that we had stalled for the last time. As his anger grew, we rushed to complete his order. You guess what happened: Everything came out all wrong. Our customer was out of time, so he accepted our delivery and used his own personnel to alter our product to make it work. After the dust settled, I called the buyer to tell him how profusely sorry we were and that we'd like another chance at some future date. He listened, but even the promise of a huge discount on a future order didn't do much to calm his anger. He let me know that he'd call us in the future; we shouldn't bother calling him. Some time later, I made it a point to be in their area and to call on them unannounced. I knew I was taking a chance, but what did I have to lose? We hadn't heard from them since the debacle; the worst they could do was decline to see me. The purchasing agent greeted me coolly in the reception area and asked what had brought me in. I looked him straight in the eye and asked him if we had any shot of being considered for a small job. As he started to respond, I could see it was going to be negative, so I cut him off. I said, "You've heard that the East Germans and the West Germans have torn that wall down that was separating them, haven't you? Are you going to tell me that these two countries can find a way of getting along after all they've gone through, but our two little companies can't call a truce?" He looked at me with his mouth agape, and then a smile came across his face as he started to laugh at the silliness of the whole matter. End result: We had a very civil conversation and did eventually work together again.

Q: THE THANK YOU AFTER THE RECEIPT OF THE ORDER—IS IT IMPORTANT?

JAMES CALLANDER
THE CUSTOMER PERSPECTIVE

I tend to think of the practice of sending formal thank yous or gifts after the receipt of an order as being from a previous era in sales. In fact, I can't remember the last time I received such a thank you. Most of the thank yous and gifts I receive from vendors are given when we first meet or when new offerings are being promoted.

I don't see sending formal thank yous or gifts as directly influencing sales success, but there are a few occasions when a formal thank-you letter or gift would be appropriate:

■ **You have been working with several people within the customer's organization to complete the quotation process:** If winning the sale required you to interact with different people in different departments within the customer's organization, a formal thank-you letter recognizing the efforts of these individuals would be appreciated. Perhaps someone in the engineering department provided you with a greater understanding of specifications or tolerances. Maybe someone in the department that will actually use the product or service gave you a tour or explained the application in which it would be used. Sometimes the buyer is unaware of assistance provided by others; a letter to the buyer recognizing their efforts serves a dual purpose: informing the buyer of the assistance received and commending those who provided it, paving the way for future working relationships. Likewise, if the buyer has done something above and beyond the call of duty to enhance the purchasing process, consider directing your thank you to his or her management. Everyone appreciates recognition for a job well done.

- **The sale is part of a larger project and/or of great importance to the customer:** If the product or service you are providing is part of a significant project or event in the customer's business, a thank you recognizing not only the sale but also the milestone reached is in order. If, for example, the customer is opening a new store or has been awarded an important new contract and gives you business associated with this event, your thank you can double as a form of congratulations. Your recognition of the importance of the project or milestone and an expression of your appreciation for being made part of it is a great way to position yourself as a business partner. A thank you of this nature lets purchasing managers like myself know that a salesperson is paying attention to what is important to me and my organization.

As for me, I make it a point to send a letter of appreciation to the manager of any salesperson who exceeds my expectations and provides above-grade support. I want to recognize that person to his or her superiors. If someone has demonstrated an understanding of our business and at every opportunity provided more than what was required, that person should be acknowledged by me and my company; a little encouragement received from my office goes a long way toward maintaining that person's support. I also like to pick up the phone and call inside salespeople who help me dodge obstructions to complete a task and compliment them right on the spot. Usually, the vendor inside person is thrilled to hear praise after a full day of grumpy calls. You can almost see their smile as they listen to my thank you.

MARVIN MILETSKY

THE SALES PERSPECTIVE

For the life of me, I cannot understand why anyone would need advice in this area. You're in sales (or trying to be). You're outgoing and comfortable with people. You possess an inner drive and confidence about what you do in your everyday life that should give you a natural advantage as you develop your selling skills. You're honest, you're sincere, you care about doing things professionally, and you look to develop relationships. If someone does something nice for you or gives you an order, what could be more natural than a warm and sincere thank you?

You've been on the receiving end and appreciated it; so too will your customers. Make the call. Stop by the customer's office. Appreciate the small and the large. Never take for granted that an order is automatically yours. Treat each order as if it is the best and unexpected.

Oh, and by the way, thanks for reading.

Q: How Do You Maintain Your Position When There Is No Business to Be Done?

JAMES CALLANDER

THE CUSTOMER PERSPECTIVE

Throughout your career in sales, you'll face tough times, when the volume of business available declines. One or more of your clients may discover their business is retracting; in response, they initiate measures to keep their business afloat. The two key areas the client can manage to reduce overhead are the items they purchase and staff they employ. Both affect the vendor who is supporting their operations. Finding yourself in this situation is no fun—nor is it time to rest on your laurels. The instinct to survive must kick in to overcome the lack of business.

When business slows down, your first move should be to ask your client whether the slowdown is just a hiccup or something more. If the slowdown is simply a hiccup, nothing really needs adjusting. Maintaining your exposure with the client is still important, however, even if you modify the frequency. If a slowdown is the beginning of a more serious reduction of business—one that may be permanent—you may have to reevaluate your exposure to the client. In that case, the concern for any salesperson becomes how you replace the lost business.

In some industries, the very nature of the business involves peaks and valleys. Take the construction industry, for example. Business volume swings by season and by project starts. At the start of a project, companies gear up by buying many components needed ahead of time. The spike in volume is very apparent, which leads to a very active response by a horde of vendors. This continues until at least 70 or 80 percent of the materials needed to complete the job have been purchased. At this point, the business begins to drop in volume, lowering the number of inquiries the contractor submits each day. Inevitably, several vendors will drop or eliminate their support at this point; they are what we refer as "elephant hunters." They live and die by the big order, ignoring all other opportunities. But the drop in business doesn't mean the salesperson should shift his or her support of the client; the salesperson can and should maintain his or her efforts to support what remains.

Even if you reduce your overall efforts due to a slowdown, your goal should involve some level of contact with your client to keep your name and face in the forefront. As a purchasing manager, I often have more time available for in-depth conversations with vendors during these slow periods than I do when business is hectic—making these lulls a great time to grow the relationship. If you continue to support the client through a lull, they will usually reward your support through their actions in the form of inquiries, increased exposure to other aspects of their business, and favorable payment terms when they pull out of their slow period. The goodwill that results from your maintaining your relationship with the client is hard to measure, but it is rarely forgotten.

If, however, you dropped the client due to their lack of business, you will have to start over when the client begins to issue new inquiries. You might not have to go through as many hurdles as you would with a brand-new client, but you will have to work at reestablishing yourself—and I can't guarantee that they'll be giddy over your newfound interest in their business. Keep this in mind when deciding whether to stick or step away when a client is going through a slowdown.

MARVIN MILETSKY

THE SALES PERSPECTIVE

There's always business to be done. But that aside, the best time to see existing customers and develop new ones is during lulls in activity. You can't realistically expect to visit a customer only in times of prosperity and expect them to receive you with open arms. (You know that old expression, "fair-weather friend.") It's during the slow times that you develop the relationships that allow you to seize the opportunities. The best time to introduce that new product of yours, discuss upcoming general or specific opportunities in a prospect's field, or even just kill some time by getting to know a prospect better is when that prospect is not busy. Downtimes represent opportunities to make calls in a more relaxed atmosphere, with the client able to spend more time with you. You might even be able to meet several others in the company who are usually otherwise tied up.

In the middle of every winter, I used to visit a client in Iron Mountain, Michigan. What a hike it was, leaving the warm offices of my company, trudging through several airports, and ultimately driving a very long way through ice and snow to reach my destination: a contractor who had no work! Each year, the amazed purchasing crew greeted me with the same disbelieving looks on their faces, thanked me for coming—and questioned my sanity. Didn't I have better things to do than travel to such a remote place, where there wasn't any business to be had for at least another three months? And each year I'd answer that I was there because I had run out of customers who would see me, or because I had heard that the area was known for its early springs. Yes, we all had a lot of fun with my visits! We'd spend two days together, during which I was introduced to many people in various departments and could discuss anything I wanted without facing a time constraint. And of course there were no looming competitors; odds were, the nearest one was enjoying his comfortably heated office. Sure, he might pick up a phone some time during the winter to check on his prospect, but that hardly compared to my personal visit! The outcome of these trips was always positive, leading to a tremendous amount of business. When the company came out of hibernation in the spring, they stayed loyal to those who had paid attention to them during those lean winter months.

Q: • SHOULD YOU EXPECT TO KNOW WHY
• YOU LOST AN ORDER AND TO WHOM?

JAMES CALLANDER
THE CUSTOMER PERSPECTIVE

↳ If there are other vendors supporting your client, you can and will lose orders, for any number of reasons. Those salespeople who fail to follow up with the client and attempt to establish *why* they lost the order—and which vendor succeeded in winning it—are doomed to repeat their mistakes. Without this information, you cannot improve your offering. Not only does obtaining this information benefit you, but it also benefits your client insofar as it enables you to better meet their needs. If you are not interested in why you lost business, odds are you won't be in sales for long.

One easy way to lose an order is to issue an incomplete proposal. As a client, I'm often given vendor proposals that are incomplete, often lacking important details. Indeed, I'd say at least one out of every three proposals is missing key information. I realize vendors have a full plate, but that is not my concern. I expect a certain level of performance from all my vendors, regardless of whether they are new or well established. I do not like having to chase down standard information I included in my original request. A vendor who fails to provide this information is already suspect in my eyes.

Beyond that, the most obvious place to look in determining the cause of a lost order is your price. I start the process of awarding an order by reviewing my bid tabulation, which is based solely on price. In addition to prices that are too high, vendors who fail to provide pricing for all items—particularly when their competitors have included this information—are likely to be avoided. After assessing price, I move on to the product offering. I'm looking for any items that are misquoted, which could throw off the price or the actual use. After I've checked the price and product offering, I move to the delivery and payment terms. If the delivery options and payment terms vary greatly among my vendors, I determine which best fit the requirements of my request.

But these aren't the only factors at play. Managing your business requires you to not only understand who your client is and how they conduct business, but possibly more importantly, how your support staff interfaces with the client. As I've mentioned, it is your responsibility to communicate the client's requirements to your support staff. Assignments in many sales offices involve the outside salesperson (you) and an inside salesperson who handles all incoming requests for quote by your clients. The insides person has a tremendous responsibility. He or she processes both quotes and orders, and is the person the client talks to for most of their requests. If the inside person does not have a proper understanding the client's expectations, you have let both your client and support staff down. If you want to succeed, you must manage the interaction between your client and support staff. You should never hear feedback from your client on issues with your support staff and their efforts or lack thereof.

It is in your best interest to contact your client and try to determine why you were not awarded an order. Otherwise, you may make assumptions that could cost you money, and may not even prevent you from losing orders in the future. For example, if you believe an order was lost solely because of your price, you might lower your sell price—but if the real issue was availability, you'll have gained nothing. Of course, whether your client accepts your request for feedback on a lost order is another matter. Not all client personnel feel inclined to share this information. Indeed, in some cases, they are bound by rules or guidelines that prohibit them from sharing this information.

If your client is a government agency, you can find the outcome to any bid. The client agency is required to make the information available to the public for a period of time after they have made their award. Anyone selling in this area has no excuse for not following up.

MARVIN MILETSKY
THE SALES PERSPECTIVE

↳ The cleanup after the loss of an order is critical to your next negotiation with this prospect or with others for similar types of products—and by "cleanup" I mean the gathering of intelligence as to why you lost the bid and who the successful bidder was. In your efforts to obtain an order from your prospect, you made an investment, and you should not allow yourself to come up empty. No order *and* no information is a really rotten combination.

Just be careful in how you approach your customer when trying to secure this information. I've mentioned the importance of tact on a few occasions; that same tact should be used as you try to elicit information from your customer. This should go a long way toward you getting the information you desire; in contrast, the bull-in-the-china-shop method could result not only in your failure to learn anything useful, but also in your opening a wound that will affect your relationship for the long haul.

Don't be surprised, however, if your target isn't terribly forthcoming with information about whom you lost an order to. For some reason, I've noticed a great reluctance by buyers to cite the name of the successful competitor. In an effort to gain at least some information, I concentrate on ascertaining the quality of the product that was chosen and whether mine met the standards of the requisition. I ask whether there was a dramatic difference in pricing or if the bidding was close, and of course whether any delivery issues were a concern. Having knowledge of the industry I am in, I can usually determine which of my competitors was successful.

Timing is also an ally in gathering the information. After some time goes by and the order becomes less of an issue, you might have a chance to casually ask some questions that your customer may have been reluctant to answer when the negotiation was fresh. This information is still of value to you, even if it takes some time to garner. Approach the questions casually, in a matter-of-fact sort of way, perhaps as an add-on to some other conversation.

One word of caution: There may be times when the information you receive might be a little tainted. That is, you might be fed erroneous information as part of an effort to force you to radically change your approach the next time you are given an opportunity. Be careful how you use any information you obtain, and be sure to analyze it properly. For example, you might be told your price was way out there, even though your knowledge of your market tells you your pricing was competitive. Chances are, you pricing wasn't way out there; rather, your customer may be setting you up to lower it next time. Your customer is trying to do the best for his company, just as you are for yours. I hope you enjoy chess, because that's what this could be all about!

Q: How Can You Tell If You Are Spreading Yourself Too Thin?

James Callander

The Customer Perspective

In their desire to grow their sales roster, salespeople often make commitments without considering how they might affect other areas of their business. But the time needed to manage your clients increases with every client you gain. This simple formula says it all:

Time spent in customer conversations (including multiple contacts in the same organization)	×	Number of clients for which you are responsible	=	Time required to manage your customers

Put another way, successfully growing your client base can ultimately lead you to spread yourself too thin. This is especially true as you gain access to more individuals throughout a client's organization. The time you must spend calling on these additional contacts is only a piece of the puzzle; also a factor is the fact that you must also respond to requests from these individuals. This is a good thing—until you multiply the effects by several clients. Then, you may find that you have become overloaded, which can result in delays in your responses or follow-up.

> This is particularly problematic if you receive multiple urgent requests. Which one do you focus on? Which one is more important?

If you have overloaded yourself with more clients than you can really handle, it will affect your ability to effectively balance all your clients' business. This will in turn lead to slower growth throughout your account package. The same holds true for your support staff. As your client base grows, your support staff will likely see a flood of activity. Their ability to process requests swiftly may be diminished—which may determine whether you continue to receive new requests from your client base.

267

Guarding against spreading yourself too thin is one of the most important things a salesperson can do. Your clients don't know how big your client base is—and more importantly, they don't care. The only indication they have of your abilities is how well you serve their account. If one of my vendors is hard to reach, I assume they are either ignoring me or they have too much going on—and neither conclusion bodes well for that vendor's continued use by my office. I'm not trying to contact the salesperson to see how his or her weekend was; I'm contacting that person because I have a request for information that requires his or her attention. Moreover, there's a good chance I'm under some sort of time restraint. If the salesperson or his or her support staff becomes difficult to reach, what choice do I have but to find another vendor who responds?

So how do you know if you are spreading yourself too thin? (Odds are at some point, you will be.) Take a hint from your clients. Some will respond to your lack of attention with a verbal barrage and increased volume. Others will calmly advise you of their dissatisfaction. Still others will simply and quietly move on to new sources. Hopefully, though, you'll be able to correct the problem promptly, making the necessary adjustments to improve the situation.

MARVIN MILETSKY

THE SALES PERSPECTIVE

The question isn't whether you're spreading yourself too thin; assume that you are. Rather, the question is *how* thin. Take the following test to determine just how thin you're spreading yourself:

- True or false: The purchasing agent you've come to see retired two years ago.

- True or false: You visit a company, only to discover that not only have they relocated, but there is now a newly constructed school on the site.

- True or false: You see the same person you saw before and he asks you what business you're in.

- True or false: Your contact asks about a sample you were going to show her that was discontinued for lack of interest several months ago.

- True or false: You've forgotten that you were forbidden to call on these people due to their refusal to pay your last invoice.

- True or false: You ask a follow-up question about a submission you made, and your contact answers that that project was completed years ago.

- True or false: You find out that another salesperson from your company has been calling on them for the past year.

- True or false: You find out that the new purchasing agent only speaks Spanish.

- True or false: You're asked to enter by way of the service entrance the next time you visit.

- True or false: The person who recommended you call on this account is not due out on parole for another six months.

Look, don't beat yourself up about it. I mean, have you really considered the monumental number of tasks ahead of you in your sales career and the amount of time it will take to accomplish each one? I can't remember *ever* leaning back on a reclining chair at the end of the day, satisfied that I was completely caught up, with nothing left to do. There's always the:

- Follow-up or thank-you phone call to be made

- Research required to answer questions that came up during a recent meeting

- Preparation for a sales meeting with a new client

- Preparation for a negotiation with an existing client

- Planning for your next trip

- Letter you have to write

- Proposal to be prepared

- Literature to be sent out

- Expense reports to be filled out so you can get reimbursed

- Call report you have to make out to keep track of the recent conversations with prospects and clients and to guide you in your next step

- Prospecting for new clients

- Keeping in touch with old clients

- Learning your company's new products or services

- Spending of time in your office to catch up on the progress of business items, share your experiences with your co-workers, and be generally involved with developing systems and products that will make your job easier

- Interfacing with your planning department to make sure that your project is understood and can be provided to your customer as promised

- Expediting of the order to make sure it's delivered as promised

- Calls to your customer to keep them aware of the progress of an order— either its completion in a timely manner or its lateness

- Clerical work that is an integral and necessary evil

- Assisting of the accounting department in contacting a customer whose payment is well overdue

- Catching up with e-mail

- Reading trade journals to keep up with current trends in your business

Compounding all this is the fact that often, while you're planning one thing for one customer, you've got to be thinking of that other requirement for another prospect who has given you the same deadline. And did you notice in that long list that there was no mention of the most important task: living your life? This could be made up of any of the things you enjoy: your family, your toys, your vacations, or any of the things you work so hard to be able to afford. Remember to always keep yourself in the equation.

After reading all this, you might reasonably be considering entering another field, but I do have some good news for you. As difficult as it may seem, you can balance all your tasks. You can complete them as required and still have time to live your life. You just need to realize that no one can possibly hope to balance everything without a plan. As with anything else you do, the better the planning, the better the result. I've managed things using the seat-of-the-pants method, and I've got the scars to show for it; here are some tips I've gathered from my experience to help you develop your own plan for avoiding spreading yourself too thin:

- Take notes—lots of them. Use a notebook or laptop or some other permanent utility; this will ensure your ability to retrieve the information. I learned the hard way not to take notes on little scraps of paper or on the backs of business cards; I can't tell you how many times I gave away or lost a business card with an important note or telephone number on it. These days, I carry around a yellow steno pad. I also avoid making my notes very cryptic. I make them as simple as I can, but without abbreviations or keywords, which I invariably forget later. Try to address any requirements spelled out in your notes as quickly as possible, while everything is fresh in your mind and other pressures don't distract you.

- Don't rely on your memory. You'll find that everything you need to do will quickly blend together, especially if a day or more goes by between when an item is discussed and when I'm actually able to attend to it. I've actually sent e-mails to myself using my BlackBerry and have called my own office phone to leave a message for myself for retrieval the next day. (I usually start these messages by complimenting myself about something so that my first message of the day is positive; this also ensures that at least one person appreciates me—even if it is myself!)

- Prioritize any tasks ahead of you for immediate completion, for completion tomorrow, and for completion in the weeks or months ahead. Admittedly, you're going to have lots to do as you grow and take on more clients and propose and receive more projects. It's not easy balancing all your tasks, especially when new ones arise that could challenge existing ones for your immediate attention. But I've found that changing priorities midstream is very inefficient and costly. Dropping one project to start another not only threatens the existing one's success, it prevents you from giving quality time to the new one. Try to keep on target with the current task to a point where you can either walk away comfortably, knowing you can return and pick it back up later without much problem, or finish it altogether and go on to the next.

- Implement other time-management techniques such as staying on focus, eliminating items that are just pipe dreams. In other words, pursue those things for which you know you have the best chance at success. Remember, you can't be all things to all people, so choose wisely which tasks you will attack. In your evaluation of those items, consider that there are short-term rewards and long-term ones. Not every task will provide immediate reward. Be patient; just make sure that whatever ends you are looking to achieve do, in fact, justify the means.

I'm no expert in time management, so you might want to check out any one of a number of time-management books out there, and even some seminars.

- Others can do an overwhelming amount of work that will otherwise consume you. You're not Superman; reach out to co-workers or subordinates to get them involved. Set up a partnership with your co-workers so they can take the same pride as you in the eventual success of the project. I offer my co-workers summaries of my recent trips and individual calls and otherwise make them part of my sales world to give them an understanding of what it will take to manage an account and make it grow. We discuss the requirements and assign parts based on who is most qualified to handle them. Just don't forget that you're the one the client will see as the responsible representative. You're the one at the helm. The buck stops with you. And never assume that someone you've assigned to a task is working as diligently as you are or that he or she isn't facing other pressures that could prevent him or her from completing your tasks. But through the proper use of personnel, your ability to multitask will be greatly improved. And although you'll probably never stop spreading yourself thin, you'll be able to control your effectiveness.

Q: • How Do You Avoid Overcommitting • and Underachieving?

JAMES CALLANDER
THE CUSTOMER PERSPECTIVE

In their zeal to please and to receive praise, many salespeople pounce on their clients—especially when asked to quote a product or service. They leave their sense at the door, agreeing to anything that gives them an opportunity to serve. This is particularly true for those new to selling. So eager to please, they typically don't stop selling long enough for me to respond to questions. Their fever pitch drowns out all hope of them actually gathering any information about our business. Rookie salesperson frequently make commitments believing they can handle the request. But this often backfires for both parties involved, with the client expecting a standard conclusion to their award but finding empty promises and the vendor scrambling to correct the issues that inevitably arise.

During one project, which we sourced daily for materials needed by the electricians, one of our vendors changed the salesperson responsible for our account. New to his position, this person was eager to shine both for his manager and for us, his client. Every inquiry I sent him was met with enthusiasm; after the normal jitters that accompany the start of any new job, it seemed he was off to an impressive start. His prices were in line with or better than his competitors', his lead times appeared to be acceptable, and he was offering the brands we had selected. The trouble came when materials failed to show up as requested. It turned out the salesperson was not as knowledgeable about the ordering system as he thought, and rather than asking for help, he pushed forward the best he could. As a result, the orders were messed up, along with the invoicing (which took even longer to fix). Expediting resulted in only minor delays, which at the time were acceptable—but after several more dates for delivery came and went, and work on our project began to back up due to these late deliveries (a no-no in my book), the calls from my office began to take a different tone. Eventually, I instructed my staff to stop sending the vendor any inquiries, and I was forced to contact this salesperson's manager to untangle the mess. The situation was rectified in short order, but not before we lost precious time on the job.

As a result, the vendor lost any hope of managing a large portion of our business. He overcommitted himself and his company and underachieved beyond belief. He should have asked for help, but didn't. If our system of following up were not in place, those late deliveries could have become even worse. I'm sure this young man will one day make a good salesperson in the electrical industry—if he learns a little humility.

You must find the balance needed to meet or exceed your client's expectations—but not at the cost of your good name. I would rather a vendor tell me they cannot support my request based on what is required than accept my order and hope they can perform. I believe you should commit only to what you know you can deliver and communicate when you are unsure. The client can determine whether they will accept or reject your proposal based on its merits. A lot of your success in sales will have to do with your ability to manage your clients' expectations. One trick that many veteran salespeople employ is to pad their offering when it comes to the availability of products or services, particularly with long–lead-time items. If the item in question normally ships in four weeks, the veteran salesperson will quote six. Why? Simple. They've been burned in the past by unforeseen delays, which were an irritant to both the salesperson and the client. By padding the time, neither party will be adversely affected by a delivery that takes longer than normal.

MARVIN MILETSKY
THE SALES PERSPECTIVE

You've been with me from the beginning of this book, so I'd like to repay your loyalty by offering you an opportunity to purchase a brand-new product that's certain to change your life and the lives of those around you. The name of the product is SupremaCreama, the anti-everything salve that will defy your wildest imagination! Rub it on your scalp, and instantly re-grow hair in areas you've given up on for years. Rub it over your eyes and face, and watch those lines just disappear. How about those unsightly tattoos, the products of your lost youth? Rub a small dab of SupremaCreama on your shoulder and watch as it totally erases the name of your first love from your shoulder (you know, the one your wife always points to when the two of you are having a disagreement). These are just some of the uses of this miracle salve! And the best part is, one 12-ounce tube will last you a lifetime, as the best is yet to be shared with you: When the tube is half empty, the miracle SupremaCreama regenerates itself. Within minutes, you'll have a full tube, and be ready to explore its many uses in cooking recipes. Please watch for your chance to order this cream later in the book.

Okay, now where were we? Oh, I know—we were starting a conversation about how to avoid overcommitting and underachieving. Once again, we have returned to that area known as "relationship building," the single-most important thing in continued success in selling. And most relationships have as their main ingredient that little five-letter word: T-R-U-S-T. It's actually very simple: Set the bar for your representation of both your company and their products at a level that is as high as you can comfortably attain and don't go beyond. If anything, a little understatement might be the key; that way, when the customer actually experiences delivery of his project, his or her expectations are exceeded.

Q: DO YOU SELL FROM THE TOP DOWN OR START AT THE BOTTOM AND WORK YOUR WAY UP?

JAMES CALLANDER
THE CUSTOMER PERSPECTIVE

Depending on what you are selling, whom you are selling for, and who your clients are will for the most part determine your selling approach. For example, clients that are maintenance-focused are good candidates for bottom-up selling. The decision-makers are usually found close to the actual use of the items or heavily influence the use of certain products and services. This is not to say that management is not involved; it's just that those who benefit directly from the service tend to have a strong voice in what is bought and from whom. In contrast, the top-down selling method tends to apply to large clients with multiple locations. Here, working with the client's senior management to purchase goods or services for the entire company rather than having multiple locations make decisions specific to their own needs allows for a company-wide improvement in costs, efficiency, or both.

> If you capture a large commitment from a client in a top-down scenario, you still have to execute the action needed to meet the client's needs. This part of the selling process is one of the toughest to manage. The client's various locations may not be as receptive to the new contract as you might think. The client's senior management should help champion the shift with their employers, but the actual execution is left to the vendor.

Both methods allow you to extend coverage throughout the client's organization, but there are differences between them that need to be explored:

- Selling from the bottom up starts at the user level and spreads out from this point. Your main contacts are the buyer and the production staff. Your sales calls typically focus on selection of those products and services that match existing applications for your client.

- Initially, the frequency of visits when selling from the bottom up is usually much higher than with selling from the top down. As time permits, the salesperson must branch out to the other departments at the client, scheduling appointments with management personnel, engineering, etc. The flow of information quickens as each new contact is cultivated. This is the approach I see most vendors use in their efforts to establish a relationship and to serve my business.

- Selling from the top down typically involves focusing on one or two individuals on the client's management or senior management team. Compared to bottom-up selling, the frequency of visits is reduced—at least initially. This narrow focus is required because you are, at this stage, selling a concept. Once successful, however, the salesperson must expand his or her visits throughout the client to promote the new contract. The effort to schedule appointments, review the merits of the contract, and discuss the benefits of the contract to the different departments and staff becomes a full-time job.

Clients will react differently to these two selling methods. Top-down selling may foster animosity on the part of individuals within the client, as they are told exactly whom they can use for products and services. The ensuing hostile environment will require the salesperson to spend valuable time soothing the wounds inflicted. The opposite reaction may be observed when you engage the client from the bottom. Your success can be quickly measured by the acceptance of those you are contacting. If you do meet resistance, it will likely be immediate, possibly somewhere at the management or senior-management level, but by the time a salesperson begins calling on these two areas, he or she will already be well-established with the base of the client.

MARVIN MILETSKY

THE SALES PERSPECTIVE

In my answer to Question 31, "How Should You Identify the Actual Decision-Maker and All Players Within the Company?" I discussed the importance of identifying and targeting the actual decision-maker. In smaller, more streamlined companies with only a few employees, you might identify that the president is also the planner, the packager, and the purchasing manager. In other words, not only is this person the "top," he's also the "bottom." He's the chief cook and the bottle washer. As such, he's the one who makes the final decisions about everything that goes on. Things aren't so simple in larger companies, however—meaning that it's of the utmost importance that you identify the decision-maker.

Notice we're discussing the decision-maker here, not where that person's position is within the company. Make the best sales pitch of your career to the wrong person, and what have you gotten for your efforts? If the person at the top of the company turns out to be the decision-maker, then that's who you should target. But make no mistake: Targeting the upper echelons in a company in an effort to market your products but leaving out those at the lower level is tantamount to committing sales suicide. That lower-level corporate person you've chosen to ignore will always wind up with the last laugh; he'll be the one placing an order with your competitor as you are out to lunch with the president.

Let's bottom line this: You must identify that person within the organization, regardless of his or her title or position, who has the ultimate authority to enter into a contract with you. That person is the one you're after; that's who your main focus should be on.

Q: HOW DOES CUSTOMER SERVICE AFFECT THE SALES EFFORT? ARE THE TWO DEPENDENT ON EACH OTHER?

JAMES CALLANDER
THE CUSTOMER PERSPECTIVE

Strong salespeople can and will gain opportunities for their companies, but a strong customer-service group must be in place to back that salesperson up. Likewise, a strong customer-service group can only grow with solidly performing salespeople making client calls every day. They can maintain business, but without someone selling, they cannot grow business.

Customer service plays a reduced role in initial sales—unless the customer has had previous experience with your company. Customer service is critical, however, to repeat business. The "valued add" of customer service becomes a key selling point in future sales, especially in very time-sensitive businesses. It's important to convey to your client that you believe your company offers superior customer service and support, but your client will ultimately determine to what extent he or she agrees with you.

What a wonderful world it would be if every sale went from order to delivery to payment without a hitch—but that's just not reality. Clients know things can go wrong. Even when the salesperson has done everything right, clients realize that something unexpected can cause problems. Your client wants to know that when things go wrong, you can and will do everything possible to make them right. With that knowledge will come your client's confidence in you.

Your client's confidence is further increased by knowing you have a knowledgeable support staff that is capable of assisting them when you aren't available. You don't have to work for a huge company with a full-blown customer-service organization to provide support; an inside salesperson or even a receptionist will do the trick—provided that person recognizes the importance of customer service and is committed to supporting your customers. These aren't the only company representatives who must be committed to customer service; delivery personnel, accounts receivable, and so on all play a role. They may not be the main focus for your client, but each represents another spoke in the wheel that helps support your client. When your co-workers take a vested interest in customer service, your clients will notice.

As a customer, I have no interest in vendors who can't supply me with customer service when I need it. For this reason, I view sales and customer support as interdependent. Most selling and customer-service work is based on reacting to the client. When the client calls, everyone jumps to attention. Over the years, those vendors who have responded—and done so quickly—with accurate information have usually landed either at the top of my list of vendors or are steadily climbing upward. If, however, I find myself waiting on support from a vendor—especially if other vendors have already responded—then it becomes difficult for me to continue to request support.

MARVIN MILETSKY
THE SALES PERSPECTIVE

The perfect guy to answer this question is Dante Longo, who is a regional sales support manager for the Petroleum/C-store division of VeriFone Inc., a leading manufacturer of point-of-sale equipment. In this role, which he has held for five years, Dante is responsible for overall quality of service available to end users of VeriFone Petroleum products from Maine to Florida. Job activities range from general management of the nearly 200 authorized service organizations in his region to maintaining direct relations with major customers and key corporate accounts.

GUEST PERSPECTIVE: DANTE LONGO

I should begin by pointing out that there is a distinction to be made between customer service, meaning the entity, and customer service, meaning the description of any pro-customer activity. Coming from a background rooted in technical service, my response is geared more towards the impact of the customer service as an entity.

The interdependence of "sales" and "service" is a bit more straightforward, so I will answer that question first. Being that they are both customer-facing entities, sales and service make likely bedfellows and often travel together. Often, these two groups are the only customer-facing entities in a company; that's because almost anyone who interacts with a customer could be thought of as a representative of one discipline or the other. This mindset is often echoed in the repetition of such catchphrases as "We are all salespeople for our company or product" or "We are all here to provide excellent service." I rarely hear phrases like "We are all here for credit and collections!" There is a good reason for this.

Sales and service are two of the de facto standards established by the society of consumers to judge us and our products.

I believe there is a fairly universal perception that the two forces are at odds with each other—that somehow, together, they have a yin-yang type of balance. This perception works on the surface, but only because many people perceive sales as the "taking of money" more than "providing the goods or services that come in exchange." It's part of human nature and part of why a salesman needs to establish trust to become successful. Service is perceived as something that should be or is "given back" in addition to the goods on which the money was spent.

To underscore this point, I would like to consider the actions of a single individual whose title and primary role is that of a "salesperson." If that individual, in the course of his normal routine, were to make a concession to a customer or go out of his way for that customer, we would refer to that as an act of customer service. Even if this action had been something that most of us would consider a basic job requirement for the salesperson's role, we would still refer to it as customer service. To further the point, a salesperson who fails to deliver almost anything to the customer is guilty of poor customer service. Failure to gather from the customer and deliver to the company, however, is considered poor salesmanship. These perceptions are rooted in instinct and have a deep psychological impact on our dealings with a customer.

Based on this, we can see that sales and service are interdependent, but it is important to recognize that the relationship is not fair and balanced. Service must rely on sales to set and maintain reasonable expectations, but to do so, sales must act graciously or risk offense to the customer. Good customer service from sales involves becoming a customer advocate without crossing the line. Sales, on the other hand, must rely on service to properly evaluate and respond to the customers' needs to the best of their abilities. This is the point at which things become interesting.

Almost every "for profit" organization exists by the grace of the revenue generated by the sale of its products or services. The whole organism depends on revenue as its means of survival—and the sales organization is the primary, if not sole, provider of that revenue. From this high-level point of view, it is common sense that all divisions in the company are wholly dependent upon sales for their existence. To this end, the entity of customer service must support sales. That said, they cannot be completely subordinate to them. They must support sales strategically, which may sometimes put them at odds tactically. The name of customer service cannot be invoked sell the whole organism short for one deal. It might be good customer service to allow a customer 365-day terms instead of 30 or 60, but someone has to look out for the company and say no.

What is the impact of customer service on sales? It is important to recognize that this will vary greatly depending on the nature of the product and the manner of its distribution. With few exceptions, most goods and many services sold to an end user will have been resold through layers of distribution, each with its own unique service needs. I will identify those echelons I have defined through my own experience, but I don't expect that I can claim to be complete in my listing. The takeaway from this should be that failures at each echelon of service are likely to affect the sales effort in different ways—all of them negative. At least in our society, people have come to expect their own vision of service as a birthright. Great customer service is almost always expected, and is thus less likely to gain a sale than poor customer service is to lose it.

For a manufacturer of goods, the customer-service support chain is the longest and most convoluted. Customer service may be deemed to include all customer-facing interactions, and for a manufacturer, "customers" may range from wholesalers and distributors, to resellers or retailers, to the end users themselves. For the highest levels of this chain, service issues are likely to revolve around pricing, discounting, quantities, terms, exclusivity, special processes, and the processes of ordering and delivery. The next level of the chain is the retailer, who is likely to interact on such issues as marketing materials, training on products they are selling, handling of warranty or returns for customers, and perhaps rebates or incentives. The last stop is the end user or consumer. Interaction with the end user is likely to revolve around calls for product support or product performance. For wholesalers and the retailers, relationships with their customers will echo this outline.

Having identified some of the common provider/consumer relationships, I will not delve too deeply into the ways in which they are all different. That discussion could fill many more pages. It is enough for the reader to be aware that there is a bigger picture and that no matter which level they work on, they are likely to be only a small piece of the picture. While this comment may sound negative at first, there is a point to be made by it. Be you sales or service, you must address each customer interaction in the most customer-friendly way possible, balancing your interactions with departmental goals. Every individual and department has a job to do; chances are, if you are not putting the needs of your department first, no one is. You must focus on what is best for your customers. You must keep them as happy you can, and you must avoid giving them a reason not to come back.

So you ask again what is the impact of service on sales? To answer truthfully, I must admit that there is no one answer to be given in this short a space. Consumers at every one of the different levels I defined previously are driven by many factors. There are some buyers for whom service is a priority, but it is mere rhetoric to assert that service itself is more than one factor out of many. Cost, availability, familiarity, desire, and good old-fashioned laziness are just a few of the many factors sales must deal with to gain and maintain a loyal customer.

Customer service is so important because it is the one aspect of the customer interaction in which we all have some degree of control, no matter what our role. People are more accepting of flaws in products than in people. It is harder to get angry at an inanimate object for breaking or at an organization for its policies than at a person for not performing. Consumers almost expect a small percentage of products or services to be flawed. They can live with that. But no one likes to accept people as flawed. If you make a mistake, fail to accommodate, or act improperly, the consumer will react negatively.

We come from a society of instant gratification. The task for the customer-service entity is to build an infrastructure that can simultaneously meet the needs of as many different customers as possible with the lowest cost and highest efficiency. Great customer service is like insurance: Nobody wants to pay for it, but everyone wants the protection to be there when they need it. Even if there is no charge for a service, the customer will equate the purchase of the product with the purchase of a service and will expect that service to be in place and up to their standards. Anything short of this lofty goal can and will result in lost sales potential.

No one needs to look very far or think very hard to come up with a company, product, or store that has so offended us that we will never patronize it again. What was it that put you over the edge? In my personal life, I am a consumer of technology above all other things. I tend to make high-dollar purchases on items I have chosen primarily because they have tickled my fancy in some fashion. In these interactions, I have found two major retailers that always frustrate me in my attempts to make purchases. I have said on more than one occasion that it should *be* this hard to get someone to take my money! I of course swore off these retailers, only to recant from time to time when the sale was good or the item was exclusive. These retailers became my last choice, but did not lose my business altogether due to circumstance. In any event, as of today, one of those retailers is gone and the other is in the midst of going-out-of business sales. The retailer that won my loyalty years ago appears to be going strong, however, and I am still willing to pay a reasonable premium to shop there. I leave it to the reader to determine the likelihood that my experience with those failed retailers was common enough to be a factor in their downfall. I suspect that it was.

Q: • HOW IMPORTANT IS IT TO LOOK
• FOR WAYS TO IMPROVE EACH YEAR?

JAMES CALLANDER
THE CUSTOMER PERSPECTIVE

If you are not improving as a salesperson—indeed, as a *person*—I believe you are on a slippery slope to disaster. Salespeople who believe they have nothing to learn, who are totally satisfied with their effort, will one day find themselves playing second fiddle to a competitor's up-and-coming salesperson. I believe all salespeople must reflect on their past performance to find areas where they can improve. It's easy to see your accomplishments, measured in sales and margin achieved. But these accomplishments aren't the whole story, and conducting such a lopsided review will do little to help the client.

During the course of the year, you may have lost some business you really wanted, even though you were sure you would be awarded it. Obviously, the client evaluation didn't go the way you intended or expected. Did you follow up to identify why? If not, I suggest you take a moment to write down any proposals you lost and to contact those clients and ask them why. If you *did* follow up and find out why, have you altered how you develop your proposal? If not, why? Reviewing your efforts daily, weekly, monthly, and yearly provides insight into how you are growing and, more importantly, what you need to do to improve.

Here are more questions you should ask yourself:

- **Have you evaluated the cause of any order errors?** Your clients would love to be able to process orders knowing you have rectified any issues that occurred with past jobs. Your efforts to remedy known issues with order entry, delivery, returns, or any number of other areas is something all clients want to hear about. These efforts show that you are paying attention and are making a conscious effort to rectify things—information that your clients will find helpful when evaluating their vendor base.

- **Did you set any goals during the past year?** If so, you need to review how you did against those goals. How realistic were they? Did you achieve them? Which goals did you miss? Why? Goals are great sources of inspiration and can come in many forms—from ones that are simple to attain to ones that require you to stretch yourself. Goals need not be of the long-range variety; many can be developed for the day or week. No doubt you'll be asked by your organization to set goals, but the ones you set for yourself each day or week can provide you with a sense of purpose with regard to the work ahead. These daily goals carry you forward to meet the larger ones you have established.

When salespeople have taken an objective look at their efforts and committed themselves to improving, I notice it immediately when they visit. The change becomes evident in the manner in which they conduct themselves and their line of questioning, and it brings my focus to the discussion. Inevitably, my interest in them begins to grow. I might even find new opportunities to submit based on their change. In tough times, when clients reduce the number of vendors they source from, they look to advantages of using one vendor over another. You might actually discover your efforts to improve each year provide you additional business.

MARVIN MILETSKY

THE SALES PERSPECTIVE

It's amazing, but after all these years of being in the business of selling, I've never actually sat back and thought specifically of ways to improve each year. I suppose the lessons I've learned have come as a sum total of all my experiences, and any improvements I've made were as a result of some failure that had occurred. After all, the term "improvement" itself connotes repairing some failure, no matter what the degree.

Let's just give this some thought: Do you know how long it's taken me to get to this point? The lessons I had to learn through lost and failed orders? The lack of attention to detail that created larger-than-life problems that took up far more of my time than I had ever budgeted for? What about the lack of understanding between myself and my clients and co-worker that prevented projects from getting out on time, at the profit we expected? And what *didn't* I spot in myself that, if caught earlier, could have led to a greater success rate?

The answers in this book represent the sum total of a life on the road facing the everyday challenges of a career in sales. That's great news for you. Your very act of picking up this book shows a desire to get ahead and investigate methods of attaining your goals while circumventing the school of hard knocks that I attended. Congratulations! Keep doing exactly what you're doing. I think you're on the right path.

In lots of other occupations, there are continuing-education classes meant to keep professionals updated on advancements in their fields. Some of these courses are required to meet licensing requirements, such as with doctors, lawyers, and accountants, to mention a few. Not so with sales! But what a novel idea: actually attending a class or seminar to help you improve on what you've been doing. Attend those seminars, go to the trade shows, take a course in the power of positive thinking, network with older, more experienced people in your company. Don't be afraid to learn from a customer; I've actually asked customers how others in sales have failed to answer their needs. And keep reading. Maintain that thirst for knowledge. As you budget time for everything else in your life that's important, dedicate some to improving your skills. (By the way, this question talks about improving each year, but you don't have to wait a year before you find a way to improve what you did last week.)

Your sales career should always be a work in progress. Never think of it as a job; it's your career. Keep investing in it, and never *never* think you've learned it all.

Q: Is the Customer Always Right?

What's your perspective on this question? Let us know at
PerspectivesOnSales.com.

James Callander
The Customer Perspective

Eventually, you will hear someone utter these words, either from a teaching point of view or out of total disgust. And even if the customer *isn't* right, this is the unwritten rule that governs vendor-client relations—especially when challenges arise.

An example: During the quote phase, I make it a point to inform vendors that I will not accept a separate charge for freight. If the salesperson has to offset the cost of the delivery, then he or she needs to bury that cost in the pricing of the items I am requesting. It's a simple request, one that can easily be followed, and yet I frequently see freight charges applied at the time of invoicing. (These charges, I might add, often are not mentioned in the vendor proposal.) Inevitably, when I follow up with the vendor, the response is, "We charge freight." Whether or not their proposal included freight charges, the fact that I specifically instructed the vendor to bury those costs is driven home during my call. So as the customer, am I right? Some would say no; I should pay for the freight. But from my point of view, the issue is whether the vendor should demand $10 worth of freight costs that might jeopardize thousands of dollars in future sales. Because the fact is, if a vendor continues to insist on payment of the freight cost, I will make my dissatisfaction known in the volume and type of opportunities that vendor sees down the road.

Of course, in reality, problems that arise aren't always the vendor's fault. Say the client is late ordering items they need, and must solicit and award a large order with minimum delay. Although the client knows the delivery time is eight weeks, they need the items in seven. After receiving proposals quoting an eight-week delivery from various vendors, the client has you on top for the award—but insists you can and must accommodate this shortened delivery time. In the back of your mind, you know how this will go down; sure enough, the seventh week comes and goes, and the client is livid. Even though the delivery is made in week eight as quoted, the client is left wondering why they awarded you the order in the first place. You did nothing wrong; you attempted to support the requirement, even though from the outset it was doomed to fail. But now you are seen by the client as the worst vendor they could have picked. The customer heaps the criticism on you, when it was their own short sightedness that led to the situation. How fair is that? Of course, it's not fair at all. But if the customer is always right, then you can expect to wind up on the short end of the stick in these situations. The sad fact is, clients are not normally interested in making your life easier.

As a salesperson, you will from time to time run aground on the banks of The Customer Is Always Right Island. Sometimes, the issue will be nothing more than a minor screw-up on the client's end that spills over into your lap; other times, there will be real issues that require real solutions. Hopefully, the situation won't be so dire that you can't manage it; either way, handling the information presented by the client and making good decisions for all parties is the best you can do. All this being said, those vendors who live by this unwritten rule in their daily management of clients do so with the understanding that the upside business potential must outweigh the short-term effect of making things right for the client. If not, the vendor will typically be less inclined to support any and all client demands—especially if the vendor believes the client is in the wrong.

MARVIN MILETSKY

THE SALES PERSPECTIVE

↳ Even when the customer's wrong, he's right—sort of. What I really mean is that even if the customer is wrong, you may need to pretend he's right. It's all in the way it's handled. (Ever hear of the word "tact," my friend?)

If you're faced with a customer who is wrong, you'll need to assess the benefits of proving yourself right and the customer wrong. Ask yourself, what do you have to gain by doing so? Proving a customer wrong at the expense of a relationship or order does not really contribute toward your success, so think hard before you do it. We've discussed that ego all us salespeople have and when to toss it out.

More than once, I've been on the receiving end of a complaint where I told a customer something but he forgot or he insists he told me one thing and I know he told me something else. And while each time I thought to myself that the guy had lost his marbles or marveled at his selective memory, he was the *customer*. Proving him wrong would have gained me nothing, and none of the misunderstandings were so serious that I couldn't make adjustments without getting hurt, so I just swallowed hard, made the change to the order, and went on with my life.

There may be times, however, where the disagreement might really have a dramatic effect on the order or project you're working on and turning your head could be costly. That's why my best advice for this situation is to *put everything you discuss in writing*. Leave nothing to chance. This takes any question of memory out of the equation and will serve as the end-all to any argument. There you have it, in black and white: the proof of your contention. Still, no gloating when you prove your case. Try to be accommodating so the customer is not alone in his or her mistake and you both share in finding the fix.

All that being said, there is one scenario where you'll be doing your customer a favor by pointing out (tactfully) that he or she is wrong. Often customers try to insinuate themselves into your business, going beyond their knowledge of exactly what it takes to produce your product or service. Put another way, they want to put their two cents in where it doesn't belong. Many feel because they're the recipient of the product, they know everything about its production—but they don't. If they did, they'd work for *your* company. Of course, you should listen to them (some patience will be required here). But after you digest their idea or suggestion, thank them, and then politely remind them that your company has been hired to produce the item they specify, not the other way around. Obviously, they need to spell out the details of what they want as a finished product, but after that, they need to stop and let you do what you do best.

As your relationships start to evolve, interacting with your client should get easier. Your ability to have disagreements and even argue a little with them will increase. Your past efforts will have proven to be in their best interests, so they'll probably be a little more accepting of your comments. But if you realize the argument is getting you nowhere, back off and go on to something else. Once, a customer of mine, with whom I have a wonderful and friendly relationship, was arguing with me about something that I absolutely knew he was wrong about. As the argument deepened in intensity, I realized it was getting me nowhere, so I conceded the point to him by saying "Okay, I give up. You are not wrong, but you certainly are not as right as you normally are!" Our relationship was strong enough to survive this sort of fun; before you open your mouth, make sure yours is, too.

PART FIVE
Just for Fun

Q: What Was Your Worst-Ever Order?

Marvin Miletsky
The Sales Perspective

↳ I have a friend who, when asked how he's feeling, says "I feel absolutely great…but that can't last." Likewise, things may be going great at work—but that can't last. Defecation happens. While I've always exuded an air of confidence about what I do and the company I represent, I'm always ready for the shit to hit the fan. I may think I've seen it all, but for all I know, my worst-ever order is waiting for me just around the corner. I've probably had about a dozen that could tie for worst order ever, and still another dozen that deserve honorable mention. Here are just a few:

- The time we shipped the material we were supposed to have manufactured ourselves before we realized the name of the *actual* manufacturer was inscribed inside each unit.

- The shipment that was ready on time—but shipped to the wrong customer (I've had quite a number of these).

- The shipment that was supposed to be made on a specific date in the future that actually shipped the day the order was entered, six months early.

- The order that was shipped directly to our customer's customer with the original invoice included—meaning the end user could see the real cost to their supplier. (That actually wouldn't have been so bad if not for the fact that the profit margin was so high for the middle man that his end user cancelled the order on him, after which he immediately cancelled on us, never to favor us with an order again.)

- The times (yes, more than once, in my formative years) that I promised the customer we'd ship on Thursday but forgot to enter the order until Friday.

Yeah, they've happened to me, and they're probably going to happen to you, too. It's all part of doing business. Expect these things to happen, and expect them to happen at the most inconvenient time to your most important customer. Just be ready for the eventuality and have a plan for rectifying the situation.

You are probably noticing that I didn't really answer the question about my worst-ever order. Well, there actually was a "worst ever," and believe it or not, I was both the seller and recipient of the order. Without further do, I offer the following for your reading pleasure: It was about a month before a trade show in Minneapolis—the most important one in our industry, held every three years, which attracted an international audience. It was the big one. We'd rented our booth space long in advance and made the necessary arrangements for travel, car rental, and hotel. The display-booth company had finished our display and shipped it to the convention center in plenty of time. All that was left to do was order the samples, products, and literature that would fill our display booth. We entered the order into our system like any other, except that for this one, the customer was actually our own sales department and the consignee was this same department, care of the convention center in Minnesota. We then made sure the shipping department understood the importance of this material arriving on time and of packing carefully so that nothing would be damaged.

Fast-forward to the convention: We arrived at the convention center on a Friday morning to allow enough time to set up and be ready for the Sunday opening of the convention. The temperature inside the hall was extremely hot, so the owners of the building, rather than run air-conditioning during the weekend, opened every door they could, including the overhead garage doors, in an attempt to circulate the air. Well, that did the trick; they actually created a wind-tunnel effect throughout the hall, which had a wonderful cooling effect on us all.

But the best was yet to come: Our order was delivered to our booth in two huge wooden crates, probably five feet cubed. I can only imagine how our faces looked as we viewed these crates and wondered how we were going to open them; the gold in Fort Knox would have been safe inside these containers. Somehow, we were able to obtain a crowbar, and after what seemed an endless amount of time, we were finally able to pry the first one open. Slowly, carefully, we removed the crate's side panel—and that's when we got the shock of our lives: Everything inside was packed in Styrofoam peanuts, which, you guessed it, got swept up by the wind and transported to every corner of the venue, showering every booth within 100 feet of ours. What a spectacle! Apparently, our shipping department had taken our caution about packaging to heart.

Wait, that wasn't all: When we carefully opened the other crate—this time managing to keep the peanuts under control—and started to unpack them, we realized that many of the products on our order were not to be found. Was there perhaps another crate that we were missing? At about that time, we discovered the packing slip. There, in the boldest of letters, was a list of items that were *backordered*. Yes, our own company's shipping department backordered material that was meant for a three-day trade show. The computer-generated slip advised that the backordered material would be shipped within three weeks—putting it at the convention center just four weeks after the end of the convention. You just can't make these things up!

Look at it this way: The more problems you encounter, the more selling you're doing. Or, conversely, the more you sell, the more you open yourself to the possibility of things going wrong. On a percentage basis, if three orders out of 100 wind up with a story to tell, the rate of problems would be 3 percent. Doubling your orders will also probably double the quantity of problems, but probably not the rate—which, at 3 percent, will result in the failure of just six orders. Not too terrible a price to pay for such an increase in sales!

JAMES CALLANDER

THE CUSTOMER PERSPECTIVE

It is hard to imagine any one single order standing out as the worst ever. With all the preparation that goes into submitting a request for quote (RFQ), establishing requirements for these requests, reviewing submitted proposals, making the award, following up with the vendor, confirming delivery, verifying receipt, and finally validating the invoice, anything can go wrong. Despite all our best efforts, each step or combination of steps can turn the whole process on its head and thwart all good intentions. The fact is, *anything* that slows down the process is the worst thing that can happen.

I have dealt with vendors who thought they were quoting the correct item but quoted the wrong one, received the order based on the correct item, delivered the wrong item, confirmed they screwed up, and found out they do not even carry the item we requested—after several weeks. This probably falls under the "worst order" category.

I have placed orders with wire vendors for specification quantities of wire on each reel and shown up at the job site to find the reels tagged with the correct wire length, only to discover that the actual length of the wire was not even close to the lengths noted. Oh, and the wire was custom made, requiring a very long lead time, and crews were scheduled to use the wire based on the delivery. This, too, should probably fall under the "worst order" category.

I have dealt with vendors manufacturing custom parts who exacerbate an already long delivery schedule by failing to obtain the raw materials they use every day, forcing me to track down the raw materials for their production. Where were their buyers? How was I able to find the raw materials but somehow they could not? I believe this might fall under the "worst order" category.

In one instance, a rush order was delayed because the driver of the truck carrying materials we needed refused to surrender his driver's license (as required to enter our secure area), thereby failing to deliver the goods—*on three consecutive days*. It was later revealed that the carrier's dispatcher scheduled drivers knowing they would refuse to relinquish their licenses. Definitely a "worst order."

Q: HAVE YOU EVER REALLY GOTTEN INTO A SALESPERSON'S OR CLIENT'S FACE?

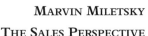

MARVIN MILETSKY
THE SALES PERSPECTIVE

I've never been involved in a face-to-face, body-to-body confrontation with anyone in my life, least of all with a customer. I have, though, witnessed two physical confrontations between a sales manager at a company I was working for and the vice president of purchasing. Both times, a mere conversation about the expected delivery of components escalated to some heated words and eventually shouting. With each exchange, their bodies grew closer until they were both in each other's face. The shoving that ensued at that point escalated immediately into an exchange of punches and then into an all-out battle, which had to be broken up by several witnesses. After the incident, they made their peace with each other and continued to function in their respective positions—although always with an air of suspicion. All was well until sometime later, when another shouting match appeared to be igniting another battle, and upper management decided they'd had enough of their inability to get along and of the effect their continued bickering was having on the spirit of the personnel within the company and terminated both. It wound up being a loss in both areas of the company, but it had to be done for the overall health and future of the organization. The best part of this story is that some years later, they actually wound up employed in the same positions they had held and for the exact same company. We all expected to pick up a newspaper someday and read about a shooting.

I have been involved in some serious incidents that could have escalated into something ugly had they not occurred over the telephone. Once, when a purchasing agent screamed at me over the phone, he got personal. There was taunting, cursing, and even personal threats; clearly, he was over the top. I don't remember what had led to this behavior, but I do remember losing my temper. I shouted back at him, pounded my desk, and grabbed the object nearest to me—which happened to be a catalog that weighed several pounds—and threw it across my office. I then proceeded to hang up the phone. That was my one and only time; just relating the story to you has gotten my blood boiling once again!

I had let the customer get to me—not just my external business-person self, but into the inner me, which I really do protect.

I've never taken an order I knew I couldn't fill or made a promise I knew I couldn't keep that would put my clients' business in jeopardy or have any negative effect on their personal life. Still, there've been times—and I expect there'll be others—where circumstances beyond my control have created problems I could not have predicted. But one thing is for sure: No matter what the circumstance, I will never again accept anyone screaming at or getting personal with me. When a situation appears to be turning ugly, I attempt to diffuse it by simply asking, in a non-challenging fashion, that my contact lower his or her voice, noting that I'm having trouble hearing him correctly. If this fails, I politely tell the person that I am going to hang up and let some time pass so everyone can cool off. No slamming of the phone, no screaming—just a low-key, polite disconnect. And although I've been tempted to, I've never put any of my thoughts on such a matter in writing, such as in the form of an e-mail to my contact. That actually could come back to bite me.

I encourage you to serve your customers well, which will entail being the recipient of some complaints, perhaps even at elevated voice levels. But once these escalate into a personal attack, remember that in the end, you've got to answer to yourself. Respect yourself. Don't allow any of this to consume you. You really must weigh those things that are important in your life.

JAMES CALLANDER
THE CUSTOMER PERSPECTIVE

Recently, we placed a large order with a vendor knowing we were already behind schedule to install the material. The lead time was four weeks, and we were running smack-dab into a deadline for completion of work. Compounding the problem was the fact that the material was made to order, not off the shelf. We immediately began expediting and demanding improvement on the delivery schedule, but with every hour that went by, our efforts were dashed, our every request met with rejection. It seemed no matter what the vendor did, we could not be pleased. Then we caught an unexpected break: The vendor informed us we would receive a small production run early. Everyone felt relieved, broadcasting the scheduled delivery—until it was discovered that the vendor had misspoken. The delivery wouldn't be *this* Friday; it would be *next* Friday. At this point, my co-workers called the vendor in to discuss this disappointing news, or "got into the vendor's face," so to speak. They expressed their frustration in a most urgent fashion and requested immediate contact with the vendor's manager, who assured them that they (the vendor) were doing everything in their power to provide the material as quickly as humanly possible. A couple days later, we were able to secure acceptable delivery dates and carrier information for tracking and to proceed with our installation.

Pressure and tension are part of conducting business; how you deal with it becomes the key. We are all human (or so I've been led to believe), and we all have emotions that seep into our daily lives—even when we're conducting business. Time-sensitive situations in particular cause stress for all parties, not least of which the client. When things go wrong, we tend to get worked up about it. When vendors do not communicate quickly or provide information about how an order is proceeding, you can bet they'll get an earful if and when the client finds out that something's gone wrong. This may be just another order to the vendor, but the client likely has scheduled work or production based on the availability of the items ordered. When the order is delayed or, worse, wrong, you may find yourself across the desk from some very upset people.

Your client can and will be pushy at times—forceful or even belligerent. No doubt, you will be tempted to reach across the desk and strangle that person. I'm sure you'll be able to hold back long enough to allow yourself to interject a more reasonable response. If, as a salesperson, you get in your client's face, you'd better start looking for a new client soon thereafter. The knife doesn't cut both ways in this relationship. While it isn't fair or proper for a client to engage in such practices, that doesn't mean it won't happen—but for a salesperson, attempting to communicate with your client in this manner is not the way to go. You will not have any further success dealing with a client if you step over the line of professionalism to prove a point.

Q: WHO WAS YOUR MOST MEMORABLE CHARACTER YOU'VE EVER HAD TO WORK WITH?

MARVIN MILETSKY

THE SALES PERSPECTIVE

There's a song that I can't help but sing to myself as I respond to this question. It goes something like this: "Bless them all, bless them all/Bless the long and the short and the tall" (at least, I think that's how it goes). That song comes to mind because people come in all sizes and shapes, races and religions, males and females (and some of indeterminate gender)—yet they are characters all, each with something a little different, many with quirks that have made them stand out beyond the crowd. We're all characters in one way or another, and it's the adjustments we have to make to communicate with each type that have made my sales career so much fun.

Okay, enough with the philosophy. You asked and I'm answering: The most memorable character I've worked with is a guy who's in sales. I've witnessed first-hand some of the trouble he's gotten himself into through the use of his quick mouth and biting sense of humor, which is not always understood by those with whom he is interfacing. Here are just a few examples:

- The time he answered the phone and told a customer who was trying to enter an order—tongue in cheek, of course—that he would rather the customer call the competition, as his company was a little too busy at the moment to service his needs. The stunned customer asked in disbelief for the salesman to repeat himself, and the salesman said, "Thanks for calling us instead of the competition. We're never too busy for you!"

- Then there was the customer who called to see if he could get a rush delivery on a product, but wanted to know if he could get special holes drilled in place of the standard ones that were usually provided. "Absolutely!" was the answer. The salesman went on to inform the customer that not only could he have that done, but that the holes could be sent out in advance of the product via fax. "What size hole did the customer want?" he asked, before disconnecting with the customer. The customer then called back, asking whether he had heard that part about the holes correctly.

- The salesman was with his superior out of town. They had an early-morning appointment downtown and another appointment scheduled for mid-morning on the other side of town. After the first meeting ended, they rushed to make their next one. Realizing there was no time to spare if they were to make it on time, the sweat began to pour as they approached their destination. When they arrived, the guard in the lobby told them the company they were looking for had moved. He gave them the address—which turned out to be the exact same building they had just rushed from, clear back on the other side of town. Our friend the salesman did the "old soft shoe," attempting to get the guard to confirm that the company had just moved that very morning; much to his chagrin, however, the company had actually moved more than a year earlier. It's amazing my friend still had a job after that little episode.

- During a particularly tedious and boring meeting that he was required to attend, there finally came a non-technical question that was directed at him. Without batting an eyelash or missing a beat, he looked up and answered very firmly, "23 across." All eyes were on him, all ears open wide, as the other attendees waited for him to explain what he meant; it was then that he apologized, explaining that he had been trying to figure out the answer to 23 across in his crossword puzzle when he was asked the question. Oops!

He's my nominee. It's really a wonder he has any customers at all.

JAMES CALLANDER
THE CUSTOMER PERSPECTIVE

I have worked with so many people, but one person comes to mind: Jeff Silver, a sales representative who called on me for a manufacturer rep firm. I'm sorry to say I've lost touch with Jeff over the years; he was a very pleasant fellow with tremendous bottled-up energy. If Jeff made a visit to your office, you'd be wise to move everything off your desk, shut your monitor off, and not take any calls; Jeff was like a human vacuum, sucking up any information lying on your desk or from your phone conversations. He was a very inquisitive person. Like many salespeople, Jeff had an amazing ability to read upside-down print.

At first, I was taken aback by how Jeff conducted himself. He always seemed fidgety; I honestly believe he was incapable of sitting still. The first few times I met Jeff, I felt like I'd had a workout. When he did sit down, he would plant himself right in my space, hovering over my work. He'd ask questions as his eyes flitted across my desk; it was like he was searching for some hidden treasure you'd buried there. (Knowing how he liked to work my desk, I often placed a request for quote on it in such a way that he would have to make an effort to find it. Usually, I would give in and just hand it to him, but surprisingly, he could find it at times. I also enjoyed watching his eyes to see where they were focused and then start shuffling papers and moving stuff around.) This was also true when he showed off new products or literature that had recently been updated. He'd skim my desk without missing a beat of his pitch. In fact, he could tell a joke, answer a question, write down notes—and *still* manage to scan my whole work area, including the walls, pictures, books, magazines, and other items sitting out. And when he found something that piqued his interest, he didn't beat around the bush; he'd ask me about it.

Many of Jeff's clients didn't appreciate his curious nature. But to me, Jeff was a warm and friendly person with a big heart to match those oversized eyes. He wanted so much to serve and to do a good job. He gave himself to his work. You knew when he said something, it was golden. Sure, it took a while to get comfortable with his style—but once I knew he was coming to visit, I could easily prepare. With any distractions off my desk, we could focus directly on why he was there or why I had asked him to come see me.

I believe they broke the mold after Jeff, since I have never met another person quite like him. I wouldn't recommend emulating his techniques; most clients wouldn't put up with this behavior from a salesperson. I guess it was a flaw in me to give Jeff the opportunity to serve after our first few encounters. I'm okay with that; I can look back and appreciate Jeff for who he was and how he helped make my life and my work a little easier—and more fun.

Q: What Sage Advice Would You Pass On to Others Looking to Build a Career in Sales?

Marvin Miletsky
The Sales Perspective

⤷ As you move forward in your sales career, always take the time to look back upon your accomplishments and take pride in your success—but never forget where you came from and how you arrived at this point.

Throughout your career, you've had help. You didn't go it alone. You were trained by a mentor; remember that person. Your first order was given to you by someone who stuck his or her neck out and gave you your first chance; don't ever forget that customer. The support group that helped prepare your bids—recognize them. The lathe operator who made the sample that convinced the buyer to place an order is not to be forgotten. The inside sales group that processed the order and made it flow, praise them. Those manufacturing people who worked in the heat and cold and got the order out, or those who worked night and day designing that new advertising plan, share with them your pride. The accounting units who sent the invoice and collected the money, which allowed you to sell again, let them know that they, too, were an integral part of the overall picture.

Your assistants, secretaries, co-workers—those above and those below—encouraged you, helped you thrive, and eased your burden. They've got to be given the recognition they have earned. Then there's the porter who cleaned your office and emptied your trash; he was always there with that smiling face as he took an interest in all of your road-warrior stories. Even when no one else around you was sympathetic, he was; let him know that he's been as important to the formula as all the rest. And your company—the company that hired you and enabled you to become who you are, that saw your potential and gave you a stage on which to perform—stay loyal to them and never, never forget the debt that's owed them.

And of course, there are those outside influences that allowed you to flourish: your family, friends, and teachers—all those who listened and stood with you while the world was caving in and helped you to not only survive, but thrive.

There's also thanks due to those with whom you were *not* successful: They taught you what not to do and what not to say. By learning the lessons from these failures, you became a better person. (I actually would not call them directly at this point to thank them, but remember them anyway.)

You did not do this by yourself. Remember that.

JAMES CALLANDER

THE CUSTOMER PERSPECTIVE

A career in sales is never easy but it can be very satisfying and fulfilling. If you're considering a career in this field, here's my advice to you:

- You must be willing to lose more than you win. Rejection is commonplace, and you'll meet resistance with your every opportunity for success.

- Perseverance is a state of mind. You must persevere daily through all of the ups and downs dealing with your clients. Likewise, service is not a buzz-word to be handed out like business cards; it should become your creed—something you instill in everything you do.

- Read all you can about selling. Always seek to learn something new about your offering.

- If you want to be the expert your clients turn to, you must apply yourself to constantly improve.

- Ask yourself where you want to be in 20 years. You probably won't have an absolute answer, but write it down anyway. Then break down that long-range goal by asking where you need to be in 15 years to meet that 20-year goal. Next, ask where you need to be in 10 years to be on track, and then where you need to be in five years. Sometimes, to reach our goals, we must start at the end and work our way back. This is true for all aspects of your life, at work and at home.

- Find people you can ask for counsel; they will provide you important guidance that you will need to become better each year. For example, you might seek counsel from a colleague, a manager, someone from a company you represent, or even one of your clients. Seeking counsel from people with differing backgrounds provides you with a broader spectrum of knowledge that you can tap into and expand your understanding of sales and business. Whoever you choose to approach, make sure that person understands why you have chosen to approach him or her and what you hope to gain from his or her insight. As an added bonus, you may find that a friendship will develop, which could lead you to other successes in life.

- Stay away from gossip and busy talk as much as possible. The petty differences people have will be like poison, affecting your thinking and your reactions toward others. If a person or group confronts you, intent on spewing negative views about others, excuse yourself and move on. You will find it much healthier to keep your distance from the negative talk.

- Say what you mean, and mean what you say. Too many people in sales are timid, even though they should not be. Instead of explaining to a client exactly what has gone wrong and how they are working to correct the problem, they skirt the issue, dodging any negative comments from the client. If you are going to be in sales and want to be successful, you need to communicate well both internally at your company and with your clients.

MARVIN MILETSKY

It's been a long time since that first lemonade stand I talked about in my opening remarks to where I am at today. But I've never lost sight of how lucky I've been to be a member of this noble profession. I've been able to travel both locally and nationally, eat good meals, stay in nice places, talk to a vast and varied audience, and all the time getting paid as well! What a world. I probably would have done it for free, if they'd only asked me to.

This truly has been a labor of love that continues to this day. I return to my place of business after being awarded a contract to witness the activity of my co-workers as they put into motion the various components required to satisfy the new order. And I take pride in knowing that I've been an integral part of the process that gets the product from the drawing board into the hands of my customers.

I hope you've picked up some advice from reading this book and several ideas on which to base some of your own solutions to the challenges ahead. Enjoy those challenges. Fight those fights. You're a salesperson, after all!

JAMES CALLANDER

I have enjoyed working with so many different people, both vendors and clients, it becomes hard to believe how quickly time moves. Over the years, I've been blessed to have some great people guide me. This is probably the main reason I've always enjoyed teaching others—especially people new to sales—the little things they can do or say to improve themselves as they deal with clients. In writing this book, it was my goal was to put together information I have collected from others and through my own experience in a format that might provide some guidance for those interested in a sales career.

My hope for you, the reader of this book, is success. If the information presented here will help you attain that, then I am pleased. The questions answered were developed from the real-life situations that vendors and clients commonly find themselves in. Sales covers so many different industries and markets, it's difficult to provide a broad-based answer to a few of the questions; my goal was to provide with a common-sense approach to clients that could cross over to markets beyond the industry I serve.

Sales is a great profession that allows for creativity, friendship, and loyalty to flourish. Once established, the mutual trust between client and salesperson is very rewarding. I sincerely hope that your career in sales will follow a path marked with achievement and hard work. Give yourself every opportunity to learn. Always plan your day, and then work your plan. Never overcommit, no matter how badly your client insists. In closing, I leave you with this quote from Robert E. Lee:

"Do your duty in all things.
You cannot do more; you should never wish to do less."

INDEX

A

achievement, 272–274

advancement, 283–285

advice, sales career, 299–301

agreement, verbal, 206–208

animated introductory, multimedia, 128

annoyance, 34–36

appearance. *See* dress code

appointment. *See also* meeting

    canceling, 75–76

    rescheduling, 75–76

    showing up without, 72–74

appreciation, 259–260

attitude

    assessing the customer through, 90–91

    as reason for halting business, 123

author, as improving ability to sell, 49–51

authority, 180–182

availability

    as benefit offer to customer, 151

    bluffs about, 219

B

backtracking, 217–219

bad presentation, 187–191

balance

    overcommitting, 272–274

    spreading yourself too thin, 267–271

believing in product or service, 13–15

benefit

    availability as, 151

    payment practice as, 150

    reliability as, 152

    technical support as, 151

    time management as, 152

Benrubi, Jack, 133

bid process, 167

blogging, 128–129

bluffs, 217–219

body language

    assessing the customer through, 90

    reading chances of negotiation through, 144

booth, trade show, 77–78

bottom up approach, 275–277

brand

    preferred *versus* off-brand products, 46–48

    as sales decision based on, 145

breaks, 79

bribes, 168–169

brochure, 114

buddy system, cold-calling, 68

business card, 80, 114

business volume swings, 261–263

buyer

    establishing relationship with, 94–95

    home office visits, 158

    untrained, 130–131

C

cancellation, appointment, 75–76

canned presentation, 185–186

career in sales advice, 299–301

cash rebate program, 132–134

casual dress code, 7–9

catalog, 86, 114

checklist, 143–144

checks, rebate program, 135

client. *See also* prospects

    approaching multiple, 102–104

    befriending, 234–235

    customer base, targeting, 108–110

    customer business, importance of knowing and understanding, 59–61

    customer is always right concept, 286–288

    halting business with, 123–125

    identifying roles of, 94–96

    key players, identifying the, 94–96

    learning about and identifying with, 18

    managing expectations of, 52–54

    most memorable character example, 296–298

    name, importance of remembering, 97–98

    old, staying in touch with, 269

    one-time only, 111–112

    payment practices, 60

    pledging yourself to, 2–4

    as referral, 65

    taking advantage of, 170–172

    walking away from, 213–216

clothing. *See* dress code

cold-calling

    buddy system, 68

    in person, 68–69

    by phone, 67–69

    rejection, 67

    unsolicited approach, 70–71

college education, 29–30

follow-up, 58
    after demonstration meeting, 88
    after signed contract, 225–227
    after trade show, 81
    technical representation, 96
follow-up questions, 21
formal dress code, 7–9
friendship, client-vendor, 234–235

G

gifts, 259–260
goals, salesperson improvement, 284
golf outings, 142
gossip, negative discussion, 120–122

H

handouts, 114–115
higher authority, jumping to next level of, 180–182
home office visits, 156–159
honesty, 36–38
humility, 24–26
humor
    as icebreaker, 22
    overusing, 23
    when to use, 22–23

I

iContact Web site, 128
improvement, salesperson, 283–285
incentives, 132–135
incomplete proposal, 264–266
influencer, 94–96
initial meetings, 57
instant rebate program, 134
Internet importance, 126
introductions, meeting, 92

J–K

jewelry, dress code, 5

keychain, as promotional material, 114
kickbacks, 168–169
knowledge, customer business, 59–61

L

lack of business, 261–263
letter, thank-you, 259–260
licensing, 285
LinkedIn, 129
listening skills, 40
literature
    attaching business card to, 114
    presentation, 188
    as promotion material, 114
    trade show, 81
Longo, Dante, 279
losing orders, 264–266
low points, helping through tough times, 247–249
loyalty, 239–241
lunch, as relationship builder, 140–142

M

meals, as relationship builder, 140–142
meeting. *See also* appointment
    demonstration, 85–88
    duration, 89–93
    follow-up, 58
    initial, 57
    introductions, 92
    length of, 57
    presentation, 58
    secondary, 57
    timing considerations, 56–57
    Web *versus* face-to-face, 231–233
membership, trade association, 82–83
mistake
    customer is always right concept, 286–288
    price, 253–255
mugs, as promotional material, 114
multimedia
    animated introductory, 128
    blogging, 128–129
    correct use of, 127
    e-mail, 128
    overview presentation, 128
    printed advertising, 126
    as promotional material, 126–129
    social networking, 129
    Webinar, 129

N

names, importance of remembering, 97–98
negative discussion, gossip, 120–122
negotiation
  bid process, 167
  how to judge, 144
  misleading statements and hidden agendas, 149
  payment practices, 150
  power and authority of final deal, 166–167
  price, 147–149
nervousness, 45
new employee, how to approach, 130–131
note taking, 270

O

obnoxious, 24
old client, staying in touch with, 269
one-time only customer, 111–112
open-ended questions, 21
orders
  direct approach of asking for, 163–165
  failed, 256–258
  inability to furnish, 197–199
  letting go to competition, 182–184
  losing, 264–266
  worst order examples, 290–292
overcommitting, 272–274
overload, spreading yourself too thin, 267–271

P

passing the buck, 250–252
payment practices, 60
  negotiation, 150
  special payment terms, 150
payment schedule, in fine print, 202
pen, as promotional material, 114
pencil, as promotional material, 114
persistence, 34–36
personal appearance. See dress code
personal information sharing, 236–238
personality
  calm and relaxed approach to, 28
  introvert, 27
  staying true to yourself, 27–28
personality conflicts, 242–243
phone, cold-calling by, 67–69

pitfalls, presentation, 190–191
points program, 132–135
poor product or service, 250–252
premiums, 115
presentation
  bad, 187–191
  dress code for, 188
  literature, 188
  negative effects of, 189
  one-on-one, 189
  pitfalls, 190–191
  preparation for, 187–188
  samples, 191
  technical problems, 191
  unorganized, 190
  visual aids, 188
  welcome greeting, 188
pressure and tension, 293–295
price
  as benefit offer to customer, 151
  bluffs about, 219
  mistakes, 253–255
  negotiation, 147–149
  rush requirement based, 173–175
  as sales decision based on, 145
prioritization, 271
problem solving, 39–42
product or service
  customized, 244–246
  importance of believing in, 13–15
  importance of learning about, 16–18
  limited knowledge about, 17
  poor, 250–252
  tailoring to customer, 244–246
  time-sensitive request, 175
  unneeded, 170–172
project meeting, 229–231
promotional materials
  brochure, 114
  catalog, 114
  client-specific, 113
  confirming receipt of, 115
  effectiveness/ineffectiveness, 113
  entertainment, 142
  flyers, 113–114
  hand-delivery, 114–115
  handouts, 114
  keychains, 114
  literature, 114
  mugs, 114
  multimedia as, 126–129

Here is a preview of five
questions from another book
in the *Perspectives On...* series

Now available!

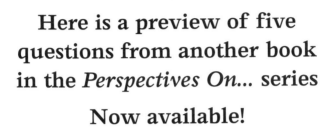

PERSPECTIVES™ ON
MANAGING
EMPLOYEES

- Improve your business by sharpening your managerial skills
- Topics include working with new hires, celebrating the individual, managing through issues and more
- Hear what the management expert and the employees have to say—authors have not collaborated

THE MANAGEMENT PERSPECTIVE
MICHAEL A. FINA

THE EMPLOYEE PERSPECTIVE
SELECTED EMPLOYEES

Q: A SIMPLE GOOGLE SEARCH CAN REVEAL A LOT ABOUT AN EMPLOYEE, A MANAGER, OR A COMPANY. WHAT SHOULD EVERYONE DO TO BE PREPARED AND PROTECTED?

MICHAEL FINA

THE MANAGEMENT PERSPECTIVE

↳ Every day, I find myself fascinated by what you can find on the Internet. The information available—both true and not—is endless. Using the Internet, I have found out so much about my competitors, my customers, and my employees, it's scary, not to mention sobering.

On the Internet, I have found pictures of the inside of competitors' offices, blogs that talk about what it's like to work for my competition, nice stories from happy customers, and statistics about my customers that enable us to propose new ways to better serve them. I've also found loads of information that people have posted online about themselves—much of it inappropriate. Thanks to social-networking Web sites, blogs, and other online collaborative resources, people can share anything and everything about their lives, both inside and outside work. And amazingly, very few people apply any sort of filter when posting information about themselves online, as if they have some expectation of privacy.

It's very simple: If you wouldn't want someone—your parents, boss, kids, clergy, customers, competitors, employees, or the person who will be interviewing you for a job you really want—to see something or know something, don't post it. Also, you should periodically search for your own name and see what comes up. Unless you have an overly common name (e.g., Joe Smith), you will either discover that there is nothing outrageous about you posted online or find less-than-flattering facts that you will want to address. (You might also find some interesting people with the same name as you.) In any case, you will be well informed, and you will be confident that when others search for your name, they will see the same things as you. If you find yourself looking to change jobs, keep this in mind as you begin your process; any hiring managers you speak to may be searching your name already.

Recruiters and hiring managers should think of searching candidates' names as another form of reference-checking, which may reveal an inconsistency in a candidate's resume. That is, if the information about a candidate that you find online doesn't match the candidate's resume or personality, or if it gives you cause for concern for some other reason, raise the red flag and consider yourself informed. Of course, you can't trust everything you read online, so be sure to keep an open mind.

> Although I love that professional networking sites enable users to stay in touch with people, candidates and hiring managers alike should fight the temptation to overuse them. Be careful what you share. What may be an innocent attempt to connect with a business partner can alert others who you would prefer not find out.

Companies typically don't need to worry about what appears on their own Web site. That information has no doubt been reviewed and approved by the legal and communication teams. What companies should be more concerned about are unaffiliated Web sites where unhappy customers and employees may post their less-than-sterling opinions. Fortunately, most companies have both legal and public-relations strategies for addressing this, in addition to policies that restrict personnel from representing themselves as company employees in public communications. As managers, it is our responsibility to educate our employees to follow these policies, as well as apply a smart filter when posting online.

STEVE, AGE 36, VIDEO EDITOR
THE EMPLOYEE PERSPECTIVE

These days, finding information about everything and everyone is as easy as running a simple search. The best way to deal with this is to counteract it by simply coming to the interview prepared.

- **Look the part:** Keep in mind the type of job and company you're interviewing for and modify your sartorial choices accordingly. A suit and tie might work wonders if the company is conservative, but a creative position might call for more casual garb. If the company fosters a "sandals and T-shirts" environment, the suit won't do as much for your chances as a pair of khakis, a button-up shirt, and a comfortable sports coat. Never go *too* casual, however! Make an effort to look good, no matter what the dress.

- **Dress for success:** On a related note, finding out you are no longer a 44L on the morning of an interview is no way to launch your career with a company. Make sure your shirt and your suit, if appropriate for the type of job you're interviewing for, are cleaned, are pressed, and fit!

- **Culture club:** Corporate culture is the most difficult thing to ascertain about a potential employer. No Web search or phone call can tell you if everyone is in dress shirts and itchy pants or jeans and polo shirts. Stopping by an office the afternoon before your interview, however, may offer some insight into the type of environment you're about to walk into and can certainly help you understand how to best impress.

- **Shave and a haircut, two bits:** Don't go for a trim on the day of or the day before your interview! This relates more to your confidence in your appearance than your appearance itself. You want to be comfortable, not just groomed. Plan to get a haircut the week prior so you'll have time to get used to it. Once you've had a few days to work with the new cut, you'll have confidence in how you look, and you won't catch yourself checking or adjusting it.

- **Go surfing:** While you don't need to go too crazy with this, you should take the time to locate and read through the Web site for the company you're interviewing with. Make sure you know what they do—what products or services they provide. Chances are you're not going to get quizzed on this, but doing your homework will show that you've put in some effort and actually care about getting the job. Despite claims to the contrary, there *is* such a thing as a stupid question; asking "So, what exactly do you guys do here?" will make it pretty clear you didn't bother to take five minutes to answer that basic question for yourself. There's usually a lot of information floating around the Web about any company you'll be interviewing with. Read reviews, editorials, or anything else you can find; it'll be pretty impressive if you can show that you have a real strong understanding of what the company is about.

- **No smoking:** Smell is among the most potent of the five senses. Of course, you know to arrive showered, possibly with a dash of a neutral perfume or after-shave. But if you're a smoker, you may not realize just how strongly that scent can linger in your clothes. Once the interview outfit goes on, stay smoke-free.

- **Know thyself:** Know what you bring to the table, where your strengths lie, and how to keep those pesky "what are your weaknesses" questions from overshadowing your positive side. Personality and confidence can often overcome a slim resume and skill set. Show intelligence, interest, and an eagerness to interact—and *always* show that you know who you are.

- **Would the real interviewee please stand up:** Many people forget that an interview is a two-way street. Determining whether a company is right for you is nearly as important as convincing the company that you are right for them. Turning the interview around, reversing roles such that *you* interview *them*, shows the kind of initiative most managers are looking for.

Q: • SHOULD THE MANAGER BE A BOSS • OR A COACH? IS THERE A DIFFERENCE?

SHELLY, AGE 47, PARALEGAL

THE EMPLOYEE PERSPECTIVE

A boss expects employees to do things for him or her—accomplish tasks and reach goals. Bosses tell their employees what to do, and the employees do it. With a coach, however, I think employees learn something while they're doing their work. I don't just mean learning about the computer systems or how things get filed—although that's definitely part of it. I mean learning more philosophical lessons. I see a coach as being able to pass along wisdom to his or her employees.

I think it's a really good thing when a manager is a coach. Working with a coach is more motivating. It helps keep my attitude and spirits up at work—something I don't see a boss doing as much. Sometimes employees need to be energized, and they can learn a lot from their managers. And it's reassuring to know there's someone there who's ready to give you that extra, added pick-me-up when you need it (and when you run out of coffee).

But I don't think managers can be coaches right away. Before my manager can be my coach, he or she needs to earn my respect as my boss. Like a lot of people, I learn best from people I trust and respect, and that requires time to develop. If my manager at a new job acted like a coach right off the bat, I don't think I'd get a lot out of it. I'd go through the motions and listen—and maybe I'd learn something—but it would be forced. I think it's better when the coaching or mentoring comes naturally, not when it's planned out so much. Better to be a really good boss first—to get your employees into a groove, to let them feel like you have a real handle on things, to have a strong sense of what's going on, to be accessible for questions, to be reasonable with deadlines, to be rational when dealing with issues, and to be level-headed with emergencies. Then, little by little, as respect is earned (sorry, we don't just come in on day one with respect—it has to be earned), managers can make the transformation from boss to coach.

MICHAEL FINA

THE MANAGEMENT PERSPECTIVE

↳   If asked, most employees will consider a boss to be very different from a coach. In the world of management, however, they are viewed as the same person. A manager *must* be both a boss and a coach. Effective managers need to have both skill sets, play both roles, and know how and when to balance the two.

Ideally, bosses provide direction, guidance, order, fair treatment, and clarity. These are all great things for employees who like to work within an established structure. For even the most creative contributor, a boss can be a great asset to keep projects on schedule, expenses in line, and expectations in focus. Bosses also provide a path of escalation for questions or problems that require more attention. I like to think of the role of a manager as a "tie-breaker"; when employees are faced with a dilemma about which two or more parties have opposing views, it is up to the boss to cast the deciding vote. It's not always an enviable position, but management is all about making decisions. As a boss, the effective manager will work tirelessly to make employees consider him or her a great boss. When a new employee is asked by friends or family, "So, how is your new boss?" the response should be nothing less than "Fantastic!"

The term "boss" brings with it a negative connotation, however—which I believe is often unjustified. When we think of a boss, we usually imagine a harsh, loud dictator type who hovers next to the time clock to be sure that every employee punches in and out on schedule. I think most leaders will agree that the days of tyrannical bosses are gone. We have been repeatedly exposed to the employee-retention principle that warns that "Employees don't leave companies; they leave their boss." Let us not forget that bosses are not just people who sit in the offices with the big chairs. These are people who have accepted a responsibility to deliver on a commitment. Whether the delivery of that commitment is profitability, satisfaction, efficiency, or productivity, it requires people to make it happen. If the commitment is not met and the delivery fails, the boss is the person who will be held responsible—by his or her boss. Just as we all serve "customers" (refer to my answer to Question #11, "Is It True That Every Employee in Every Company Delivers an Experience to the Customer, Regardless of His or Her Position? Or Is That Just Something Managers Like to Say?" for more), everyone has a boss.

In contrast, coaching—good coaching—enables managers to elevate employees with great potential to great heights. While some managers consider coaching a daunting task, I like to think of it as being like navigation. A coach is your compass (or, for you Gen Y readers, your GPS), helping keep travelers (employees) on course. When you drift off course—which, thanks to the ever-growing array of distractions and commitments in our personal and professional lives, is easier today than ever before—your coach helps bring you back.

There is no one right way to coach; different coaching styles work for different people. Effective coaching is done in the context of a given situation and modulated as circumstances dictate. But there are a few key points that apply across the board:

- **Sincerity is crucial:** An employee will consider your coaching utterly meaningless if it is perceived as insincere.

- **Coaching should not be forced:** An employee who is not open to coaching and a manager who is insistent on it is a recipe for disaster. If the time is not right, back off. Even the best message will be interpreted poorly if the recipient is not willing to listen.

- **Don't be discouraged if your coaching is not received well:** Think of coaching as being like sales. Not every customer is going to buy, but some will turn out to be repeat customers.

- **Your approach must change if circumstances dictate:** When coaching goes beyond course correction and moves to discipline or policy enforcement, then the communication style and protocol must change. If you are not sure which side of the line you are on, look for some internal coaching for yourself from a senior leader or HR professional.

Even though I can't actually juggle, if I were interviewing for a management job today, I would definitely put it on my resume. I'm not advocating untruthful statements; I'm just saying that these days, management is very much about juggling. In addition to juggling responsibilities, managers must juggle the attributes of a great boss with those of an effective coach. Some managers make it look easy, while others visibly struggle. The fact is, we can't always clearly see the line between the two roles. When in doubt, let instincts and sincerity prevail.

Q: • WHERE DOES FOLLOW-UP END • AND MICROMANAGEMENT BEGIN?

LILLY, AGE 24, EXECUTIVE ASSISTANT

THE EMPLOYEE PERSPECTIVE

Micromanagement is when your manager or boss does the work for you or stands over your shoulder and tells you what to do at every step (which is the same as just doing it for you, only worse). It's really hard to get any work done this way, because not everybody works at the same pace or takes the same route to complete their tasks. For example, my boss frequently gives me lists of things to do. Typically, I want to do the tasks on a list in a certain order or in a certain way. But he'll watch me work and constantly ask, "Why are you doing it that way?" and say, "You should do it this way instead." It makes me feel like there's really no point in even coming to the office because he'd be better off just doing the work himself.

I do understand that it can be hard to let go and give someone else the reins. That's never easy. And everyone always thinks they can do a job better than anybody else can do it. But my manager hired me for a reason: to help him do work that he doesn't have time for so he can work on other, more important things. So I think he should trust his own hiring skills. He should trust that I'll do a good job for him and give me a little room to work. That goes for all the employees he supervises, since he micromanages all of us. Managers need to trust that they hired certain people for a reason, and that we're competent enough to do our jobs well and on time.

The best way for everyone to get as much done as possible is for managers to give us assignments or goals and then let us do them on our own. We should have the ability to ask our manager questions when we need to (without having to worry that asking a simple question is going to prompt them to stand over our shoulder and watch us work), and then report back to them on the progress that we've made either at the end of each day or each week. This way, the employees feel like we've got the trust of our managers, have a little more freedom to do our jobs, and feel a little more motivated to get our jobs done well.

We'd feel like we're more a part of the team because we're actually contributing. When the manager stands over the employees' shoulder, I think we stop being part of a team and start being just mindless button-pushers.

MICHAEL FINA

THE MANAGEMENT PERSPECTIVE

There are many management styles in the workplace—one of which is micromanagement. After decades of discussion, this management style is now almost universally considered to be the absolute worst. Nonetheless, it's still out there. There are still managers who insist on making every decision, overseeing every task, taking a lead role in every project, being an authority in every conversation, retaining all responsibility and delegating none, and hovering over employees to ensure that work is done "the right way." The micromanager does not encourage problem solving, creativity, original thinking, or self-confidence. This manager is overly controlling and creates a stressful atmosphere for employees.

This manager does, however, have some positive attributes. He pays attention to detail, is hard-working, is committed to success, and is passionate. He knows that an important job of any manager is to follow up. These are all good qualities—but there is a fine line between follow-up and micromanagement. Follow-up, definitely a core responsibility of management, can easily turn into micromanagement if the following conditions emerge:

- Employees are not trusted to work independently.
- Employees are trusted to work independently only on meaningless tasks.
- Work is taken away when errors are found.
- Employees must consult the manager before making decisions.
- Details are more important than strategic direction.
- There is no focus on developing employee skills to allow for growth and future opportunities.
- Employee confidence erodes.

I'm sure there are some employees who can deal with this management style, but I've never met one. People want to work in an environment where they can succeed. Success grows from making decisions and learning from them. Some decisions will be good and some will not, but we evolve as people, as employees, and as managers through learning. Being able to make decisions requires responsibility. It is up to the manager to delegate effectively and appropriately to allow others to take on responsibility and make decisions.

To ensure that following up doesn't cross over to micromanaging, managers should try these approaches:

- When you delegate work, come to an early agreement with the employee on when you will follow up. By setting milestones, you set the expectation for "when."

- Set the expectation for "what." Agree on what you will be looking for when you follow up.

- Define what success and failure look like.

- Be thorough in your follow-up. Don't throw your arms in the air and give up at the first sign of a mistake. Make an effort to see the complete picture.

- Find the good and the bad. Nobody is perfect. Everyone will make mistakes. But focusing on the positives as well as the negatives will make the follow-up more effective.

- Stay strategic and aligned to the vision. (For more on vision see the answer to Question #21, "Is It Important for New Employees to Know the Manager's Vision and the Vision of the Company?")

- Be nimble. If, when you follow up on an initiative, you find that the project's timeline or deliverables have drifted (with good reason), be open to adjusting the final expectations accordingly.

- Don't always give away the answers. When an employee working on a project gets stuck and comes to you for help, resist the temptation to give away the answer. Make the employee think and try to figure it out independently.

- Be supportive. Being a mentor and a sounding board through open communication will help employees grow and do better work in the future.

- Celebrate success. When expectations are met and projects are completed, celebrate with your employees.

The difference between micromanagement and follow-up is leadership. Are you going to be a leader or just a boss? Are you going to develop a talent pool that is driven to succeed, or are you going to manage a revolving door of workers who do as you say? Are you going to focus on working in alignment with the organization's vision, or are you only focused on your personal vision?

Q:

WHEN IT COMES TO REWARDS, GIFTS AND NOTES ARE NICE, BUT ISN'T CASH THE KING?

MICHAEL FINA

THE MANAGEMENT PERSPECTIVE

 I learned long ago that the world is full of uncertainties. But there is one thing that managers can be sure of: If you ask an employee if he or she wants more money, the answer will always be *yes*. I have yet to meet the employee who would not like to receive more cash. If you are simply looking for the fastest, easiest way to celebrate employees, give 'em money. That said, this approach is proven to be the *least* effective way to promote loyalty, motivation, or trust. You cannot build a caring professional relationship with money, nor can you express true gratitude with money.

For decades, theorists have put forth opinions as to why cash is not an effective motivator. Most theories link cash to the basic human need for safety, security, and survival. In other words, people associate cash with these needs because you need money to stay alive. Increases in compensation, then, are associated with these needs, *not* with recognition for performance.

> Our inherent need for recognition, praise, and gratitude can be satisfied only if our need for security, safety, and survival has been met. Celebrations that focus on achievements and contributions are effective motivators—assuming basic compensation is in place.

Here are a few other theories:

- Cash cannot reinforce a brand or a culture. Companies looking to get employees engaged and committed to their brand cannot do it through cash. It is only through the culture and messages from trusted leaders that people will become passionate about a company. It is trust and relationships that result in people getting engaged and staying engaged. When an employee chooses to do something great, that person will most likely do so because of his or her commitment to the culture and the organization.

- More money cannot make your organization stand out among the competition. Cash is a commodity, not a differentiator. Employees are more willing to brag about non-cash rewards than money, which is perceived to be a part of compensation. The true differentiators are the intangibles that really make a difference in an organization's culture—the ways that the organization and its leaders use recognition and rewards to engage employees and build relationships.

- Cash programs inevitably end up becoming entitlements and are therefore hard to take away. You must have the flexibility to change your organization's reward structure when necessary, and cash programs make this difficult. Any company that has used cash as a reward and later tried to change its reward structure has felt the pain of this type of change.

- Cash has no trophy value. It is not memorable. Most people cannot remember what they spent their last bonus on. Even when we receive personal gifts of money, we usually forget how much we received and what we did with the money. Sure, an employee might use a cash reward to buy something memorable, but most current evidence indicates that cash rewards just go to pay bills and debt.

Regardless of how much money a company spends annually on employee rewards, if employees are not celebrated in a meaningful way by a trusted manager, these individual rewards will be meaningless. For more about what types of non-cash rewards are most effective, see my answer to Question #56, "What Types of Gifts Are Appropriate for a Workplace Celebration?"

YVETTE, AGE 26, RETAILER

THE EMPLOYEE PERSPECTIVE

If I were receiving a reward and had a choice between a physical gift, a gift certificate, or cash, I would choose cash.

A physical gift can be limiting, for there are just a few things that one can receive. It cannot be traded for other services or materials, and it is also individualistic in the sense that it can only be used by one person at the time which it is received. A physical gift provides only temporary gratification.

A gift certificate can only be used at a particular establishment, meaning the recipient is limited to purchasing something within the confines of the merchandise available. It's also a pain to spend all the money on the card since there is always tax included in any purchase—meaning the recipient will either have to pay any overage out of their own pocket or waste whatever small amount remains on the card after the purchase has been made. So even though a gift card provides a little more flexibility than a physical gift, it still has a lot of limitations.

Cash, however, can be used for anything and everything: food, materials, expendables, and even the unheard of. It's the best reward anyone can receive. One could invest in the future with stocks and bonds or buy merchandise. It can be used to buy gifts or even donated to a charity. Every business accepts cash, but not all accept credit cards or gift certificates. Although the downside to cash is that many people may be more inclined to use it to pay a bill or put it in the bank than to spend it on something nice for himself or herself, this would not deter me from preferring to receive cash as a reward.

I do think, though, that no matter what I get from my manager—whether it's cash, a gift card, or a physical gift—I would appreciate it for what it is and be happy that my work and contribution to the company have been recognized.

Q: Why Do Some Managers Deliver Discipline More Effectively Than Others?

JAVIER, AGE 29, TRANSCRIPTIONIST
THE EMPLOYEE PERSPECTIVE

Power trip, man, pure and simple. Good managers manage from the heart, and they don't look down their noses at their employees. They see the people who work for them as human beings, not as machines that can be easily replaced. So when managers like that discipline an employee, it sucks—but it's okay. They make sure the employee understands why he or she is being disciplined, they don't just yell for the sake of raising their voice, and employees respect them for it. (At least, they do later on, even if it's hard to take at first.)

Bad managers, though, get some sort of secret thrill out of reprimanding their employees, and that's just not right. Discipline should be given because someone is doing something wrong that needs to be fixed, not because a manager gets off on puffing out his chest and showing off how tough he is. We know who's in charge; there's no need to prove it. Reprimand with a reason, and make sure that the employee who's in trouble knows what he or she has done wrong and understands what to do to avoid making those same mistakes again.

One of the easiest ways to tell a good manager from a bad manager is by noting where they do their disciplining. A good manager takes employees behind closed doors and speaks to that person firmly but without yelling so that nobody outside can hear what's going on. That's the more human way of doing it; it gets the point across without embarrassing anyone. In contrast, a bad manager reprimands employees in front of their co-workers or by pulling them into a private office and then yelling so loudly that everyone outside the door can hear, making everyone feel uncomfortable and humiliating the person being scolded. That's not right. Humiliation isn't a part of healthy or productive discipline; employees are adults who sometimes make mistakes, not children who need to be taught hard lessons. If a manager reprimands an employee in front of others, that employee won't learn anything from it; he or she will be focused on how embarrassing the situation is and on just getting it over with. And afterward, that employee will probably just save face by talking shit about the manager as soon as the manager leaves, which won't do much to bolster that manager's reputation among other employees.

MICHAEL FINA
THE MANAGEMENT PERSPECTIVE

 This is like asking why some people are better at dating, interviewing, or selling than others. Some people are just inherently better communicators. Their personality and character enable them to easily engage in conversations, in a way that makes others feel important in the dialog. They are adept at expressing good news, delivering bad news, and persuading people to take action. But while there are these individuals who have natural talent, most people need to rely on more concrete skills and attributes to deliver hard messages.

Anyone can become more effective at handling discipline and delivering difficult messages. It simply requires understanding some of the factors that contribute to delivering effective messages. The most important of these is experience. Speaking is a skill, and delivering tough messages effectively takes experience. You can't expect to be great the first time. For many managers, it takes years to refine their technique. This is a skill that must be developed through real situations and experiences that you will encounter.

Whether your message is perceived by others to have been delivered well or delivered poorly is a subjective matter. Just as a television commercial may inspire me to buy something, that same commercial may have no effect on another person. The same is true for messages in business conversations. I may hear or read a message from someone that is perceived very differently by someone else. It's important to realize, then, that the goal is not to deliver the right message, but to deliver a message that will be *perceived* the right way by your audience. This means adjusting your message for every conversation. Professional communicators possess this talent and skill and use their experience to alter their message precisely to fit each situation.

Confidence will play a major role in how your message is perceived. A tough message must be delivered by a person who has confidence in the message, the reason for the message, and his or her authority to deliver it. You must approach the conversation knowing that your message is important and accurate; your firm belief in this will translate into confidence that is obvious to the other person. It is always more difficult to disagree with a person who appears confident and unwavering in his or her message than with someone who shows signs of uncertainty.

The quality of the relationships you build with employees will also drive the effectiveness of your tough messages. If you have built trusting and caring relationships with employees, they will be more likely to accept tough messages from you. Even if it's a message they don't like or don't want to hear, they will be more willing to do so if they know they can trust you and you have displayed care for them in the past. When you have consistently celebrated successes and reinforced positive behaviors, employees will accept that sometimes your job is to deliver unfavorable messages.

As discussed in my answers to Question #79, "When Managing an Employee Issue, How Critical Is Choosing the Right Words to Deliver the Message?" and Question #80, "Does Body Language Really Matter If the Manager's Message Is Clear and Direct?" carefully selecting your words and using the right body language will make your delivery of the message more effective. Think of the steps you take to carefully craft your message as planning. As with anything in your career, planning is critical to success. You cannot enter a disciplinary conversation and hope that you will find the right words to convey your message. (As my co-workers often remind me, "Hope is not a plan.") You must take some time to plan the message and consider your words. Body language is a major element of the execution of your plan. When you are conducting the conversation, pay attention to how you use body language to deliver the message. Also pay attention to the other person's body language and how it changes during your conversation. Use this to adjust your message appropriately. Don't lose sight of the fact that tough messages are hard to deliver and are also difficult to hear. Be compassionate. Show empathy for the other person. Your message must be clear and direct but conveyed with a tone and an attitude that demonstrates that you understand the other person's perspective. Even if you don't agree with or support his or her viewpoint, you should be aware of it.

Don't expect delivering discipline and tough messages to ever be easy. You may become more effective at delivering the message, but it's normal if you never stop feeling like it's a hard and uncomfortable part of your job. It is of course unavoidable; learn from the past, be confident, plan, execute, and be empathetic.

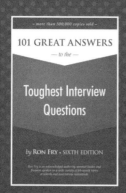

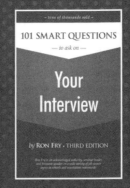